Lina Hug

Switzerland

Lina Hug

Switzerland

ISBN/EAN: 9783337152055

Printed in Europe, USA, Canada, Australia, Japan

Cover: Foto ©Andreas Hilbeck / pixelio.de

More available books at **www.hansebooks.com**

ANCIENT SWISS LAKE DWELLINGS, ZURICH LAKE. (*From Design by Dr. F. Keller.*)

SWITZERLAND

BY
MRS. LINA HUG
AND
RICHARD STEAD
AUTHOR OF "HOLDERNESS AND THE HOLDERNESSIANS," ETC.

London
T. FISHER UNWIN
PATERNOSTER SQUARE
NEW YORK: G. P. PUTNAM'S SONS
MDCCCXC

RESPECTFULLY DEDICATED

TO

PROFESSOR GEORG VON WYSS

AND

PROFESSOR G. MEYER VON KNONAU

PREFACE.

FOR many reasons, some of which are obvious to the least thoughtful, the history of Switzerland is peculiarly interesting, and not least so to English-speaking peoples. In the first place, the "playground of Europe" is every year visited by large numbers of British and Americans, some of whom indeed are familiar with almost every corner of it. Then to the Anglo-Saxon race the grand spectacle of a handful of freemen nobly struggling for and maintaining their freedom, often amidst enormous difficulties, and against appalling odds, cannot but be heart-stirring. To the citizen of the great American republic a study of the constitution of the little European republic should bring both interest and profit—a constitution resembling in many points that of his own country, and yet in many other respects so different. And few readers, of whatever nationality, can, we think, peruse this story without a feeling of admiration for a gallant people who have fought against oppression as the Swiss have fought, who have loved freedom as they have loved it, and who have performed the well-nigh incredible feats of arms the Switzers have performed. And as Sir Francis O. Adams and Mr. Cunningham well point out in their recently published work on the Swiss Confederation, as a study in constitutional history, the value of the story of the development of the Confederation can hardly be over-estimated.

Few of the existing accounts of Swiss history which have appeared in the English language go back beyond the year 1291 A.D., the date of the earliest Swiss League, and of course Switzerland as a nation cannot boast of an earlier origin. But surely some account should be given of the previous history of the men who founded the League. For a country which has been occupied at different periods by lakemen, Helvetians, and Romans; where Alamanni, Burgundians, and Franks have played their parts; where Charlemagne lived and ruled, and Charles the Bold fought; where the great families of the Zaerings, the Kyburgs, and Savoy struggled; and whence the now mighty house of Habsburg sprang (and domineered)—all this before 1291—a country with such a story to tell of its earlier times, we say, should not have that story left untold. Accordingly in this volume the history of the period before the formation of the Confederation has been dwelt upon at some little length. It should be mentioned, too, that in view of the very general interest caused by the remarkable discovery of the Swiss lake settlements a few years ago, a chapter has been devoted to the subject.

Mindful, however, of the superior importance of the

formation and progress of the Confederation, an endeavour has been made to trace that progress step by step, showing how men differing in race, in language, in creed, and in mode of life, combined to resist the common enemy, and to build up the compact little state, we now see playing its part on the European stage. The whole teaching of the history of the country may be summed up in Mr. Coolidge's words, in his "History of the Swiss Confederation" (p. 65). "Swiss history teaches us, all the way through, that Swiss liberty has been won by a close union of many small states." And Mr. Coolidge adds an opinion that "it will be best preserved by the same means, and not by obliterating all local peculiarities, nowhere so striking, nowhere so historically important as in Switzerland."

It remains to add a few words as to the authorities consulted by the writers of this little volume. The standard Swiss histories have naturally been largely used, such as those of Dr. Carl Dändliker, Dierauer, Vulliemin, Daguet, Strickler, Vögelin, and Weber ("Universal History"). Amongst other histories and miscellaneous writings—essays, pamphlets, and what not—may be mentioned those of Dr. Ferdinand Keller, Wartmann, Heer, Heierli, Von Arx, Mommsen, Burkhardt, Morel, Marquardt, Dahn, Büdinger, Secretan, Von Wyss, Meyer von Knonau, Schweizer, Finsler, Roget, Bächtold, Marcmonnier, Rambert, Hettner, Scherer, Roquette, Freytag, Pestalozzi, Schulze, and Kern. Amongst the English works consulted are Freeman's writings, the Letters of the Parker Society, Adams and Cunningham's "Swiss Confederation," Coolidge's reprint from the "Encyclopædia Britannica" of the article on the "History of the Swiss Confederation," Bryce's "Holy Roman Empire," &c.

The authors are indebted for most kind and valuable assistance to several eminent Swiss scholars. To Prof. Georg von Wyss and Prof. Meyer von Knonau special thanks are due, whilst Prof. Kesselring, Herr J. Heierli, and others, have shown much helpful interest in the progress of the work. They also owe many thanks to Dr. Imhoof, who has most kindly furnished them with casts from his famous collection of coins; and to the eminent sculptors, Vela and Lanz, who have given permission to use photographs of their latest works for illustration purposes.

ZURICH and FOLKESTONE, *July*, 1890.

CONTENTS.

	PAGE
PREFACE	ix
TABLE OF CANTONS	xiii
TABLE SHOWING NAMES, AREAS, AND POPULATIONS OF CANTONS	xxiv

I.

THE LAKE DWELLERS 1–12

Discovery of Lake Settlements—Dr. Ferdinand Keller's explorations—Three distinct epochs—Daily life of the Lakemen—Lake Settlements in East Yorkshire.

II.

THE HELVETIANS 13–28

Extent of their territory—Their government and mode of life—Orgetorix—Divico beats the Roman forces—Cæsar routs Helvetians—Vercingetorix—Valisians—Rhætians.

III.

HELVETIA UNDER THE ROMANS . . . 29–43

Cæsar's mode of dealing with Helvetia—Augustus—Helvetia incorporated into Gaul — Vespasian — Alamanni and Burgundians—Christianity introduced.

IV.

THE ANCESTORS OF THE SWISS NATION . . 44–57

The Huns and their ravages—Alamanni—Burgundians—"The Nibelungenlied"—The Franks subdue both Alamanni and Burgundians—Irish monks preach in Switzerland.

V.

THE CAROLINGIANS—CHARLEMAGNE . . . 58–70

Pepin le Bref—Charlemagne—His connection with Zurich.

VI.

THE KINGDOM OF BURGUNDY; THE DUCHY OF SWABIA; AND THE GERMAN EMPIRE . . 71–82

Division of Charlemagne's territory into three—Rudolf the Guelf—Swabian Dukes—Genealogical tables.

VII.

BURGUNDY AND SWABIA UNDER THE GERMAN EMPERORS 85–94

Bertha, the "Spinning Queen"—Her son Conrad—Helvetia in close connection with Germany—Henry III.—Struggle with the Papal power.

VIII.

THE REIGN OF THE HOUSE OF ZAERINGEN . 95–100

Their orgin—Freiburg and other towns founded—Bern founded—Defeated by Savoy—The Crusades.

IX.

THE HOUSES OF KYBURG, SAVOY, AND HABSBURG 101–117

Fall of the Zaerings—Kyburg dynasty—Growth of Feudalism—The Hohenstaufen—Savoy—Rise of the Habsburgs—Rudolf.

X.

THE CONFEDERATION, OR EIDGENOSSENSCHAFT 118–130

The Forest Cantons—The Oath on the Rütli—Rudolf oppresses the Waldstätten—Tell and the apple—Investigation as to the facts relating to the foundation of the League.

XI.

THE BATTLE OF MORGARTEN . . . 131–137

Attempt on Zurich by the Habsburgs—Albrecht—Gathering of the Wald peoples—Austrian defeat.

XII.

THE LEAGUE OF THE EIGHT STATES . . 139–146

Lucerne joins the League—Zurich follows—War with Austria—Glarus attached to the League as an inferior or protected State—Zug joins the Union—Bern.

XIII.

ZURICH AN EXAMPLE OF A SWISS TOWN IN THE MIDDLE AGES 147–157

Abbey Church of our Lady—Influence of the Lady Abbess—Citizens in three classes—They gradually gain freedom—Trade of the city—Zurich a literary centre—Uprising of the working classes—A new constitution.

XIV.

BERN CRUSHES THE NOBILITY: GREAT VICTORY OF LAUPEN 158–166

Bern of a military bent—Forms a West Swiss Union—Siege of Solothurn—Bern opposes the Habsburgs—Acquires Laupen—Victory at Laupen—League of the Eight States completed.

XV.

THE BATTLES OF SEMPACH AND NAEFELS . 167–178

Opposition to Austria—Leopold III., Character of—His plans—Defeat and death at Sempach—Winkelried—Battle of Naefels.

XVI.

HOW SWITZERLAND CAME TO HAVE SUBJECT LANDS 179–189

Acquisition of surrounding territories desirable—Appenzell—Valais—Graubünden—Aargau—Quarrels with Milan.

XVII.

WAR BETWEEN ZURICH AND SCHWYZ . . 190–199

Dispute concerning Toggenburg lands—Stüssi of Zurich and Von Reding of Schwyz—Zurich worsted—Makes alliance with Austria—France joins the alliance—Battle of St. Jacques.

XVIII.

BURGUNDIAN WARS 200–216

Charles the Bold—Louis XI. of France—Causes which led to the war—Policy of Bern—Commencement of hostilities—Battle of Grandson—Morat—Siege of Nancy and death of Charles.

XIX.

MEETING AT STANZ, &c. 217–229

Prestige gained by the League—Disputes respecting the admission of Freiburg and Solothurn—Diet at Stanz—Nicolas von der Flue—Covenant of Stanz—Waldmann—His execution.

XX.

THE LEAGUE OF THE THIRTEEN CANTONS COMPLETED 230–242

Maximilian—Swabian War—Separation of Switzerland from the Empire—Basel joins the League—Schaffhausen—Appenzell—Italian wars—Siege of Novara—Battle of Marignano—St. Gall.

XXI.

THE GREAT COUNCILS, LANDSGEMEINDE, AND DIET, &c. 243–253

Two kinds of Canton—Constitution of Bern and of Zurich—Landsgemeinde—Tagsatzung—Intellectual and literary life.

XXII.

THE REFORMATION IN GERMAN SWITZERLAND   254–268

Zwingli—His early life—His desire for a reformation—Appointed to Zurich—A national Reformed Church established—Spread of the new faith—The Kappeler Milchsuppe—Disputes between Luther and Zwingli—Second quarrel with the Forest—Zwingli killed.

XXIII.

THE REFORMATION IN WEST SWITZERLAND   269–278

Political condition of Vaud and Geneva—Charles III. and Geneva—The "Ladle Squires"—Bonivard thrown into Chillon—Reformed faith preached in French Switzerland by Farel—Treaty of St. Julien—Operations in Savoy.

XXIV.

GENEVA AND CALVIN   279–290

Calvin—His "Institutes"—His Confession of Faith—Banishment from Geneva—His return—The *Consistoire*—The "Children of Geneva"—Servetus burnt—The Academy founded—Calvin's death.

XXV.

THE CATHOLIC REACTION   291–302

Droit d'asile—Pfyffer—Carlo Borromeo, Archbishop of Milan—Borromean League—Protestants driven from Locarno—Switzerland an asylum for religious refugees—Effect of Swiss Reformation on England—Revival of learning—Escalade of Geneva.

XXVI.

THE ARISTOCRATIC PERIOD   303–314

Thirty Years' War—Graubünden and its difficulties—Massacre in Valtellina—Rohan—Jenatsch—Peasants' Revolt—Treaty with France.

XXVII.

Political Matters in the Eighteenth Century 315–323

Aristocracy and plebeians—French League—Massacre at Greifensee—Davel's plot—Bern—Its three castes—Constitutional struggles in Geneva—Affray in Neuchâtel.

XXVIII.

Switzerland and the Renaissance: Influence of Voltaire and Rousseau . . 324–342

Voltaire — Residence at Ferney — No special influence on Geneva — Rousseau — Madame de Staël — Swiss savants — Zurich a Poets' Corner — Breitinger, Bodmer, Haller, Klopstock, &c.—Pestalozzi—Lavater—The Helvetic Society.

XXIX.

The French Revolution and Switzerland 343–359

Swiss Guards massacred in Paris—Insurrection of Stäfa—Treaty of Campo Formio—The Paris Helvetic Club—The "Lemanic Republic"—Surrender of Bern—Helvetic Republic proclaimed—Opposition by Schwyz, Stanz, &c.

XXX.

The "One and Undivided Helvetic Republic" 357–368

A levy ordered by France—Franco-Helvetic alliance—Austrian occupation — Russian occupation—Battle of Zurich — Suwarow's extraordinary marches—Heavy French requisitions—Rengger and Stapfer,—Centralists and Federalists—Napoleon as mediator.

XXXI.

The Mediation Act and Napoleon . 369–381

Conference in Paris on Swiss matters—Mediation Act signed—The Bockenkrieg—Six new cantons formed—Material and intellectual progress—Extinction of Diet—The " Long Diet "—Congress of Vienna—Completion of twenty-two cantons.

XXXII.

SWITZERLAND UNDER THE CONSTITUTION OF 1815–48 382–394

Dissatisfaction with results of Vienna Congress—The French revolution of 1830—The "Day of Uster"—The Siebner Concordat—Catholic League—Progress of education—Political refugees in Switzerland—Louis Philippe—Louis Napoleon—Disturbances in Zurich by the Anti-Nationalists—The Sonderbund War.

XXXIII.

UNDER THE CONSTITUTION OF 1848 . . 395–407

New Federal Constitution—Federal Assembly—Federal Council—Federal Tribunal—Powers of the individual cantons—Military service—Neuchâtel troubles—Federal Pact amended—The Initiative—The Referendum.

XXXIV.

INDUSTRY, COMMERCE, RAILWAYS, EDUCATION. THE "RIGHT OF ASYLUM" 408–421

Extent of trade—Exports and imports—Railways—Education—Keller the poet—The Geneva Convention—International Postal Union—International Labour Congress—Switzerland as a political asylum—Franco-German War—Summary of population statistics.

GENEALOGICAL TABLES 83, 84

INDEX 423

LIST OF ILLUSTRATIONS.

	PAGE
LAKE DWELLINGS, ZURICH LAKE, FROM A DESIGN BY DR. FERDINAND KELLER	*Frontispiece*
MAP, SHOWING LAKE SETTLEMENTS AROUND ZURICH LAKE, BY MR. HEIERLI	2
(1) DECORATION ON SWORD HILT; (2 AND 3), STONE CELTS FOUND IN SWISS LAKE DWELLINGS (COPIED BY PERMISSION FROM "HARPER'S MAGAZINE")	4
(1) VESSEL; (2) SPECIMENS OF WOVEN FABRICS FOUND IN SWISS LAKE DWELLINGS (COPIED BY PERMISSION FROM "HARPER'S MAGAZINE")	7
SPECIMENS OF POTTERY FOUND IN SWISS LAKE DWELLINGS (COPIED BY PERMISSION FROM "HARPER'S MAGAZINE")	10
JOHANNISSTEIN, WITH RUINS OF CASTLE OF "HOHEN-RHÆTIA," NEAR THUSIS, GRAUBÜNDEN	16
HOUSE (FORMERLY CHAPEL) IN ROMAUNSH STYLE, AT SCHULS, LOWER ENGADINE, GRAUBÜNDEN	27
SILVER COIN, VERCINGETORIX (DR. IMHOOF, WINTERTHUR)	29

LIST OF ILLUSTRATIONS.

	PAGE
GOLD COIN, VESPASIAN [VESPASIANUS IMPERATOR-AETERNITAS] (DR. IMHOOF)	34
GOLD COIN OF SIXTEENTH CENTURY [ST. FELIX, ST. REGULA–SANCTUS CAROLUS] (DR. IMHOOF)	42
THE EIGER	52
GREAT MINSTER AND WASSERKIRCHE, ZURICH (APPENZELLER, ZURICH)	67
FURKA PASS	79
CATHEDRAL (EXTERIOR), LAUSANNE	92
CHÂTEAU DE VUFFLENS, VAUD (FOURTEENTH CENTURY)	102
BRONZE FIGURES FROM MAXIMILIAN MONUMENT, INNSBRUCK (ARTHUR OF THE ROUND TABLE, BRITAIN; THEODOBERT, DUKE OF BURGUNDY; ERNEST, DUKE OF AUSTRIA; THEODORIC, KING OF THE OSTROGOTHS)	106
THE OLD HABSBURG CASTLE, CANTON AARGAU	112
THALER OF THE THREE CANTONS (URI, SCHWYZ, AND UNTERWALDEN)	120
MAP OF OLD SWITZERLAND	138
UPPER FALL OF THE REICHENBACH (MEYRINGEN)	160
PORCH OF BERN MINSTER, WITH STATUE OF RUDOLF VON ERLACH	165
WINKELRIED'S MONUMENT, STANZ	174
ARMS OF URI	189
ST. JACQUES MONUMENT, BASEL, BY SCHLÖTH	196
ARMS OF SCHWYZ	198
ELIZABETH, WIFE OF ALBERT II.; MARIA OF BURGUNDY; ELEANOR OF PORTUGAL; KUNIGUNDE, SISTER OF MAXIMILIAN (FROM MAXIMILIAN MONUMENT, INNSBRUCK)	201

	PAGE
MAP OF GRANDSON	210
OLD WEAPONS AND ARMOUR IN ZURICH ARSENAL	214
INNER COURT OF THE ABBEY OF OUR LADY. LUTH CHAPTER OF ZURICH	220
ARMS OF UNTERWALDEN	229
MARBLE RELIEVI, MAXIMILIAN MONUMENT, INNSBRUCK	231
CITY WALLS OF MURTEN	235
CUSTOM-HOUSE, FREIBURG	240
SARNEN, BERN	244
CITY WALLS, LUCERNE	246
ULRICH ZWINGLI	256
MINSTER, BERN	270
THALER OF 1564 (ST. GALL)	289
HIGH ALTAR, CHUR CATHEDRAL	306
ROUSSEAU	329
PESTALOZZI	330
HALLER	333
LAVATER	340
THE LION OF LUCERNE	344
LA HARPE	348
REDING	354
DILIGENCE CROSSING THE SIMPLON PASS	362
INTERLAKEN, FROM THE FELSENEGG	386
POLYTECHNIKUM AT ZURICH	397
VIEW OF SION	404
LAW COURTS AT LAUSANNE	407
"VICTIMS OF THE WORK," ST. GOTHARD TUNNEL, FROM A BAS-RELIEF BY VELA (BY SPECIAL PERMISSION OF SCULPTOR)	411
PORTRAIT OF GOTFRIED KELLER, THE POET	413
INTERIOR OF LAUSANNE CATHEDRAL	419

TABLE

SHOWING NAMES (GERMAN AND FRENCH), AREAS, AND POPULATIONS OF CANTONS.

German Name.	French Name.	Area in Square Miles.	Population (approximate) Dec. 1, 1888.
1. Aargau	Argovie	543	193,000
2. Appenzell { Ausser Rhoden	Appenzell { Rhodes Extérieures	100	54,000
{ Inner Rhoden	{ Rhodes Intérieures	60	13,000
3. Basel Stadt	Bâle-Ville	14	74,000
,, Land	,, Campagne	163	62,000
4. Bern	Berne	2,660	539,000
5. Freiburg	Fribourg	644	119,000
6. St. Gallen	St. Gall	779	229,000
7. Genf	Genève (Geneva)	109	107,000
8. Glarus	Glaris	267	33,000
9. Graubünden	Grisons	2,774	96,000
10. Luzern	Lucerne	579	135,000
11. Neuenburg	Neuchâtel	312	109,000
12. Schaffhausen	Schafthouse	116	37,000
13. Schwyz	Schwyz (Schwytz)	351	50,000
14. Solothurn	Soleure	303	85,000
15. Tessin	Tessin (Italian, Ticino)	1,095	127,000
16. Thurgau	Thurgovie	381	105,000
17. Unterwalden { ObdemWald	Unterwalden { Le Haut	183	15,000
{ Mid dem ,,	{ Le Bas	112	12,000
18. Uri	Uri	415	17,000
19. Wallis	Valais	2,026	102,000
20. Waadt	Vaud	1,244	251,000
21. Zug	Zoug	92	23,000
22. Zürich	Zurich	665	332,000
	Total	15,987	2,920,723[1]

[1] This grand total of the population, on Dec. 1, 1888, is taken from the provisional Census Tables issued by the Swiss Government in 1889.

THE STORY OF SWITZERLAND.

I.

THE LAKE DWELLERS.

WHO first lived in this country of ours? What and what manner of men were they who who first settled on its virgin soil and made it "home"? These questions naturally present themselves every now and then to most thoughtful people. And the man with any pretensions to culture feels an interest in the history of other countries besides his own.

But however interesting these questions as to primary colonizations may be, they are usually exactly the most difficult of answer that the history of a country presents. Now and then indeed we may know tolerably well the story of some early Greek immigration, or we may possess full accounts of the modern settlement of a Pitcairn Island; but in far the greater number of instances we can but dimly surmise or rashly guess who and what were the earliest inhabitants of any given region.

In the case of Switzerland, however, we are particularly fortunate. "Every schoolboy" has heard of

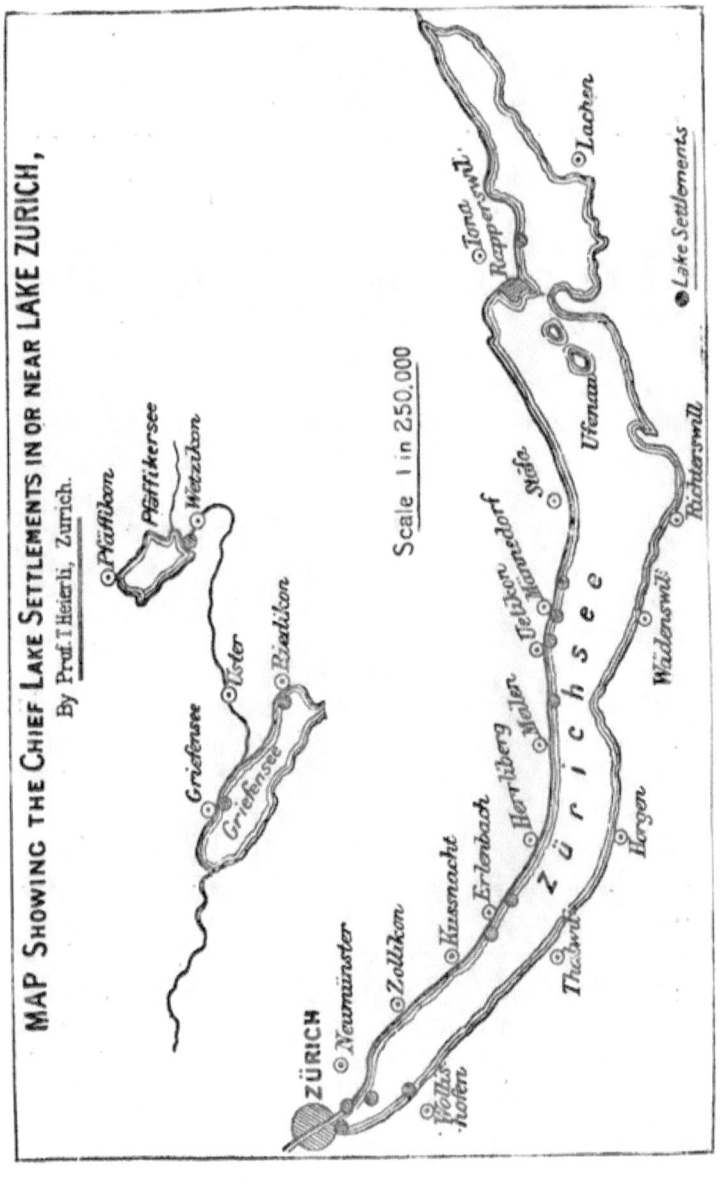

the wonderful discoveries made on the shores of the beautiful Swiss lakes during the last few years, and the same schoolboy even understands, if somewhat hazily, the importance attaching to these discoveries. Nevertheless, some short account of the earliest inhabitants of the rugged Helvetia must occupy this first chapter. And to the general reader some little information as to what was found, and how it was found, on the lake shores, may not come amiss.

In the winter of 1853, the waters of Zurich lake sank so low that a wide stretch of mud was laid bare along the shores. The people of Meilen, a large village some twelve miles from the town of Zurich, took advantage of this unusual state of things to effect certain improvements, and during the operations the workmen's tools struck against some obstacles, which proved to be great wooden props, or piles. These piles, the tops of which were but a few inches below the surface of the mud, were found to be planted in rows and squares, and the number of them seemed to be enormous. And then there were picked out of the mud large numbers of bones, antlers, weapons, implements of various kinds, and what not. Dr. Ferdinand Keller, a great authority on Helvetian antiquities, was sent from Zurich to examine the spot, and he pronounced it to be a lake settlement, probably of some very ancient Celtic tribe. Many marks of a prehistoric occupation had previously been found, but hitherto no traces of dwellings. Naturally the news of this important discovery of lake habitations caused a great sensation, and gave a great impulse to archæological studies. Dr. Keller called

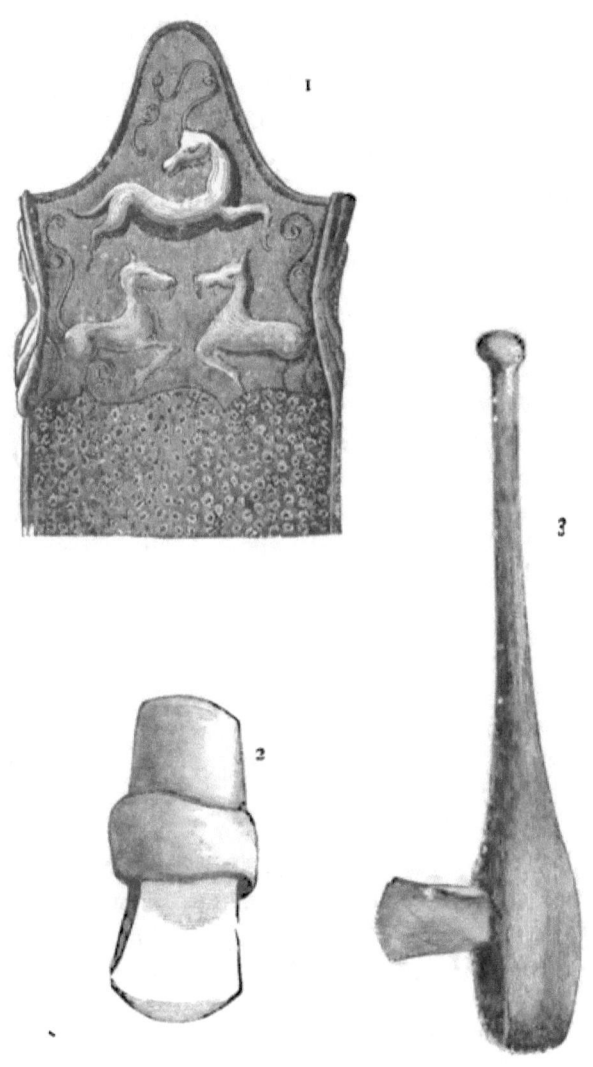

(1) DECORATION ON SWORD HILT; (2 AND 3) STONE CELTS, FOUND IN SWISS LAKE DWELLINGS.
(*Copied by permission from "Harper's Magazine."*)

these early settlers *Pfahl-bauer*, or pile-builders, from their peculiar mode of building their houses.

During the course of the last thirty years, over two hundred of these aquatic villages have been discovered—on the shores of the lakes of Constance, Geneva, Zurich, Neuchâtel, Bienne, Morat, and other smaller lakes, and on certain rivers and swampy spots which had once been lakes or quasi-lakes. The Alpine lakes, however, with their steep and often inaccessible banks, show no trace of lake settlements.

The lake dwellings are mostly[1] placed on piles driven some 10 feet into the bed of the lake, and as many as thirty or forty thousand of these piles have been found in a single settlement. The houses themselves were made of hurdlework, and thatched with straw or rushes. Layers of wattles and clay alternating formed the floors, and the walls seem to have been rendered more weather-proof by a covering of clay, or else of bulrushes or straw. A railing of wickerwork ran round each hut, partly no doubt to keep off the wash of the lake, and partly as a protection to the children. Light bridges, or gangways easily moved, connected the huts with each other and with the shore. Each house contained two rooms at least, and some of the dwellings measured as much as 27 feet by 22 feet. Hearthstones blackened by fire often remain to show where the kitchens had been. Mats of bast, straw, and reeds abound in the settlements, and show that the lakemen had their notions of cosiness and comfort. Large crescent-

---

[1] There are two distinct kinds of settlement, but we are here dealing with the first or earlier kind.

shaped talismans, carved on one side, were hung over the entrances to the huts, showing pretty clearly that the moon-goddess was worshipped. The prehistoric collections in the public museums at Zurich, Berne, Bienne, Neuchâtel, and Geneva, not to speak of private collections, are very extensive and very fine, containing tools, handsome weapons, knives of most exquisite shape and carving, women's ornaments, some of them of the most elegant kind. A "lady of the lake" in full dress would seem to have made an imposing show. An undergarment of fine linen was girded at the waist by a broad belt of inlaid or embossed bronze work. Over the shoulders was thrown a woollen cloak fastened with bronze clasps, or pins, whilst neck, arms, and ankles were decked with a great store of trinkets—necklaces, anklets, bracelets, rings, spangles, and so forth. The whole was set off by a diadem of long pins with large heads beautifully chiselled, and inlaid with beads of metal or glass, these pins being stuck through a sort of leathern fillet which bound up the hair. So beautiful are some of the trinkets, that imitations of them in gold are in request by the ladies of to-day.

It is curious to find that one of the most extensive lake colonies in Switzerland is situated in and spread over the vast marshes of Robenhausen (Zurich) which once formed part of Lake Pfäffikon. The visitor who is not deterred by the inconvenience of a descent into a damp and muddy pit some 11 feet deep, where excavations are still being carried on, finds himself facing three successive settlements, one above another, and all belonging to the remote stone age. Between

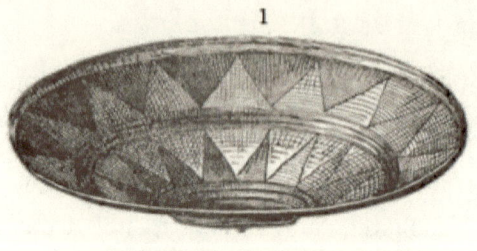

(1) VESSEL; (2) SPECIMENS OF WOVEN FABRICS FOUND IN SWISS LAKE DWELLINGS.
(*Copied by permission from "Harper's Magazine."*)

the successive settlements are layers of turf, some 3 feet thick, the growth of many centuries. The turf itself is covered by a stratum of sticky matter, 4 inches thick. In this are numbers of relics embedded, both destructible and indestructible objects being perfectly well preserved, the former kept from decay through having been charred by fire. The late Professor Heer discovered and analysed remains of more than a hundred different kinds of plants. Grains, and even whole ears of wheat and barley, seeds of strawberries and raspberries, dried apples, textile fabrics, implements, hatchets of nephrite—this mineral and the Oriental cereals show clearly enough that the lake-men traded with the East, though no doubt through the Mediterranean peoples—spinning-wheels, corn-squeezers, floorings, fragmentary walls—all these are found in plenty, in each of the three layers. The topmost settlement, however, contains no destructible matters, such as corn, fruits, &c. This is to be accounted for by the fact that the two lower settlements were destroyed by fire, and the uppermost one by the growth of the turf, or by the rising marshes. In the latter case there was no friendly action of fire to preserve the various objects.

The scholar's mind is at once carried back to the account given by Herodotus of Thrakian lake-dwellers.[1] The people of this tribe, he tells us, built their houses over water, so as to gain facilities for fishing. They used to let down baskets through trap-doors in the floors of their huts, and these baskets rapidly filled with all kinds of fish that had gathered around, tempted by the droppings of food.

[1] Herod. v. 16.

Though the lakemen depended chiefly on the water for their supply of food, yet they were hunters, and great tillers of the ground as well as fishermen. They grew wheat and barley, and kept horses, cattle, sheep, and goats. The women spun flax and wool, and wove them into fabrics for clothing. Their crockery was at first of a very primitive description, being made of black clay, and showing but little finish or artistic design. But the children were not forgotten, for they were supplied with tiny mugs and cups.[1]

With regard to the date when the immigration of lakemen began the savants are hopelessly at variance. Nor do they agree any better as to the dates of the stone and bronze epochs into which the history of the lake settlements divides itself. But as in some of the marshy stations these two epochs reach on to the age of iron, it is assumed by many authorities that the lake dwellers lived on to historical times. This is particularly shown in the alluvial soil and marshes between the lakes of Neuchâtel and Bienne, Préfargier being one of the chief stations, where settlements

---

[1] The lake tribes of the bronze age, however, not only understood the use of copper and bronze, but were far more proficient in the arts than their predecessors. Some of the textile fabrics found are of the most complicated weaving, and some of the bronze articles are of most exquisite chiselling, though these were probably imported from Italy, with which country the lake dwellers would seem to have had considerable traffic. The earliest specimens of pottery are usually ornamented by mere rude nail scratchings, but those of the bronze period have had their straight lines and curves made by a graving tool. In fact, the later tribes had become lovers of art for its own sake, and even the smallest articles of manufacture were decorated with designs of more or less elaboration and finish.

SPECIMENS OF POTTERY FOUND IN SWISS LAKE DWELLINGS.
(*Copied by permission from "Harper's Magazine."*)

belonging to the stone, bronze, and iron ages are found ranged one above another in chronological order. In the topmost stratum or colony, the lakemen's wares are found mingling pell-mell with iron and bronze objects of Helvetian and Roman make, a fact sufficient, probably, to show that the lake dwellers associated with historical peoples. It would be useless as well as tedious to set forth at length all the theories prevailing as to the origin and age of the lake dwellings. Suffice it to say that, by some authorities, the commencement of the stone period is placed at six thousand, and by others at three thousand years before the Christian era, the latter being probably nearest the truth. As to the age of bronze, we may safely assign it to 1100–1000 B.C., for Professor Heer proves conclusively that the time of Homer—the Greek age of bronze—was contemporary with the bronze epoch of the lakemen.[1]

The Lake period would seem to have drawn to a close about 600–700 B.C., when the age of bronze was superseded by that of iron. According to the most painstaking investigations made by Mr. Heierli, of

---

[1] The products of the soil seem to have been the same amongst the lakemen as amongst Homer's people. Both knew barley and wheat, and neither of them knew rye. In their mode of dressing and preparing barley for food the two peoples concurred. It was not made into bread, but roasted to bring off the husk. And roasted barley is still favourite article of diet in the Lower Engadine. The Greeks ate it at their sacrifices, and always took supplies of it when starting on a journey. So Telemachus asks his old nurse Eurykleia to fill his goat skin with roasted barley when he sets out in search of his father. And young Greek brides were required to complete the stock of household belongings by providing on their marriage day a roasting vessel for barley.

Zurich, now the greatest authority on the subject in Switzerland, the lakemen left their watery settlements about the date just given, and began to fix their habitations on *terra firma*. Various tombs already found on land would bear witness to this change. When these peculiar people had once come on shore to live they would be gradually absorbed into neighbouring and succeeding races, no doubt into some of the Celtic tribes, and most likely into the Helvetian peoples. Thus they have their part, however small it may be, in the history of the Swiss nation. It must be added that the Pfahl-bauer are no longer held to have been a Celtic people, but are thought to have belonged to some previous race, though which has not as yet been ascertained.

But enough has been written on the subject, perhaps. Yet, on the other hand, it would have been impossible to pass over the lakemen in silence, especially now when the important discoveries of similar lake settlements in East Yorkshire have drawn to the subject the attention of all intelligent English-speaking people.[1]

[1] Those who wish to see pretty well all that can be said on the matter should read the valuable article in *The Westminster Review*, for June, 1887.

II.

THE HELVETIANS.

THE history of a country often includes the history of many peoples, for history is a stage on which nations and peoples figure like individual characters, playing their parts and making their exits, others stepping into their places. And so the Swiss soil has been trodden by many possessors—Celts, Rhætians, Alamanni, Burgundians, Franks. These have all made their mark upon and contributed to the history of the Swiss nation, and must all figure in the earlier portions of our story.

Dim are the glimpses we catch of the early condition of the Helvetians, but the mist that enshrouds this people clears, though slowly, at the end of the second century before Christ, when they came into close contact with the Romans who chronicled their deeds. The Helvetians themselves, indeed, though not ignorant of the art of writing, were far too much occupied in warfare to be painstaking annalists. At the Celto-Roman period of which we are treating, Helvetia comprised all the territory lying between Mount Jura, Lake Geneva, and Lake Constance, with the exception of Basle, which included Graubünden, and reached into St. Gall and Glarus. It was parcelled out amongst many tribes, even as it is in our own day. The Helvetians, who had previously occupied all the land between the Rhine and the Main, had been driven south by the advancing Germans, and had colonized the fertile plains and the lower hill grounds of Switzerland, leaving to others the more difficult Alpine regions. They split into four tribes, of which we know the names of three —the Tigurini, Toygeni, and Verbigeni. The first named seem to have settled about Lake Morat, with Aventicum (Avenches) as their capital. Basle was the seat of the Rauraci; to the west of Neuchâtel was that of the Sequani; whilst Geneva belonged to the wild Allobroges. The Valais[1] district was inhabited by four different clans, and was known as the "Pœnine valley," on account of the worship of Pœninus on the Great St. Bernard, where was a temple to the deity. In the Ticino were the Lepontines, a Ligurian tribe whose name still lingers in "Lepontine Alps." The mountain fastnesses of the Grisons (Graubünden) were held by the hardy Rhætians, a Tuscan tribe, who, once overcome by the Romans, speedily adopted their speech and customs. Romansh, a corrupt Latin, holds its own to this day in the higher and remoter valleys of that canton.

All these tribes, except the two last mentioned, belonged to the great and martial family of the Celts, and of them all the wealthiest, the most valiant, and

[1] Valais (German, *Wallis*) means valley, and is so called from its being a long narrow dale or vale hemmed in by lofty mountains.

the most conspicuous were the Helvetians.[1] Of the life and disposition of these Helvetians we know but little, but no doubt they bore the general stamp of the Celts. They managed the javelin more skilfully than the plough, and to their personal courage it is rather than to their skill in tactics that they owe their reputation as great warriors. But in course of time their character was greatly modified, and, owing probably to their secluded position, they settled down into more peaceful habits, and rose to wealth and honour, combining with their great powers a certain amount of culture. They practised the art of writing, having adopted the Greek alphabet, and gold, which was possibly found in their rivers, circulated freely amongst them. To judge from the relics found in Helvetian tumuli the Helvetians were fond of luxuries in the way of ornaments and fine armour, and they excelled in the art of working metals, especially bronze. They had made some progress in agriculture, and in the construction of their houses, and more especially of the walls that guarded their towns, which struck the Romans by their neatness and practicalness. Nor would this be to be wondered at if the old legends could be trusted, which tell us that Hercules himself taught the Helvetians to build, and likewise gave them their laws; an allusion, no doubt, to the fact that culture came to them from the east, from the peoples around the Mediterranean. Besides many hamlets, they had founded no fewer than four hundred villages and twelve towns, and seem to have been well able to select for their settlements the most

[1] Mommsen, "Roman History," vol. ii. p. 166.

JOHANNISSTEIN, WITH RUINS OF CASTLE OF "HOHEN-RHÆTIA," NEAR THUSIS, GRAUBÜNDEN.
(*From a Photograph.*)

picturesque and convenient spots. For many of their place-names have come down to us, in some cases but little changed. Thus of colonies we have Zuricum (Zurich), Salodurum (Soleure), Vindonissa (Windisch), Lousonium (Lausanne), and Geneva; of rivers navigable or otherwise useful, Rhine, Rhone, Aar, Reuss, Thur; of mountains, Jura and perhaps Camor. Disliking the hardships of Alpine life the Helvetians left the giant mountains to a sturdier race.

The nature of their political code was republican, yet it was largely tinctured with elements of an aristocratic kind. Their nobles were wealthy landed proprietors, with numerous vassals, attendants, and slaves. In case their lord was impeached these retainers would take his part before the popular tribunal. The case of Orgetorix may be cited. He was a dynastic leader, and head over one hundred valley settlements; his name appears on Helvetian silver coins as Orcitrix. He was brought to trial on a charge of aspiring to the kingship, and no fewer than a thousand followers appeared at the court to clear him, but *vox populi vox dei*, and the popular vote prevailed. Orgetorix was sentenced to die by fire, a punishment awarded to all who encroached upon the popular rights.

Their form of religion was most probably that common to all the Celts, Druidical worship. Invested with power, civil and spiritual, the Druids held absolute sway over the superstitious Celtic tribes. Proud as the Celts were of their independence, they yet were incapable of governing themselves because of the perpetual dissensions amongst the tribes; and they were overawed by the intellectual superiority of a priesthood that professed all the sciences of the age—medicine, astrology, soothsaying, necromancy—and had taken into its hands the education of the young. The common people were mere blind devotees, and rendered unquestioning obedience to the decrees of the Druids. Druidism was, in fact, the only power which could move the whole Celtic race, and could knit together the Celts of the Thames and those of the Garonne and Rhone, when they met at the great yearly convocation at Chartres, then the "Metropolis of the Earth." Human sacrifice was one of the most cruel and revolting features of the Druidical religion.

The Celts were a peculiarly gifted people, though differing greatly from the contemporary Greeks and Romans. They had been a governing race before the Romans appeared on the stage, and wrested from them the leading part. They had overrun the whole world, so to speak, casting about for a fixed home, and spread as far as the British Isles, making Gaul their religious and political centre, and settled down into more peaceful habits. Driven by excess of population, or their unquenchable thirst for war, or simply their nomadic habits—one cannot otherwise account for their retrogression—they migrated eastwards whence they came—to Italy, Greece, and Asia Minor—demanding territory, and striking terror into every nation they approached by their warlike habits. They knocked at the gates of Rome, and the Galatians were conspicuous by their atrocities.[1] Brilliant

[1] "Story of Alexander's Empire," by Mahaffy, p. 79.

qualities and great national faults had been their peculiar characteristics. Quick-witted they were, highly intelligent, ingenious, frank, versatile; attaching much value to *gloire*, and *esprit;* susceptible of and accessible to every impression, skilled handicraftsmen; but inclined to be vain, boastful, and fickle-minded, averse to order and discipline, and lacking in perseverance and moral energy. This, according to both ancient and modern writers, was their character. They failed to create a united empire, and to resist their deadly enemy, Rome.

What they did excel in was fighting. Dressed in gaudy costume—wide tunic, bright plaid, and toga embroidered with silver and gold—the Celtic noble would fight by preference in single combat, to show off to personal advantage, but in the brunt of battle he threw away his clothing to fight unimpeded. Bituitus, king of the Arverni, attired in magnificent style, mounts his silver chariot, and, preceded by a harper and a pack of hounds, goes to meet Cæsar in battle, and win his respect and admiration.

The Helvetians were peaceful neighbours to Italy so long as they did not come into direct contact with the Romans, but on the Rhine they were engaged in daily feuds with the German tribes, who had driven them from their settlements in the Black Forest, and had continued their raids beyond the river. For the sake of plunder, or from mere restless habits, the Germans had left their northern homes on the Baltic and North Seas, the Cimbri, and their brethren, the Teutons and others, and were slowly moving southward, repelling or being in turn repelled. The most daring crossed the Rhine, and made their way straight through the lands of the Belgians and Helvetians towards the South, thereby anticipating the great dislocation of peoples which was to take place but five hundred years later, when the Roman Empire, sapped at the root, crumbled to pieces, unable longer to resist the tide of barbarian invasion.

On one of these expeditions the Cimbri, giving a glowing account of sunny Gaul, and the booty to be obtained there, were joined by the Helvetian Tigurini, whose leader was the young and fiery Divico (B.C. 107). They started with the intention of founding a new home in the province of the Nitiobroges in Southern Gaul; but when they had reached that territory they were suddenly stopped on the banks of the Garonne by a Roman army under the consul Cassius and his lieutenant Piso. But, little impressed by the military fame of the Romans, the Tigurini, lying in ambush, gave battle to the forces of great Rome, and utterly routed them at Agen, on the Garonne, between Bordeaux and Toulouse. It was a brilliant victory; both the Roman leaders and the greater part of their men were slain, and the rest begged for their lives. The proud Romans were under the humiliating necessity of giving hostages and passing under the yoke—a stain on the Roman honour not to be forgotten; but the victors, being anything but diplomats, knew no better use to make of their splendid victory than to wander about for a time and then go home again.

A few years later (102 and 101 B.C.) the Tigurini, Toygeni, Cimbri, and Teutons joined their forces on a last expedition southwards. The expedition ended in the destruction of these German tribes. The Toygeni perished in the fearful carnage at Aquæ Sextiæ, and the Cimbri later on at Vercellæ. When the Tigurini heard of this last-mentioned disaster they returned home.

Cæsar had been appointed governor of the Province (Provence) which extended to Geneva, the very door of Helvetia; on the Rhine the Germans continued to make their terrible inroads. Thus there was but little scope for the stirring Helvetians, and the soil afforded but a scanty supply of food; so they turned their eyes wistfully in the direction of fair Gaul. Meeting in council they decided on a general migration, leaving their country to whoever might like to take it. Then rose up Orgetorix, one of their wealthiest nobles, and supported the plan, volunteering to secure a free passage through the neighbouring provinces of the Allobroges and Ædui. The 28th of March, B.C. 58, was the day fixed for the departure, and Geneva was to be the meeting-place; thence they were to proceed through the territory of the Allobroges. For two years previously they were to get ready their provisions, and to collect carts, horses, and oxen, but before the period had expired Orgetorix was accused of treason, and being unable to clear himself, put an end to his own life to escape public obloquy. This episode made no difference in the general plan. The Helvetians, indeed, insisted on its being carried out. Setting fire to their towns and villages to prevent men from returning, they started on their adventurous journey on that spring morn of

58 B.C. Cæsar's figures seem very large, but, if he is to be trusted, the tribes numbered some 368,000 men, of which 263,000 were Helvetians, the rest being neighbours of theirs. But 93,000 were capable of bearing arms.

A curious yet thrilling sight must have been that motley caravan of prodigious proportions—ten thousand carts drawn by forty thousand oxen, carrying women, children, and the old men; riders and armour-bearers alongside, toiling painfully through woods and fords, and up and down rugged hills; behind the emigrants the smoking and smoulderings ruins of the homes they were leaving with but little regret. Yet they were no mere adventurers, but looked forward with swelling hearts to a brighter time and a more prosperous home. Arriving at Geneva they found the bridge over the Rhone broken up by Cæsar's order. Cæsar was, in truth, a factor they had not reckoned upon, and, after useless attempts to make headway, they turned their steps towards Mount Jura, and whilst they were toiling over the steep and rugged Pas de l'Ecluse, Cæsar returned to Italy to gather together his legions. Returning to Gaul he arrived just in time to see the Helvetians cross the Arar (Saône) with the utmost difficulty. The Tigurini were the last to cross. And on them Cæsar fell and cut them down, thus avenging the death of Piso—the great-grandfather of Cæsar's wife—and wiping out the stain on the honour of the Roman arms. His legions crossed the Saône in twenty-four hours, and this performance so excited the admiration of the Helvetians, who had themselves taken twenty days to cross, that they condescended to send legates to treat with Cæsar for a free passage. They promised him that they would do no harm to any one if he would comply with the request, but threatened that if he should intercept them he might have to see something of their ancient bravery. No threats or entreaties were of avail, however, with such a man as Cæsar, who, smiling at their naïve simplicity, asked them to gives hostages as a sign of confirmation of their promise. "Hostages!" cried Divico, the hero of of Agen, in a rage, "the Helvetians are not accustomed to give hostages; they have been taught by their fathers to receive hostages, and this the Romans must well remember." So saying he walked away.

The Helvetians continued their march, Cæsar following at a distance, watching for an opportunity of attacking them. At Bibracte, an important city of Gaul (now Mont Beuvray), west of Autun in Burgundy, the opportunity offered itself. Cæsar seized a hill and posted his troops there, and charged the enemy with his cavalry. The Helvetians fiercely repulsed the attack, and poured on the Roman front, but were quite unable to stand against the showers of the Roman pila, which often penetrated several shields at once, and thus fastened them together so that they could not be disentangled. Disconcerted by this unexpected result, the Helvetians were soon discomfited by the sharp attack with swords which instantly followed. Retiring for a while to a hill close by, the barbarians again drew up in battle order, and again descended to combat. Long and fierce was the struggle which followed; the Helvetians fighting like lions till the evening, never once turning their backs on the enemy. This is Cæsar's own report. But barbarian heroism was no match for the regular, well-organized, and highly-trained Roman army, and once more driven back, they withdrew to the hill where had been left their wives and children with the baggage. From this place they ventured to make a last resistance, and they drew up their carts in the form of a deep square, leaving room in the middle for the non-combatants and the baggage. Then mounting their extemporized fort—the so-called Wagenburg—the Helvetian men commenced the fray, even their women and children hurling javelins at the enemy. Not till midnight did the Romans seize and enter on the rude rampart, and when they did the clashing of arms had ceased. All the valiant defenders lay slain at their feet, and the spirit of bold independence of the Helvetians was crushed for ever.

After this fearful disaster the rest of the emigrants, to the number of 110,000, continued their march through Gaul, but lacking both food and capable leaders, and being moreover ill-used by the Gauls, they sent to Cæsar for help. He demanded hostages, and ordered them to return home and rebuild their towns and villages. And, further, he supplied them with food for the journey, and requested the Allobroges to do the same when the Helvetians should arrive in their province. Cæsar admits that this apparent generosity on his part was dictated not by compassion, but by policy. It was to his interest that these barbarians should re-occupy Helvetia, because they would keep watch on the Rhine, and prevent the irruption of the Germans into the country. In their condition now, he calls the Helvetians ASSOCIATES (*fœderati*), and not SUBJECTS, and leaves them their own constitution, and, to some extent, their freedom. But they did not relish this forced friendship, which was indeed more like bondage; and when the Celts of Gaul rose in revolt under the noble and beloved Vercingetorix, who had been a friend of Cæsar, they joined their brethren (52 B.C.), and were again vanquished. On the defeat of the Helvetians at Bibracte followed that of the Valisians, in 57 B.C. To establish a direct communication between Central Gaul and Italy, Cæsar took those same measures which Napoleon I. employed long afterwards; he conquered the Valais (by his lieutenant Galba), that he might secure the passage of the Great St. Bernard. A splendid road was formed over Mount Pœninus, and a temple erected to Jupiter Pœninus, where the traveller left votive tablets as a thanksgiving offering after a fortunate ascent.

The subjugation of Rhætia was delayed for more than a generation. To guard the empire against the Eastern hordes; against the mountain robbers of Graubünden and the Tyrol, who descended into the valleys of the Po, ravaging the country as far as Milan, and no doubt liberally paying back in their own coin, the Romans who had made from time to time such havoc in the Alpine homes—to guard against these, and the wild Vindelicians of Bavaria, Augustus sent the two imperial princes to reduce them to subjection. Drusus marched into the Tyrol, whilst Tiberius advanced on Lake Constance, where even the Rhætian women engaged in the conflict, and, in default of missiles, hurled their sucking children into the face of the conquerors, through sheer exasperation. Their savage courage availed them nothing, however; the incursions from the East were repressed; and once the Rhætians were overcome, they became the most useful of auxiliaries to the Roman army. Horace's ode to Drusus alludes to the Rhætian campaign.

The Rhæto-Roman inhabitants of Graubünden—for they still occupy the high valleys of the Engadine and of the Vorder-Rhine—present much interest in point of language and antiquities. The sturdy Rhætians belonged to the art-loving Etruscan race, whose proficiency in the *amphora-technic* we so highly value. An old legend calls their ancestor Rætus a Tuscan. And not without show of reason, says Mommsen, for the early dwellers of Graubünden and the Tyrol were Tuscans, and spoke a dialect agreeing with that of the district of Mantua, a Tuscan colony in the time of Livy. In Graubünden and Ticino were found, some thirty years ago, stones bearing inscriptions in that dialect. The Rhætians may have dropped behind in these Alpine regions on the immigration of Etruscans into the valleys of the Po; or, they may just as likely have fled there on the advent of the Celts, when that warlike race seized on the fertile plains of the river, and drove the Etruscans from their home southward and northward. Be that as it may, however, it is certain that the Rhætians, once blended with the Romans, have preserved the Latin tongue

HOUSE (FORMERLY CHAPLE) IN THE ROMAUNSH STYLE, AT SCHULS, LOWER ENGADINE, GRAUBÜNDEN.
(*After a Photograph by Guler.*)

and customs to this day, for Romaunsh a corrupt Latin, with no doubt some admixture of Tuscan, is still spoken by more than one-third of the population of the Grisons.

III.

HELVETIA UNDER THE ROMANS.

ON the surrender of the noble Vercingetorix, a valiant knight, but no statesman—he delivered himself up to Cæsar, trusting in his generosity on the plea of former friendship, and died a prisoner of Rome—the war with Gaul was virtually at an end.

SILVER COIN, VERCINGETORIX.
(*Dr. Imhoof, Winterthur.*)

The sporadic risings that followed lacked the spirit of union, and led to no results of any consequence. During the seven years of his governorship in Gaul (58–51 B.C.), Cæsar had completed the subjection of the entire country, with the exception of the province of Narbonensis, whose conquest was of more ancient date. He followed up his victories, and secured their results by organizing a line of secure defences on the northern boundary of Gaul, along the Rhine, creating thereby a new system of open defences—defences offensive, so to speak—which he sketched out with full details, and made Gaul herself a bulwark against the inroads of the aggressive Germans. To secure peace and voluntary submission, he also regulated the internal affairs of the new province, leaving her, however, most of her old national institutions, hoping by conciliatory measures to gradually bring her under Roman influences, and win her to side with Rome. But it was left to others to carry out his plans, the Emperor Augustus being the first to put them into practice; for civil war was again threatening Italy, and Cæsar returned home to carry on his great contest with Pompey for supremacy in the State.

Although Cæsar's plans were but a sketch they were faithfully carried out, and the Gallic conquest proved to be more, and aimed higher, than the mere subjection of the Celts. Cæsar was not only a great general, but also a far-seeing politician. He had clearly understood that the barbarian Germans might well prove more than a match for the Greek-Latin world if they came into close contact with it. His defeat of Ariovistus, who was on the point of forming a German kingdom in Gaul, and his wise measures of defence, kept the barbarian hordes at bay for centuries, and thus there was ample time given for the Greek-Latin culture to take root throughout the West. It happened consequently that when Rome could no longer offer any serious resistance, and the Germans poured into her lands, the people of the West were already Romanized, and those of Gaul,

Britain, and Spain, became the medium of transmitting to the Germans the spirit of classicism, by which they would otherwise have hardly been affected; and those nations became the connecting link between the classical age and the German era which absorbed its high-wrought culture. If Alexander may be said to have spread Hellenism over the East; Cæsar may be taken to have done as much, and indeed vastly more for the West, for it is owing to him, though we can scarcely realize the fact in our day, that the German race is imbued with the spirit of classical antiquity.

The fall of Cæsar, and the state of anarchy that followed again, delayed the work of pacification, and Helvetia was left to take care of herself. But when Augustus was firmly seated on the imperial throne, he resumed the task which had been bequeathed to him. The organization of Gaul was chiefly his work, and it required an energetic yet moderate policy, The old Narbonensis district, which had long been moulded into a Roman province, was placed under senatorial control. New Gaul, or Gallia Comata (*Gaule Chevelue*), as the whole territory was called which Cæsar had conquered, was submitted to imperial authority, and treated more adequately in accordance with the ancient constitutions of the various tribes. To facilitate taxation and administration New Gaul was divided into three provinces, each ruled by a Roman governor. Of these three provinces, one was Belgica, extending from the Seine and the mouth of the Rhine to Lake Constance, thus including Helvetia proper. Belgica, on account of its size, was subdivided into three commands, in one of which, that of Upper

Germany, Helvetia found itself placed. Thus we find Helvetia incorporated with Gaul.

The political capital of the Tres Galliæ, or Three Gauls, was Lugdunum (Lyons), owing to its central position, and it seems to have been a very important city. Here Drusus had raised an altar to his imperial father, Augustus, and the Genius of the City. Here met the representatives of the sixty-four Gallic states (including those of the Helvetians and the Rauraci) on the anniversary of the emperor. Here, too, was the seat of the Gallic Diet; and here, in the amphitheatre, took place rhetorical contests, the Celts holding eloquence in high honour.

Eastern Switzerland, that is, Graubünden, and the land around Lake Wallenstatt, as far as Lake Constance, was joined with Rhætia, which likewise included, amongst other districts, the Tyrol and Southern Bavaria. The whole of this territory was ruled by a governor residing at Augusta Vindelicorum (Augsburg). The Valais district was joined to some part of Savoy, and ruled by the procurator of the Pœnine Alps. Ticino does not concern us here, as it remained a portion of Italy down to the sixteenth century.

Yet though thus arbitrarily made a part of Gaul, Helvetia formed a province of itself, and had its own history and kept its own constitution, thanks to Cæsar's wise and generous policy, by which he provided that the Celts should not be interfered with in their method of governing by tribes (*pagi* or *civitates*), nor in their constitution, so long as it did not clash with the Roman laws. When Cæsar had defeated the

Helvetians he sent them back to rebuild their old homes, and they re-occupied their ancient territory, with the exception of that portion which stretches from Fort l'Ecluse to Geneva and Aubonne, and borders on Mount Jura. This portion was wrenched away and given to the Equestrian Julian colony settled at Noviodunum (Nyon) on Geneva lake, to keep the passes of the mountain (43 B.C.). The Jura range separated Helvetia from the territory of the Rauraci, where another veteran colony was about the same time established as a safeguard for the Rhine, to check the incursions of the Germans. The Colonia Rauracorum was afterwards called Augusta Rauracorum in honour of the emperor. The colonists of these two settlements were mostly Romans, or had been admitted to Roman citizenship, and occupied a different position from the inhabitants of the country generally, for they were allowed Roman privileges and favours—exemption from taxation most likely amongst others—but, on the other hand, they were entirely dependent on the Roman Government.

The laborious investigations of the learned Mommsen and Charles Morel go to show that the Helvetians were mildly treated by their masters. They had been received into the Roman pale as friends (*fœderati*), and as such lived on favourable terms with these, and enjoyed as high a degree of liberty and autonomy as was compatible with their position as Roman subjects. The Rhætians had been taken from their country; the Helvetii, on the contrary, had been sent back home and entrusted with the guardianship of the Rhine, merely being required to furnish a contingent for service abroad. They were allowed to maintain garrisons of their own—that of Tenedo on the Rhine, for instance—to build forts, to raise militia in case of war. And, as has before been mentioned, their religious worship was not interfered with, nor their traditional division into *pagi*, or tribes, and they were allowed a national representative at the Gallic capital, Lyons. Helvetia took the rank of a state (*Civitas Helvetiorum*), its chief seat (*chef-lieu*) being Aventicum, which was also the centre of government. So long as Helvetia conformed to the regulations imposed by the imperial government she

GOLD COIN, VESPASIAN (VESPASIANUS IMPERATOR-AETERNITAS).
(*By Dr. Imhoof, Winterthur.*)

was allowed to manage her own local affairs. Latin was made the official language, though the native tongue was not prohibited.

A.D. 69-79. Under Vespasian, however, a great change took place. Thanks to the munificence of that emperor, who had a great liking for Aventicum, this city lost its Celtic character, and was made a splendid city after the Italian type. He had sent there his befriended and faithful Flavian colony of the Helvetians to live, giving her the lengthy title of Colonia Pia Flavia Constans Emerita Helvetiorum Fœderata in return for services, for she had staunchly supported his party against Vitellius when the latter contended with Galba for the imperial throne. The inhabitants most likely received the Latin Right (*Droit Latin*), or were considered Roman citizens, and as such were more intimately connected with Rome, and had to submit to closer control. Her institutions were assimilated to those of Italian towns. She had a senate, a council of decuriones, city magistrates, a *præfectus operum publicorum* (or special officer to attend to the construction of public buildings), Augustan flamens, or priests, and so forth.

Notwithstanding the overwhelming importance of Aventicum, a certain amount of self-government was left to the country districts, towns, and villages (*vici*). The inhabitants of Vindonissa (Windisch), Aquæ (Baden), Eburodunum (Yverdon), Salodurum (Soleure), erected public buildings of their own accord. The towns of the Valais, Octodurum (Martigny), Sedunum (Sion), &c., had their own city council and municipal officers, and received the Latin Right. In the case of the Helvetians, those of the capital and those of the provinces equally enjoyed that Right; whereas, with Augusta Rauracorum, the case was different, only the colonists within the walled cities being granted the like standing and liberties. On the whole it may be said that, though Helvetia kept many of her own peculiarities, and some of her ancient liberties, she submitted to Rome, and was greatly influenced by the advanced civilization of the empire. The Helvetians, indeed, underwent that change of speech and character, which split them into two nations, French and Germans.

One of the chief factors contributing to the Roman colonization of Helvetia was the military occupation of its northern frontier, though this occupation weighed heavily on the country. The great object of Rome was to keep back the Germans, who were for ever threatening to break into the empire. Vindonissa was one of the military headquarters, and its selection for the purpose was justified by its excellent position, situated as it was on an elevated neck of land, washed by three navigable rivers, the Aare, Reuss, and Limmat, and at the junction of the two great roads connecting East and West Helvetia with Italy. A capital system of roads, too, was planned all over the country.

There would no doubt often be but little love lost between the Helvetians and the soldiery in occupation. Tacitus ("Annals") tells of one bloody episode. After the death of the madman hero, the twenty-first legion, surnamed *Rapax*, or Rapacious, no doubt for good reasons, was quartered at Vindonissa. Cæcina, a violent man, lieutenant of Vitellius, then commander of the Rhine army, marched into Helvetia to proclaim Vitellius emperor. But the Helvetians supported his opponent Galba, not knowing that he had just been murdered, and fell upon the messengers of Cæcina, and put them in prison, after first seizing their letters. The lieutenant enraged at this affront laid waste the neighbouring Aquæ (Baden near Zurich), a flourishing watering-place much frequented for its amusements, Tacitus tells us. Calling in the Rhætian cohorts, he drove them to the Bœtzberg, and cut them down by thousands in the woods and fastnesses of

Mount Jura; then, ravaging the country as he went, Cæcina marched on to Aventicum, which at once surrendered. Alpinus, a notable leader, was put to death, and the rest were left to the clemency of Vitellius. However, the Roman soldiery demanded the destruction of the nation, but Claudius Cossus, a Helvetian of great eloquence, moving them to tears by his touching words, they changed their minds, and begged that the Helvetians might be set at liberty.

However this military occupation was, after sixty years of duration, drawing to a close. Under Domitian and Trajan all the land between Strasburg and Augsburg, as far as the Main, was conquered and annexed to the Roman Empire. An artificial rampart was formed across country from the mouth of the Main to Regensburg on the Danube, and the military cordon was removed from the Swiss frontier to the new boundary line. Helvetia, now no longer the rendezvous of the Roman legionaries, quietly settled into a Roman province, where the language, customs, art, and learning of Rome were soon to be adopted.

If the military stations were starting-points of the new culture, it was the more peaceful immigrants who introduced agriculture, commerce, and wealth, or, at any rate, caused it to make progress. Gradually the Helvetians amalgamated with the Romans, adopting even their religion. Horticulture and vine-culture were introduced. A Roman farmer grew vines on a patch of ground near Cully, on Lake Geneva, and on an inscribed stone (dug up at St. Prex) begs Bacchus

(*Liber Pater Cocliensis*) to bless the vintage. He little anticipated that his plantation would be the ancestor, as it were, of the famous La Côte, now so highly valued.

Wherever the art-loving Roman fixed his abode he built his house, with the wonderful Roman masonry, and furnished it with all the luxury and art his refined taste suggested. Thus the country gradually assumed a Roman aspect. Many towns and *vici*, or village settlements, sprang up or increased in importance under Roman influence—Zurich, Aquæ (Baden near Zurich), Kloten, Vindonissa, and others.[1] Yet the eastern portion of the country could not compete in the matter of fine buildings with the western cantons. Indeed, in the eastern districts the Helvetian influence was never predominated over by the Latin influence, and the Helvetians clung to their native speech despite the Latin tongue being the official language.

But it was the mild and sunny west which most attracted the foreigner, as it still does. Wealthy Romans settled in great numbers between Mount Jura and the Pennine ranges. Every nook and corner of the Canton Vaud bears even down to our days the stamp of Roman civilization. The shores and sunny slopes of Geneva lake were strewn with villas, and the woody strip of land between Villeneuve and Lausanne and Geneva was almost as much in request for country seats by the great amongst the Romans as that delightful stretch of coast on the Bay of

[1] We know little of them, most likely they were but *vici* (village settlements). Aquæ alone we know from Tacitus was a city-like watering-place; Kloten had handsome villas, but what it was we do not know.

Naples, from Posilippo to Pozzuoli and Baiæ, where Cicero and Virgil, and many Romans of lesser mark, had their *villegiatures*.

But the most remarkable place, whether for art, learning, or opulence, was Aventicum, the Helvetian capital. Of this town some mention has been made above, and, did space permit, a full description might well be given of this truly magnificent and truly Roman city. Its theatre, academy, senate-house, courts, palaces, baths, triumphal arches, and private buildings were wonderful. Am. Marcellinus, the Roman writer, who saw Aventicum shortly after its partial destruction by the Alamanni, greatly admired its palaces and temples, even in their semi-ruinous condition. The city next in beauty and size was Augusta Rauracorum (Basel Augst), where the ruins of a vast amphitheatre still command our wondering admiration.

But this period of grandeur was followed by the gradual downfall of the empire, which was already rotten at the core. The degenerate Romans of the later times were unable to stand against the attacks of the more vigorous Germans. The story is too long to tell in detail, but a few points may be briefly noted. In 264 A.D. the Alamanni swept through the country on their way to Gaul, levelling Augusta Rauracorum with the ground, and considerably injuring Aventicum. At the end of the third century the Romans relinquished their rampart between the Rhine and the Danube, and fell back upon the old military frontier of the first century. Helvetia thus underwent a second military occupation. Yet the prestige of Rome was gone. In 305 A.D. the Alamanni again overran Helvetia, and completed the ruin of Aventicum. Weaker and weaker grew the Roman power, and when the Goths pressed into Italy the imperial troops were entirely withdrawn from Helvetia. As for the Helvetians themselves, they were quite unable to offer any resistance, and when the Alamanni once more burst into the land (406 A.D.), they were able to secure entire possession of the eastern portions. The Burgundians, another German tribe, followed suit, and in 443 A.D. fixed themselves in West Helvetia. The inaccessible fastnesses of Graubünden alone remained untouched by the tide of German invasion, which effected such changes in the neighbouring districts.

At this period of worldly grandeur and internal decay, occurs another historical event of the greatest importance, the rise of Christianity, containing the vital elements necessary for bringing about the spiritual regeneration of the world. The social and political decomposition throughout the empire, the cruel tyranny of the sovereigns, the decrepitude of the state and its institutions, the growing indifference to the national religion, which showed itself in the facile adoption of, or rather adaptation to, the Eastern forms of worship—the adoption of the deities Isis and Mithra, for example—all these and many other things unnecessary to mention, were unmistakable signs that Roman rule was drawing to its close, and they also prepared the way for the reception of the new doctrine. The belief in one God of mercy and love; of one Saviour, the Redeemer of the world; of a future life,—were startling but good tidings to the poor and oppressed, and made their influence felt also on the rich and cultivated, who saw in Christianity a tolerance, benevolence, human love, loftiness of principle and moral perfection which had not been attained by the creeds of antiquity. The passionate ardour and force of conviction amongst the Christians was such that they faced suffering and death rather than abjure their tenets or desist from preaching them to others.

The accounts of the introduction of Christianity into Switzerland are mostly legendary, yet it is generally believed that it was not the work of special missionaries. It is more likely that the new faith came to the land as part and parcel of the Roman culture. Indeed this is now the opinion most generally received. The military operations of the empire required continual changes of locality on the part of the troops; thus we find Egyptian, Numidian, and Spanish soldiers quartered on the Rhine and the Danube, and such as they would most probably be the first to bring in the new faith.

At first the Roman authorities looked upon Christians as state rebels, and fierce persecutions followed. The oldest Christian legend of this country tells of such a conflict between the state officials and the Christians, and no doubt contains some admixture of truth, as many of these stories do. A legion levied at Thebes in Egypt—hence called the *Thebaïde*—was sent to Cologne to take the place of troops required to quell a rising in Britain. Coming to the Valais, they were required by the Emperor Maximian to sacrifice to the heathen gods (A.D. 280-300), but being mostly Christians they refused, and were massacred with their chief, Mauritius. Some, however, escaped for the time, but were called upon to receive the martyr's crown later on, and in other places. Two such, Ursus and Victor, came to Soleure with sixty-six companions, and were put to death by order of Hirtæus, the Roman governor. Two others, Felix and his sister Regula, reached Zurich, where their successful conversions irritated Decius, who put them to the rack, and then beheaded them. Yet, wonderful to tell, the legend goes on, they seized their heads that had

GOLD COIN OF SIXTEENTH CENTURY (ST. FELIX, ST. REGULA—SANCTUS CAROLUS). (*By Dr Imhoof, Winterthur.*)

fallen, and, walking with them to the top of a hill close by, buried themselves, bodies and heads too. This wonderful feat was an exact counterpart of that reported to have been performed also by Ursus and Victor at Soleure. Felix and Regula became the patron saints of Zurich, and play a conspicuous part in its local history. Tradition says that Charlemagne himself in later days erected a minster on their burial spot. Thus, as ever, the blood of martyrs became the seed of the Church.

The Roman towns Geneva, St. Maurice, Augusta Rauracorum, Aventicum, Vindonissa, and Curia had been episcopal sees since the third century, though some of these sees were in process of time removed to other places. Thus, Augusta, Vindonissa, and St. Maurice were removed to Basel, Constance, and Sion respectively.

VI.

THE ANCESTORS OF THE SWISS NATION.

THE ALAMANNI; BURGUNDIANS; FRANKS; MEROVINGIANS.

THE fifth century was remarkable for what may be called the dislocation of the peoples of Europe—the migrations of the Germans into the Roman Empire, and, mightiest movement of all, the irruption of the Huns under their terrible king Attila, the "Scourge of God." The mere sight of the hideous Asiatics filled men with horror. Never afoot, but ever on their ill-shaped but rapid steeds, to whose backs they seemed as if they were glued, and on which they lived well-nigh day and night, it seemed as if man and horse had grown into one being. Their large heads ill-matched their meagre bodies; their tawny faces with deep-set eyes and high, protruding cheek-bones made them resemble rough-cut figures in stone rather than human beings. The Goths regarded them as the offspring of spirits of the desert and of witches. These masses of Asiatic barbarism, which had burst into Europe, stayed for awhile in Hungary, but soon rolled towards the West, dislodging all the peoples with whom they came in contact. Marching to the Rhine, they drove the Burgundians from their settlements in the district of Worms, a land so rich in song and saga, and entered Gaul to found a new kingdom. But the doom of the Huns was at hand, for Aëtius the Roman general, and the last defender of the empire, defeated them, A.D. 451, in a truly gigantic battle on the Catalaunian Plain, in the Champagne country. The slaughter was so terrible that the saying went abroad that the river ran high with the blood of 300,000 men.

But it was clear that the tottering empire could not defend itself against a whole world in commotion. The time had come when Rome was to leave the stage of history. The great German nation was forming. It would be tedious and profitless to mention all the German tribes beyond the Rhine and Danube, a well-nigh endless list of names, impossible to remember. Besides, the petty tribes and clans gradually formed alliances with each other for greater security, and, dropping their ancient names, took collective ones more familiar to our ears—Saxons, Franks, Thuringi, Burgundians, Alamanni, and Bavarians.

Of these the Alamanni and the Burgundians are those from whom the Swiss are descended, and thus Switzerland, like England, has to look back to Germany as its ancestral home. The tall, fair-haired, true-hearted Alamanni for whom Caracalla had such an admiration that to be like them he wore a red wig, are said to have been descendants of the Semnones, who had migrated from Lusatia on the Spree (in Silesia) to the Main. The name Alamanni is generally held by the learned to be derived from *alah*, a temple-grove, and implies a combination of various tribes, "the people of the Divine grove." The Suevi, of whom the Semnones were the most conspicuous tribe, had a sacred grove in the district of the Spree, where they met for worship. In the fifth century we find the Alamanni occupying the district from the Main to the Black Forest, East Helvetia, and Alsatia as far as the Vosges.

When this formidable horde took possession of Eastern Helvetia they found but little trouble from the Celto-Roman population, who, thinned by previous invasions, and unaccustomed to fighting, could offer no serious resistance, and sank into slaves and servants. The towns were laid in ruins, the country ravaged, and all culture trodden under foot. It seemed as if "the hand on the dial of history had been put back by centuries,"[1] and civilization had once more to begin her work. They outnumbered the natives, and were not absorbed by them, but on the contrary on the half-decayed stock of the Roman province the Alamanni were grafted as a true German people, retaining their old language, institutions, and mode of living.

The Alamanni did not at once develop into a civilized and cultivated people, but retained their fondness for war and hunting, and other characteristics of their ancient life. Their grand and majestic

[1] Green's "Smaller History of England," p. 42.

woods had stamped themselves on the intrepid, dauntless spirits, whose deep subjectiveness and truthful natures contrasts strongly with the polished artfulness of the Romans. For the mighty aspects of nature —forest, mountain, sea—play their part in moulding the character of a nation. And their impenetrable woods had influenced the destinies of the Germans in the early periods of their history—had saved them from the Roman yoke, the labyrinths of swamp and river, defying even the forces of the well-nigh all-powerful empire. Then, too, when hard fighting was afoot, and men had burnt their homesteads before the advance of the foe, the vast forest formed a safe retreat for women and children. The original house, by the way, was a mere wooden tent on four posts, and could be carried off on carts that fitted underneath. The next stage was a hut in the style of the Swiss mountain-shed, but it was still movable—was, in fact, a chattel the more to be taken along on their wanderings.[1]

Their mode of settling in their new country was curious enough, though the early settlement of England was very similar in character. Disliking walled towns of the Roman fashion, the Germans felt their freedom of movement impeded and their minds oppressed by living within the prison-like fortifications of strong cities. But loving seclusion and independence, nevertheless, they built extensive farmsteads, where each man was his own master. To the homestead were added fields, meadows, and an extensive farmyard; the whole hedged about so as

[1] Dahn, "Urgeschichte der Römanish-germanischen Völker."

to keep the owner aloof from his neighbours. Each farmer pitched his tent wherever "spring or mead, or sylvan wood tempted him," reports Tacitus. This liking for seclusion on the part of the Germans is well shown in the case of Zurich, for at one time the canton had three thousand farm homesteads, as against a hundred hamlets and twelve villages.

The mode of partitioning the land shows democratic features. It was divided amongst the community according to the size of families and herds of cattle, but one large plot was left for the common use. The large *Allmend*, or common, supplied wood for the community, and there, too, might feed every man's flocks and herds. The nobleman as such had no domains specially set apart for him, his position and privileges were honorary. He might be chosen as a high officer of a district, or even a duke, or leader of the army, in time of war. Payment for such services was unknown. Money was scarce, and indeed its use was mainly taught them by the Romans. Not only did flocks and herds form their chief wealth, but were the standard of value, each article being estimated as worth so much in cattle.

Society was from the very first sharply and clearly divided into two great classes—the landowners and the bondsmen—the "free and the unfree." The former class was again split into "lesser men," "middle men," and "first men," or Athelinge (Adelige), these last named being of noble blood, and owners of most land and the greatest number of slaves and cattle. The "unfree" were either *Hœrige* that belonged to the estate they tilled, and might be sold with it, or slaves who could call nothing their own, for whatever they saved fell to their lord at their death, if he so willed. A shire or large district was subdivided into hundreds. The whole of the free men met on some hallowed spot, under some sacred tree, with their priests and leaders. Here, besides performing religious exercises, they discussed war and peace, dispensed justice, chose their officers of state, and their leader if war was imminent. War and jurisdiction were the whole, or well-nigh the whole, of public life at that early stage. The popular assemblies, done away with by the feudal system, revived later on in the form of the famous " Landsgemeinde " of the forest district, which are still in use in some of the cantons. Blood money, or *wergild*, was exacted from wrong-doers as in Saxon times in England. The tariff drawn up for bodily injuries reveals the mercenary and brawling temper of a semi-civilized people.

At the time they settled in Switzerland the Alamanni were heathens, and worshipped nature-deities—in groves, near springs, or mountains—the names of some of which we still trace in the names of the days of the week. Their religion, which was that common to all Germany, reveals the German mind—full of reverie, deep thoughtfulness, and wild romantic fancy that leads to a tragical issue. Like most heathen people the Alamanni clothed their gods in their own flesh and blood. Woden and his attendant deities, shield-maidens—Freyr and Freya, the king and queen of the elves—dwarfs, giants, spirits—all these are well known to us, and are indeed the charm of the fairy tales of our youth. The bright spirits, the *Asen*, war against the spirit of darkness, the giants, and lose ground, for they have broken the treaties made with them. The Asen are the benevolent powers of nature, spring sunshine, and fertilizing rain, and live in bright palaces, in Walhalla, and receive the dead; the evil spirits are the sterile rock, the icy winter, the raging sea, the destructive fire. Thor destroys the rocks with his Hammer, pounding them to earth that man may grow corn. The giants scale the sky to defy the gods for assisting mankind, but Heimdallr stands watching on the rainbow-bridge that leads to Asgard—the garden of the *Asen*—and prevents their entrance. But the gods themselves are stained with guilt, and in a fight with the Giants before the gates of Walhalla, they utterly destroy each other. The columns of heaven and the rainbow-bridge break down, the universe is destroyed and the downfall of the gods is complete. But the heathen Germans could not bear the notion of entire annihilation, so in a sort of epilogue the great tragedy is followed by the dawn of brighter and better times, the gods recover their former innocence, when they used to play with golden dice without knowing the value of gold.[1] The *Götterdämmerung*, the Divine Dawn, has broken, and a new epoch has set in for gods and men. One of Wagner's musical dramas is, as is well known, founded on these myths.

To turn to the Burgundians. They became the neighbours of the Alamanni in Helvetia about 443 A.D., after a severe defeat by the Huns. This great battle

[1] Dahn.

is pictured with great power in the "Nibelungenlied." The Burgundians play a conspicuous part in that grand old epic. A wonderful blending it is of heroic myth, beautiful romance, and historic sagas attaching to the great heroes of the early Middle Ages—Theodoric the Great, Gunther of Burgundy, Attila, King of the Huns. If space permitted, the whole story might well be told, but in this place let one feat be cited as an example. Siegfried, the Dragon-slayer, a demigod, invulnerable, like Achilles, except in one place, and who could make himself invisible, woos the sweet and lovely maid of Worms. As "invisible champion," he assists her brother Gunther in his combat with the warlike Brunhilde, Queen of the North, whom Gunther wishes to obtain to wife. After years of happy married life the Queen of Worms fell to a quarrel with the Queen of Xanten on a question of precedence, and the gallant Siegfried falls a victim to Brunhilde's hatred, and her intrigue with Hagen. To avenge his death, the disconsolate widow marries the powerful Attila, and engages in a terrible battle with the Burgundians. In this battle she and her own kindred were slain. Attila and Dietrich of Verona (Theodoric the Great) are saved, however.

Aëtius gave to the Burgundians as a settlement Sabaudia (Savoy), on condition that they should protect Gaul and Italy from the incursions of the Alamanni. One-third of the lands and homesteads were made over to them by the Romans, and later two-thirds were yielded. Gradually the Burgundians advanced in the interior of Helvetia, Vaud, Valais,

EIGER IN THE BERNESE OBERLAND.

and Fribourg, and into Southern Gaul. They occupied indeed all the territory from the Vosges to the Alps and the Mediterranean. They lived on friendly terms with the previous settlers, differing considerably in character from the Alamanni. Less numerous, less vigorous, and more pliant, they were unable to Germanize the West, as the Alamanni did the East, yet were strong enough to infuse new vital force into the enervated Roman populations. A readily cultivable race the Burgundians availed themselves of the Roman civilization and advancement, and gradually blended with the previous settlers—chiefly of Latin origin— to form a new people. Thus through Roman influence and German grafting—with two distinct German grafts—two nationalities sprang up in Switzerland, and we find, as in our own day, the Germans in the north-east, and the French in the south-west.

The Roman influence over the Burgundians was greatly increased by the policy of King Gundobad (A.D. 500). He had visited Italy, and had been greatly taken with Roman institutions. There is still extant a letter of his in which he begs of Theodoric the Great a sun- or water-dial which he had seen at his Court. Gundobad's code of laws was a blending of Roman legislation with German jurisdiction. He introduced the Latin speech and chronology officially, and gave the Romans equal rights and an equal standing with the German population. Religious differences arising—the Burgundians were Arians—and conflicts ensuing between king and people, the Franks took advantage of the turmoils to bring the subjects of Gundobad under their sway.

There was no love lost between the Alamanni and their neighbours, the Burgundians; indeed the national antipathy for each other was great, but the Frankish domination did more than anything else towards bringing about a union between the hostile peoples. The reports they have left as to the character of the Franks are not flattering. They said that the Franks were capable of breaking an oath with a smiling face, and a saying ran, "Take a Frank for a friend, but never for a neighbour." Clovis, the Frankish king, had waded to the throne through the blood of his own kin. He was, however, the first to take more extended views in politics, and planned a united German kingdom after the type of the Roman Empire. To his vast scheme the Alamanni fell the first victims. A great battle was fought in which they suffered defeat. Clovis had vowed that he would embrace Christianity if he should prevail against the Alamannic Odin. Victory falling to his side, Clovis and his nobles were baptized. His conversion was a great triumph for the Church, and furnished the Merovingian kings with a pretext for the conquest of the Arian Germans, who had been led astray from the orthodox faith. To crown the work and enhance his greatness in the eyes of his Roman and German subjects, the imperial purple, and the title of Roman Patricius was bestowed on Clovis by the Greek emperor.

The subjection of Burgundy was brought about in the following reign, under Sigismund, who had been guilty of the murder of his son by the desire of the stepmother. He fled to St. Maurice, which he endowed so richly that it gave shelter to upwards of five hundred monks. However, his piety did not bring him victory, for the Burgundians were defeated by the Franks at Autun in 532, and Sigismund and his family were hurled down a well.

In the same year Chur-Rhætia was yielded to the Franks by the Goths, who required their help against the East. Rhætia, which had escaped the German invasion, had fallen to the share of the Goths of Italy, and had enjoyed the protection and munificence of their glorious king, Theodoric the Great. He defended her against her neighbours as a forepost of Italy, but left intact the Roman institutions.

Thus had Helvetia been formed into a Frankish dependency; not a vestige was left of the very name Helvetia. Yet the Frankish rule was more nominal than real. Counts were appointed to govern shires and hundreds, and, being royal governors, were elected by, and dependent on, the Frankish kings. Jurisdiction, military command, summoning to war, raising of taxes — fishing, hunting, coinage, had become royal prerogatives—and the farmers kicked against the impositions—these were the functions of the governing counts. None the less the Burgundians retained their king or patricius, and the Alamanni remained under the sway of their own duke, to whom alone they gave allegiance. Chur-Rhætia was particularly privileged. It was ruled by a royal governor, who was supreme judge, count, and *præses*, and the dignity remained for one hundred and fifty years in one powerful and wealthy native family called the Victoriden, who held likewise the ecclesiastical livings. On its extinction in 766, Bishop Tello, the last of the family, bestowed the immense wealth on the religious-houses of Disentis and Chur.

The promotion of Christianity, and the staunch support given by the Merovingian kings to the Church, were perhaps the greatest benefits resulting from the Frankish rule. Knowing the Church to be the sole means by which in that benighted age culture could be spread and civilization extended, those monarchs availed themselves of her services, and bestowed upon her in return great wealth and high prerogatives. Churches and religious-houses sprang up one could hardly tell how. In French Switzerland there were founded the bishoprics of Geneva, Lausanne, and Sion; and in the eastern half of the country those of Basel, Vindonissa (removed to Constance in the sixth century), and Chur. St. Maurice, benefited, as we have seen, by Sigismund, was a flourishing abbey town. Yet many of the Alamanni held tenaciously to their old gods, and their holy shrines and idols stood side by side with the Cross; even Christians invoked Woden, for fear he should be offended by their neglect.

The further amalgamation of heathenism and Christianity was most effectually stopped by—curious to say—a caravan of Irish monks. In fact, later tradition attributed to these monks the foundation of religious-houses, to a number which modern investigation has shown to have been greatly exaggerated. Ireland, which had so far escaped the struggle with the great Teutonic race, had given all her energies to the promotion of the new faith, and ever since the fourth century Christianity had wonderfully flourished in the island. Filled with missionary ardour, the Irish Columban conceived an intense desire to conquer Gaul and Germany, and in 610 set out on his wanderings with a staff of twelve companions. Equipped with "knotty sticks," a leather vial, a travelling pouch, a relic case, and with a spare pair of boots hung round the neck, "tatooed," wearing long waving hair,[1] the adventurous band arrived in Gaul, and founded monasteries in the Vosges district. However, they offended Queen Brunhilde by their frankness, and had to depart. Proceeding to Eastern Helvetia, they arrived at Zurich, but at length finding nothing more to do there, as we may suppose, they proceeded to Tuggen, on the Upper Zurich lake. Here they saw people engaged in an oblation of beer to the national gods. Moved with holy anger, the monks upset the vessel, and flung the idols into the lake, and won many to Christianity. We cannot here follow them in their devoted labours. Columban passed on into Italy, but left his disciple Gallus in the neighbourhood of Lake Constance. Hence sprang up the famous monastery bearing his name.

[1] Professor Rahn.

V.

THE CAROLINGIANS—CHARLEMAGNE.

UNDER the last Merovingian kings, whose character is sufficiently attested by the name of *Fainéants*—sluggards—Alamannia and Burgundy struggled to shake off the Frankish yoke. Now the wealth and power of those weak kings were passing from them to their "Mayors of the Palace." Charles Martel, one of these "Mayors," defeated the Alamanni in a great battle (A.D. 730), and Carlomann, Charlemagne's brother, had a number of Alamannic grandees put to the sword, and their lands confiscated (A.D. 746).

Charles Martel remained simple "Mayor of the Palace," but Pepin le Bref had himself crowned king, at St. Denis, by Stephen II., in 751, rewarding the Pope for this great service by the gift of a tract of land around the Holy City. By this *coup d'état* were established both the Carolingian dynasty and the temporal power of the Pope—well-nigh convertible terms. The new dynasty greatly fostered religion, and furthered the work begun by the Irish and Anglo-Saxon monks. St. Gall's cell became an abbey church and monastic school; St. Leodegar's at Lucerne was incorporated with the abbey of Murbach in Alsatia; and on the bank of the Limmat at Zurich arose a college of prebends.

Pepin le Bref was succeeded by his son, Charles the Great, or Charlemagne, as he is usually called (768-814). For nearly half a century this talented, powerful, and lofty-minded sovereign swayed the destinies of Europe with unflagging zeal, ever bearing in mind the responsibilities of his exalted position. He ruled over a vast domain, stretching from the Ebro in Spain to the Theiss in Hungary, and from Denmark to the Tiber. Saxons, Sclavonians, Avars, Lombards, and Arabs, were subject to his rule. His Court was a great intellectual centre, whence enlightenment spread to every part of his dominions. Charlemagne was great as a general, as a statesman, as a politician; he was a painstaking economist, and his humanity, and his other virtues secured for him the noble title of "Father of Europe." A brilliant figure in a benighted age, which shed its light on after times. No wonder mediæval fancy lingered fondly on his memory; and around his name gathered song and saga and legend. Charlemagne is a special favourite with the Swiss; indeed, of all the German rulers who have held sway over them, he is the one whose memory is most dear; and Switzerland has done at least her share in helping to swell the mass of legend and fiction respecting him. The impulse he gave to education in this country was alone sufficient to endear his memory to the Swiss. Basel, Geneva, Chur, and Sion, benefited by his wise administration, and Zurich quite particularly exalts him, calling him the "Fountain of her intellectual life," during the Middle Ages. It is impossible as it is unnecessary to give at length in this volume, the history of this long and brilliant reign. A few points may suffice to indicate the character of Charlemagne, and to throw some light on the times, and the condition of the country.

The ambition of the Franks to found an empire after the fashion of Rome was practically realized when Charlemagne was crowned Emperor of the West by Hadrian in A.D. 800. Yet Charles aimed less at mere outward grandeur than at the establishment of a spiritual kingdom on earth, and a kingdom that should embrace all his people in one Christian Church, upheld by a strong and well-organized state-commonwealth. The union of Church and State, yet giving the preponderance to the latter, was Charlemagne's leading idea, and well-nigh summed up his religious and political creed. The strong religious bent of this "priestly king" was revealed at the very beginning of his reign, when he took upon himself the mission of "Defender of the Holy Church, and *Coadjutor of the Apostolic See*,"[1] thus claiming, with the concurrence of the Primate, the spiritual guidance of his realm. Hadrian's congenial nature and tendencies helped to bring about this union. Yet in this matter Charles but conformed to the policy of his ancestors, and to the spirit of the age, an age remarkable for acts of piety and devotion.

[1] See Büdinger, "Von den Anfangen des Schulzwanges," Zurich, 1865, p. 10.

And the history of Switzerland is for that period rather a history of the religious movements of the time than a political chronicle. For in those early stages the Church was proportionally far more important than in our own times. *Then* she was the sole, or almost the sole, centre of intellect, of art, of letters, and represented the ideal side of life in an illiterate age. Despite her defects the Church was a blessing to mankind.

Helvetian lands had entirely lost their political independence. During this reign, the vigorous government of the monarch frustrated every attempt at insurrection, and in the end both Alamanni and Burgundians began to feel the benefits arising from the existence of a wise and firm administration. To curb their power the sovereign abolished the dignities of the mighty dukes, and parcelled out the land into smaller shires (than the old county divisions), and placed over these counts as royal governors with judicial power. The people no longer appeared *in corpore* at the shire-motes, but were represented at the lesser court by *Schœffen*, or reeves. These reeves had to bring in the verdict; if they could not agree, trial-by-ordeal was resorted to. Twice a year Charles assembled his nobles and bishops to receive their reports, and to frame laws, which were, however, submitted to the people, that is, the "freeholders" at the "real thing," when they met in May. For the control of the shire administration, and to give the people a means of appealing more directly to the king's justice, he appointed a special commission of spiritual and temporal officers (*missi dominici*).

Charlemagne's legislation, it hardly needs to be said, was highly favourable to the Church, and tended to increase her wealth largely. He allotted to her tithes of the produce of the soil, and the people of their own free will overwhelmed the ecclesiastical and monastic institutions with offerings of lands and money. In the eighth century the monastery of St. Gall already possessed 160,000 acres of land, which had been bestowed by pious donors, whilst the twelve hundred deeds-of-gift found amongst the old abbey documents testify to the zeal of the givers. Religious establishments became the largest landowners in the country, and vassalage and the feudal system sprang up.

Under the territorial subdivision Switzerland fell into the shires of Thurgau, Aargau, Genevagau, Waldgau (Vaud), &c., far larger than at present, whence are derived the names of various cantons as we have them now. Some of the Swiss would seem to have shared in Charlemagne's military glory. The "Monk of St. Gall,"[1] recently identified with Notker Balbulus (the Stammerer), the popular biographer of Charlemagne, tells in bombastic style the feats of an Alamannic hero from Thurgau. This mediæval Hercules—Eishere the Giant by name—had accompanied the emperor against the Avars, and after his return, reported that they had "mowed down the enemy like grass," and that he himself had "strung on his lance some six or eight pigmy toads of Bohemians as if they were larks, then carried them

---

[1] Professor Bächtold, "History of German Literature in Switzerland," Frauenfeld, 1887.

hither and thither, not knowing what they were grumbling out"! Notker, the chronicler, had in his youth heard the story of the military exploits of Charlemagne, from an old Thurgau soldier who had followed the emperor in his wars. And when Charles III. was on a visit to St. Gall in 883, he was so delighted with the monk's lively chat about the matchless emperor, that he requested him to write down his recollections of his illustrious ancestor. To this monkish chronicler we owe so many of the pleasant stories of Charlemagne current among us.[1]

Interesting and touching are the traits we constantly meet with in the glimpses we get of the Court and private life of the emperor. His daughters were not allowed to marry because he could not bear separation from them. Hatto of Basel, the most illustrious of his elder bishops, often inveighed against the monarch's weaknesses, yet Charlemagne not only bore the bishop's censures, but sent him on a highly honourable mission to the Court of Constantinople, and chose him as one of the witnesses to his last will. The emperor's friendship with Pope Hadrian was quite remarkable, and, in spite of many differences, was deep and lasting. On hearing the news of Hadrian's death, Charlemagne burst into tears, and eulogized him in the most flattering terms. The emperor's management of his royal estates was in the highest degree prudent, skilful, energetic, and in every way admirable. To his property he gave the

[1] Professor Bächtold, "History of German Literature in Switzerland," Frauenfeld, 1887.

closest and most constant inspection, down to the very eggs produced on his farms.

He gathered round him scholars, artists, and teachers, from Italy and Greece, and a Court school was opened by Alcuin, the Anglo-Saxon scholar—the English were then the most cultured of the German peoples—and a body of English pupils followed him to France. Alcuin became the friend, and in matters educational the counsellor, of Charlemagne, by whom he was entrusted with the revision of the Bible. Warnfried Paulus Diaconus, the famous Lombard writer, was ordered to compile a collection of homilies from the Fathers. Copies of both these remarkable manuscripts — Bible and Homilies—were presented to the church of Zurich, and one, the beautiful Alcuin Bible, is still extant and among its literary treasures. Thronging the learned circle whose poetic centre was Charles himself, with his wife and daughters, and two sisters, were Einhard the German, the confidant and biographer of the emperor; Augilhard, the knightly poet; the Goth Theobald, Bishop of Orleans, a scholar and man of the world; as well as many another illustrious man. Charlemagne's two sisters were nuns, and one of them, Gisela, was the great friend of Alcuin.[1]

Charlemagne was fond of visiting and occasionally teaching in his Court school. He took great interest in the progress of his scholars, praising the diligent and admonishing the indolent. The "Monk" informs us that on one occasion finding the compositions of the poorer boys praiseworthy, whilst those of the

[1] See Gustav Freytag's charming "Pictures of the Middle Ages."

young nobles were unsatisfactory, the emperor rose up in anger and warned these latter youths that their high birth and fine manners should not screen them from punishment if they did not get rid of their laziness. Then, turning to the poor but meritorious youths, he highly commended them, and exhorted them to be always thus diligent, promising them rewards and preferment if they continued in their good course. Charlemagne indeed gained imperishable glory by his educational efforts, through which a foundation was laid for after ages. Full of the conviction that religion and learning were essential to happiness, he yearned to spread education amongst his people, and made it the chief object of his later years. All parents ought, he says, "to send their boys to school, and let them abide there till they are well informed," a principle only imperfectly understood and acted upon even in our own day. This ideal side of his complex activity lifts him far above the other rulers of the Middle Ages. To our mind there is but one who bears comparison with him for greatness of character and lofty aims—Alfred the Great, of Wessex. Clerical colleges, and secular schools attached to them, sprang up all over the country, and the knowledge of the Scriptures, hitherto confined to the clergy, was freely placed before the people.

The bishops were charged by the emperor to take care that the priests were "well qualified as religious teachers." Theobald enjoins his clergy to open schools and "teach the children with love, and to accept no fees but what the parents choose to give."

Such was the emperor's educational zeal, that he ordains whipping and deprivation of food even for men and women if they do not know by heart the Confession of Faith and the Lord's Prayer, and are not able to repeat them in Latin to the priests. Yet he makes allowances for the dunces who are permitted to learn and repeat these exercises in their own illiterate language. He admonishes the monks to learn better grammar, and get rid of their uncouth modes of speech. He strongly reprimands a choir-boy whose wrong notes grate on his delicate ear.

Amongst the bishops of Switzerland, Hatto of Basel, and Remedius of Chur-Rhætia, were Charlemagne's chief supporters and lawgivers in their own dioceses. The latter prelate was a great friend of Alcuin, and held a brilliant Court with many vassals. The power of these theocratic governors was very great. It may be mentioned, as an example of this, that Remedius decreed that persons guilty of sacrilege should be covered with hot tar and made to ride thus on a donkey through the villages. The emperor's protection to church and school foundations was exercised in many cases in Switzerland. According to tradition, Sion was enriched with landed property; and to St. Maurice was presented a fine onyx cup adorned with beautiful Greek *relievi*, still amongst the treasures of that church. Zurich attributes her oldest churches and schools to the emperor's bounty. To him she is said to owe her minster, bearing his name and statue; the Chorherrenstift, or College of Canons, and the Carolinum, a clerical school for prebends or canons, which developed in 1832 into the

GREAT MINSTER AND WASSERKIRCHE, ZURICH.
(*Appenzeller, Zurich.*)

University and Gymnasium respectively, and finally the Wasserkirche, a chapel by the riverside, on the spot where the martyrs Felix and Regula once suffered.

Zurich was indeed, according to tradition, a favourite residence of the great monarch, and his mansion is said to have been the Haus zum Loch (hole or cavern), standing on a steep incline near the minster. Connected with this is a charming legend which reflects the character for justice he had gained amongst the people. This story may also serve as an example, the only one our space will permit us to give, of the abundant store of legend collected around the memory of Charlemagne. There was a chapel on the riverside where he had placed a bell for people to ring if they wished to appeal to justice. One day as he was at dinner with his queen this bell began to ring. None of the servants could inform him what was the matter. The bell rang a second time, and then a third. On this the emperor rose from the table, saying, "I am sure there is some poor man you don't wish me to see." So saying, he walked down the hill to the chapel, where, hanging to the bell rope, he found a large snake. The reptile crept down, moved towards him, and wagged her tail to pay her respects. Then going on in front she led Charlemagne to a tuft of nettles, and his servants examining the spot found a large toad sitting on the eggs in the serpent's nest. At once, grasping the meaning of this appeal, he sat him down in his chair of justice and passed sentence that the toad should be killed and quartered. The next day at dinner time the snake appeared in the passage, frightening the attendants grievously. However, Charles quieted them, and said, "God is wonderful, and we cannot know the meaning of this." The snake entered the hall, climbed on the table, and, beckoning the emperor to remove the lid of his golden goblet, dropped into it a beautiful jewel. Then, descending from the table, she bowed to the royal couple, and disappeared. Charles held this to be a good omen, and resolved never to part with the jewel. The moral is obvious. Charlemagne was so just, and his reputation for equity so widespread, that even the lower animals appealed to him, and not in vain.

According to another version, the stone exerted attraction like a loadstone, for where it was dropped the emperor could not leave the place. But Archbishop Turpin had dropped it into the springs of Aachen, and hence Charlemagne no more quitted that royal residence.

It would be impossible in our space, even if it were interesting to the general reader, to enter into the discussions respecting Charlemagne's foundations in and visits to Zurich. Two things, however, come out clearly; first (thanks to the labours of the learned historian, Professor Georg von Wyss), that tradition is not entirely unworthy of trust, as there is documentary evidence still extant to prove that Charlemagne reformed the College (Chorherrenstift); second, that he kept up a close connection with the city, whether he actually resided there or not.

No doubt this exaltation of Charlemagne's merits is an expression of the attachment felt for his person, and of the admiration for his marvellous educational efforts. His grandson, Louis the German, founded the Abbey of our Lady, in 853, on the site of an old convent erected to the memory of the patron saints of Zurich. Louis erected this new abbey in order to give a more brilliant church preferment to his daughter, Hildgard, Lady Principal of a small convent at Wurzburg. This Princess Abbess received the sole right of jurisdiction, and the convent rose rapidly, and with it extended the city commonwealth. (We shall show in a later chapter how this female government checked the growth of political power in that city, and yet was the making of her.)

VI.

THE KINGDOM OF BURGUNDY; THE DUCHY OF SWABIA; AND THE GERMAN EMPIRE.

(843–1100.)

THE death of the great emperor brought this realm into utter confusion, the whole fabric of his wise and firm administration falling to pieces. All the heterogeneous and often refractory elements which his stern rule had kept in check burst their bounds and gained full play during the reigns of his descendants, who grew weaker and weaker, though with here and there an exception. The pretensions of the Church, which Charlemagne's own protection and fostering care had, so to speak, ushered in and strengthened; the struggles of eminent families and dynastic houses for sovereignty in the absence of one central and undisputed power; the increase of the immunities and the growth of feudalism—all these were serious difficulties for the coming rulers to cope with.

Louis the Pious, the only surviving son of Charlemagne, and heir to his crown, was clearly quite unfit to cope with these difficulties satisfactorily. The untimely distribution of the crown lands insisted on by the imperious Judith, his second wife, in favour of her own son, and the protracted struggles between the imperial princes, steeped the realm in intestine wars, and in the end led to its dissolution. It is impossible in this short sketch to follow to his tragical end this unworthy son of a great father. The treaty of Verdun (843) settled the bloody conflicts, but split the empire into three new dominions; the East Frankish realm devolving on Louis the German: the West Frankish kingdom falling to Charles the Bald; and the middle district, including Italy and the strip of land between the two first divisions just mentioned, and comprising Provence, Burgundy, Lorraine, and the Netherlands. This last realm fell to Lothair.

The treaty of Verdun, to which the French and German States trace their origin, also effected the most sweeping changes in Helvetia, and altered greatly its political aspect. The country was rent into two halves, East Switzerland, forming the Aare, with Chur-Rhætia, being incorporated with the East Frankish kingdom; and West Helvetia and the Valais with Lorraine or the middle kingdom. This naturally tended to revive the national antagonism between the two Helvetias.

Freed from the iron hand which had crushed all attempts at insurrection, the peoples began again their struggles for the recovery of national independence and separate rule, and thence came the restoration of the kingdom of Burgundy and the Duchy of

Alamannia, or Swabia.[1] Burgundy was the first to make sure of her national freedom. On the death of Lothair in 855 his kingdom fell to pieces. Count Boso, of Vienna, his relative, founded the kingdom of Burgundy *without* Helvetia, 879 (Provence or Arles— *Arelatisches Reich*). After fruitless attempts by various Burgundian nobles to establish their sovereignty *within* Helvetia, a renowned nobleman, Rudolf, of the illustrious house of the Guelfs, set up as a pretender to Swiss Burgundy, after the precedent of Count Boso. Rudolf possessed vast estates in Swabia, on Lake Constance. He had sworn allegiance to Charles III. (the " Stout "), who, weak as he was, had, strange to say, once more united the Empire under his sceptre. On his death, in 888, Rudolf the Guelf was crowned king at St. Maurice, the venerable abbey-town in the Low-Valais, by a large assembly of Burgundian bishops and nobles. Thus was established the Helvetian kingdom of Upper or New Burgundy (*Burgundia transjurans*), which seems to have extended into Lorraine and Savoy. In 933 both Burgundies were united.

Rudolf not only maintained his independence against the aggressive spirit of intruding neighbours, but carried his victories into East Helvetia, as far as Lake Zurich, and on his death in 912 his crown passed without opposition to his son Rudolf II. This king had inherited his father's great abilities and restless habits, which engaged him in numerous wars.

[1] It is perhaps preferable to use the word *Swabia* instead of *Alamannia* so often. Freeman in his essay on the Holy Empire speaks of the Swabian Emperors, the Hohenstaufen.

His greatest martial achievement was the defeat of the Hungarians, who were making their fearful inroads into Europe. In East Helvetia, however, his advance was checked by Burkhard I., Duke of Alamannia, who routed him at Winterthur, near Zurich, in 919. Led no doubt by their mutual admiration for each other's prowess, and by common political interests, they made peace and contracted a lasting friendship. To seal the union between the two Helvetias, Burkhard gave his lovely daughter, Bertha, in marriage to the Burgundian king, and gave her as dowry the land between the Aare and the Reuss, the district for which he had been contending. He even followed Rudolf on his expedition to Italy, and fell in a skirmish whilst succouring his son-in-law. But Rudolf was unable to maintain the authority of his Italian crown, and exchanged his claim to Lombardy for the kingdom of Lower Burgundy (Provence) in 933; this arrangement was, however, much contested.

When not engaged in wars he assisted his queen in her good works. The Burgundian kings as yet had no fixed residence, and moved from place to place on their royal estates—to Lausanne, Payerne, Yverdon, Solothurn, or Lake Thun. When making these rounds Rudolf loved to do as the judges of Israel of old—to seat himself under the shade of a fine oak and deal out justice to whoever might come near and appeal to him. Yet the memory of this good king is almost eclipsed by the glory of his wife, the famous "Spinning Queen," and her wisdom and ministry amongst the poor.

Things went less pleasantly with the Alamanni.

Their efforts to restore separate or self-government—the passionate yearning for national independence innate in the German tribes has done much to bring about the division of the German Empire into its many kingdoms, principalities, and duchies—met with far steadier and more violent opposition than was the case with the Burgundians.

Under the pacific rule of Louis the German (843-876) the Alamanni enjoyed the benefits of his peaceful tendencies, and we hear of no attempts at insurrection. This sensible and practical monarch left to East Helvetia the " remembrance of him in good works." Two things brought him into close relations with this country—his founding of the Abbey of our Lady at Zurich, where he installed his daughters Hildegard and Bertha, as has been stated before; and his benefactions to St. Gall, which he freed from the overlordship of Constance. Indeed, the chronicler of this latter institution, Notker, *Monachus S. Gallensis*, would seem to have been fascinated by his personal charms and affable manners. Promoted to the position of an independent abbey, owing allegiance to none but the king himself, and enriched by continual grants of land on the part of pious donors, St. Gall developed into a flourishing monastic commonwealth. The peaceful colony of thrifty and studious monks— Benedictines they were—who, like their Irish founder, combined manual labour with learned contemplation, earnest study, and literary skill—form a society quite unique in its way. The holy men " conjure into their cells the departed spirits of classical antiquity,"[1] and

[1] Dierauer.

hold free intercourse with them; given to ecclesiastical learning, whilst not neglectful of profane studies, these learned and high-bred scholars constitute a truly mediæval university. Their life and character is vividly set before us by their chroniclers.

Arnulf of Kaernthen (887–899), grandson of Louis, kept up a close connection with St. Gall, through his chaplain, Solomon III., its abbot. He governed the East Frankish kingdom with firmness and great ability. The military glory of the Carolingians seemed to be restored when he defeated the Normans brilliantly at Lœwen on the river Dyle. Unfortunately this vigorous ruler died after a short reign, leaving his crown to his only son, Louis "the Child," then only six years of age. Through the reign of this sickly prince (900–911) the country was torn by party struggles, and the invasions of the Hungarians increased the distresses of the time. Contemporary writers seem hardly able to express the horror they felt at the very sight of the Asiatics, who appeared even loathsome to them. Arnulf was reproached with having launched them upon Europe when he led them against his enemies, the Mæhren; whilst Charlemagne's policy had been altogether opposed to this, he having shut them in by raising gigantic walls on the Danube against the Avars. These were followers of the Huns of the fifth century, and resembled them by their savage warfare and indescribable habits.

"Woe to the realm whose king is a child," writes Solomon III. to a befriended bishop; "all are at variance, count and vassals, shire and boundary neighbours; the towns rise in rebellion, the laws are trampled under foot, and we are at the mercy of the savage hordes." Such was the condition of the country at the opening of the tenth century. Solomon, who wrote these lamentations, was himself a powerful political ruler no less than a Church potentate. Next to Archbishop Hatto, of Mayence, who governed during the minority of Louis, Solomon was the most influential man at the German Court, and wielded its destinies after Hatto's death. This high-born Churchman, educated as a secular priest at St. Gall, became secretary, chaplain, and chancellor, at the German Court, and enjoyed the friendship of four successive monarchs. Promoted by Arnulf to the Abbey of St. Gall in 890, and shortly afterwards to the see of Constance, he thus combined the dignities of the two rival institutions. Subtle, versatile, and indefatigable, this high ecclesiastic was the most consummate courtier and man of the world. Handsome and magnificent, he captivated his hearers in the council by the clearness of his argument and his ready wit; and melted the people to tears by his eloquence in the pulpit. His leadership at St. Gall promoted the magnificence of the abbey, and formed it into a prominent literary and political centre. It was, however, robbed of its ascetic character, Solomon being wanting in genuine piety, for one thing.

The absolute rule of this powerful prelate greatly checked the national risings of the Swabian leaders, for he strenuously maintained the oneness of Church and State. Conrad I. (911–919), the last of the East Frankish kings, gave all his energies to the one aim of strengthening and solidifying his rule by the suppression or abolition of the dukedoms, which he saw undermined the power of the sovereign. Relying on the support of the clergy, he was strongly influenced by Solomon's insinuations when he put forth his bloody measures against the Swabian pretenders.

During the reign of Louis the Child the state of anarchy had begotten numerous national risings, which led to the establishment of the Bavarian, Frankish, and Saxon duchies. At its very close a similar attempt was ventured upon in Alamannia. Burkhard, Marquis of Chur-Rhætia, afterwards Graubünden, one of the most eminent of the Swabian grandees, put forward claims to the duchy. His sons were banished, and, it was whispered, by Solomon's machinations (911). Yet all this was no check on the aspirations of the two brothers, Erchanger and Bertold, brothers-in-law to the king, who aspired to the Duchy of Swabia. They, too, fell victims to the policy of the prelate, whose hatred was intensified when they laid hands on his person to arrest him. Conrad called a Synod to assist him, and heavy punishment was awarded the pretenders. However, the king had them beheaded, no doubt to please his chancellor.

The cruel fate of the two made a deep impression on the people. Next year, when Burkhard, son of the unfortunate marquis, returned to his country whence he had fled—for he had joined in the rising of the two brothers, and had been summoned before the Synod—he was unanimously elected by the nobility and people (917). It was no small mortifi-

THE FURKA PASS.

cation to both king and bishop to have their designs thus thwarted, the principle they had so vigorously opposed being carried out. The annals of St. Gall bear witness to the fact that Solomon was implicated in the murders, for though usually exalting his merits, they report that the mighty prelate repented of his cruel actions, since he wandered as a pilgrim to Rome, contrite, weeping and lamenting, to do penance for his sins.

Conrad I., at the close of his reign, acknowledged that his policy had been a mistaken one by giving the crown to his most powerful antagonist, the Saxon leader, Duke Henry, whose power he had striven to abrogate. Henry I., called "the Fowler" and the "City Founder" (919–936), was the first German ruler who erected a true German kingdom. With quick discernment he founded the authority of the Crown on the union of the tribes, by reconciling their leaders and enforcing their submission through the ascendency of his own powerful Saxon tribe. Binding them by oath of fealty without detracting from their honour, he met with no opposition. His son, Otho I., the "Great," obtained the imperial crown in Rome, and increased the greatness of his new kingdom. Thus we find East Helvetia with Chur-Rhætia forming part of Alamannia, and presently the whole country was absorbed into, and its destinies bound up with, the vast empire.

Burkhard I., assuming the title of "Duke of Alamannia by Divine Right," bent to Henry's royal supremacy with little objection, no doubt feeling it a safeguard to his own position. His successors likewise held to Germany, and were faithful adherents of the emperors, who in their turn strove to knit Swabia more closely with the empire. This alliance was highly valued by them; they had to pass through Chur-Rhætia on their expeditions to Italy; the Alamanni were famous for their prowess; and their religious institutions, St. Gall, Rheinau, and Reichenau, were famous centres of culture. Swabia became a highly valuable fief to be granted at the pleasure of the emperors. On the death of Burkhard, who fell in a skirmish whilst accompanying his son-in-law, Rudolf of Burgundy, to the south, as we have seen above, the duchy devolved on the son of Otho I., and then on Burkhard II. of Chur-Rhætia. He never swerved from his policy of holding to the empire, and his marriage with Otho's niece, whose beauty and courage and literary skill were celebrated in ballad and chronicle, drew the union still closer. On her husband's death, Hadwig inherited the title and his estates, but the duchy was granted to a friend of Otho II. She retired to her favourite residence, her manor on Mount Hohentwiel, near Lake Constance, where she lived in deep seclusion till her death in 994. A good Greek scholar and fond of learning, she invited young Ekkehard II. of St. Gall to her castle, and made him her chaplain and her tutor in classical studies. Hadwig is the central figure in Scheffel's brilliant novel "Ekkehard," which glows with life and sparkling humour, and is a fanciful rendering of the amusing narratives contained in the St. Gall annals. The chronicler and the poet combining have produced an immortal work, and shed a lasting glory on the cloisters of St. Gall.

Another famous monastic institution that sprung up about this time, *i.e.*, under the Saxon emperor Otto, and obtained, like Loretto, European fame as a place of pilgrimage, was that of Einsiedeln, in Canton Schwyz.

In 1024 the Duchy of Swabia was vested in Ernest II., stepson of the Emperor Conrad II. of the Salic dynasty. A fierce struggle arose on the question of the succession to the Burgundian throne. Ernest claimed through his mother, and Conrad through his wife, niece to Rudolf III. Seeing his hopes frustrated Ernest, with his friend Werner of Kyburg, and his party, fell upon the imperial troops, and bloody frays occurred. Ernest was imprisoned, and the manor of Kyburg besieged; but both friends escaped, and again combined in new opposition to Conrad. In order to break their union, the emperor promised his son installation in Burgundy if he would deliver up his friend. But this was indignantly refused, the struggle began anew, and the gallant youths fell in a skirmish in 1030. Ernest was long a chief figure in mediæval heroic poetry.

GENEALOGICAL TABLES.

I. The Carlowingians (so far as they concern this history).

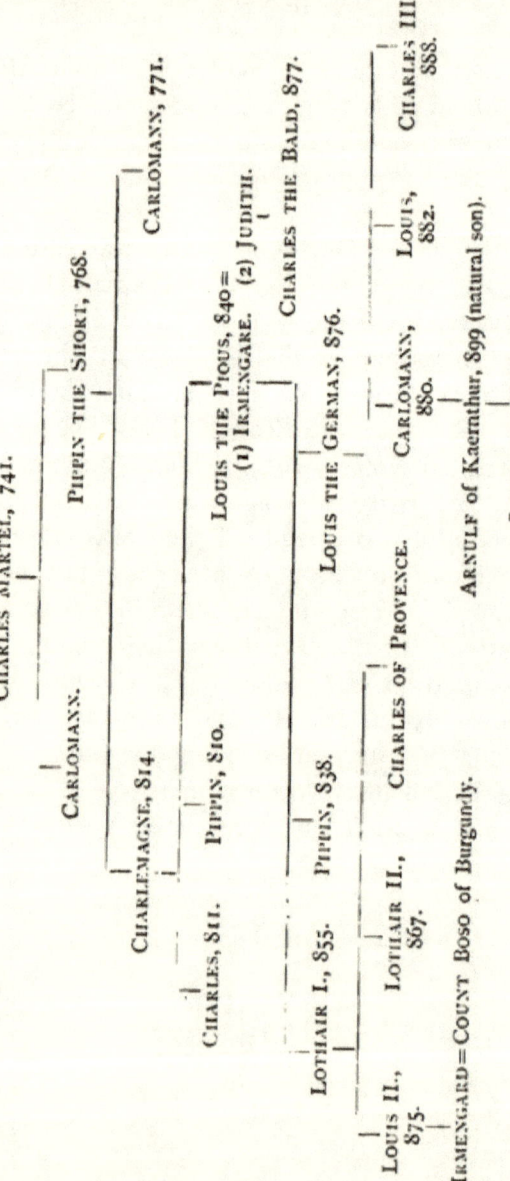

GENEALOGICAL TABLES.

II. Descent of the Saxon Emperors.

Lindolf (made Duke of part of Savoy by Louis the German).

Duke Otto, 912.

Henry I., 936 (the "Fowler").

┌──────────────┴──────────────┐
Otto I., 973 (the "Great").   Henry of Bavaria.

┌────────┬────────┤   Henry the Quarrelsome (of Bavaria), 995.
Lindolf, Duke of Swabia. Lintgarde. Otto II., Emperor, 983.
                                      Otto II., Emperor, 1002.   Henry II., Emperor, 1024.

III. Salic (Frankish) Emperors.

Conrad II., 1038 (great grandson of Lintgarde).

Henry III., 1038-1056.

Henry IV., 1056-1106.

Henry V., 1106-1125.

(The Hohenstaufen follow.)

VII.

BURGUNDY AND SWABIA UNDER THE GERMAN EMPERORS.

To return to the kingdom of Burgundy. Rudolf had greatly extended his dominions; in 919 he added to them the land between the Aare and the Reuss, and in 933 Lower Burgundy, which he had obtained in exchange for the Italian crown. The kingdom now comprised West Switzerland, Provence, Dauphiné, and Franche Comté. During the king's absence on military expeditions, and during the minority of Conrad, Bertha, the "Spinning Queen," held the reins of government. She is represented on the seal of the document founding the convent of Payerne—one of her authenticated foundations—with the spinning wheel, and the words *Bertha humilis regina* below. This Alpine queen, called by the French Swiss the "Mother of their liberties," was a model of industry and economy. Like Charlemagne, she was an excellent housekeeper, and even knew how many eggs had been laid on her estates. Humble in bearing, yet firm and strong, this lady fortified the country against the invasions of the Hungarians and Saracens. The gap between the Alps and Mount Jura was strengthened by a line of towers still to be seen, though crumbling from age, at Neuchâtel, La Molière, Moudon, Gourze. These towers were almost inaccessible, and possessed thick walls, narrow windows, and doors which, being ten feet above the ground, could only be got at by means of ladders. At the first signal of alarm, seigneur and peasantry hurried to these strongholds carrying with them whatever they were able; when they had entered, the ladders were drawn in, and there the people remained till the wild hurricane of savagery had blown over. Gradually the Burgundians rallied as regular troops to meet the hordes in open battle.

Herself always busy, Bertha hated idleness, and wherever she went she was to be found spinning, even on the road. Who has not heard of the humble and graceful queen, riding on her palfrey, spindle in hand, going from house to house, visiting castle, convent, farm, homestead, and hut, doing deeds of piety and benevolence? Once, when the Queen of Payerne, as she was often called, was on her circuits of inspection she met with a peasant girl keeping her flocks, and spinning. Delighted with the girl's industry, she gave her a handsome present. Next day all the ladies of her suite appeared before her with spindles in their hands. Smiling at the sight, she said, "My ladies, the young peasant girl, like Jacob, has been the first to receive the blessing." Space will not allow us to dwell longer on the memory of the "Spinning Queen" which is most dear to the French Swiss. It should be added, however, that the Burgundian traditions respecting this queen are doubtless mixed with mythological elements. In the German religious myths, Bertha (*Berchta, Perahta,*) means what is bright and pure and orderly: she is the Goddess of Fertility, and the Mother of the Earth, and bestows rich blessings on mankind.

On the death of his father, which had left him a mere child, Bertha's son Conrad had been educated at the Court of Otho the Great. Fearing that Burgundy might become the prey of aggressive neighbours, the emperor stepped in and made himself protector of the queen, and tutor to the children, and naturally exerted much influence on the country. Conrad, coming of age, ruled wisely, and for more than half a century (937-993), Burgundy flourished. His beautiful sister Adelheid was first Queen of Italy, but after Lothair's untimely death, became Empress of Germany, Otho I. wishing to unite Italy with his own empire, making her his wife.

The reign of Rudolf III. (993-1032) was greatly harmful to the country, which was fast declining in prestige and prosperity. Better fitted for the cloister than for the throne, he lavished his wealth and estates on the clergy, with the view of enlisting their help against the encroaching feudal vassals. In the end, indeed, he was so reduced that he was compelled to live on alms from his priests. His own incapacities drove him to seek protection from the empire. Having no children, he appointed his nephew, the Emperor Henry II., heir to his kingdom, and even during his own lifetime he arranged to give up the reigns of government to Henry. The opposition of the Burgundian nobles and the emperor's death prevented this shameful arrangement from actually coming into force. The next emperor, Conrad II., prosecuted the claim against his stepson, Ernest II., as has been told above, and was crowned king at the Cluniacensian convent, founded by Bertha at Payerne, (1033). His elevation to the Burgundian throne was confirmed in the following year by a brilliant assembly of Burgundian, German, and Italian bishops and nobles, at Geneva. Shortly before his death in 1038, he had his son Henry installed in the kingdom, and the oath of fealty to him was taken by the Burgundian nobles at the Diet of Solothurn. Switzerland was thus very closely allied with the empire; Henry III. holding the reins of government as King of Burgundy and Duke of Alamannia or Swabia. This third amalgamation with the empire told more lastingly and influentially on the country than either the Roman or the Frankish rule had done; to a great extent it stamped on the people the German character and spirit.

These external changes, these shifting scenes, these various masters and systems of government, naturally affected the internal condition of the country as well. Of the social life of the country, however, we know very little. The chroniclers of the period are monks, or noble ecclesiastics who wrote of, and for their own class, and the people did not enter into their concerns. But the political changes were very great. The Frankish county administrations fell into disuse through the increase of immunities granted to royal and ecclesiastical foundations, by which they were exempted from obedience to the county officers. The counts themselves, who had formerly held office at the sovereign's pleasure, gradually made their dignities into hereditary fiefs, which became family property in wealthy and powerful houses. Thus, at the close of the ninth and the beginning of the tenth century we already find in Switzerland a number of counts, such as the Nellenburger, in Zurichgau; the Lenzburger, in Aargau; the Burkharde, in Chur-Rhætia; the Kyburger, at Winterthur, near Zurich. The greatest changes, however, were effected by the growth of feudalism, which had arisen indeed under Charlemagne, but had to some extent been checked by him. Feudalism outgrew all other systems, and entirely disarranged the social scale. The free peasantry shrank to a small number, and there sprang up a martial nobility of high functionaries, who held offices in the army or courts of justice, and exerted much influence. On the native soil, on the very meeting-places where the old German people had assembled to deal with civil and judicial matters, eminent men founded families which grew into reigning houses. These men, combining political discernment with military ability and experience, rose above their fellows, and assumed the highest offices. The distresses, the dissensions, the intestine wars, and particularly the invasions by savage hordes, drove people to seek the protection of powerful lords, even at the risk of losing their own independence. In most cases the people became "unfree," or serfs.

Society thus was divided into distinct classes; the old German democracy gave place to a highly aristocratic order, the nobility ruling over the people. Thus, we find Switzerland, like other European countries, struggling through her age of feudalism, and centuries must yet pass before she succeeds in establishing a system of government which alone will suit her peculiar character.

At that stage of history the welfare of the country depended to a great extent on the personal character of the imperial sovereigns. They visited Swabia and Burgundy, enforcing order and discipline, holding diets at important places, and assigning prerogatives to secular and religious foundations. In truth, these imperial visits promoted greatly the development of rising cities. Of the German emperors none came so often to Switzerland as the powerful Salic ruler, Henry III. When he left Burgundy—he was often at Basel and Solothurn—the people felt, says a contemporary writer, as if the sun had gone down. Henry II. and Henry III. held imperial diets at Zurich, and the latter used to reside there for weeks together, and lavished privileges and gifts on her religious foundations. He promoted festivals in the royal palace (Pfalz), in the Lindencourt; and Zurich was the meeting-place for his Burgundian and Italian subjects, the capital of Swabia, and residence of the Swabian dukes, where they here established their mint. His wise administration tended greatly to destroy all political difference and hostile feeling between the two Helvetias.

This national concord (1057-77) was still further

strengthened by the rule of Rudolf of Rheinfelden, who for twenty years swayed the destinies of the country as "Rector of Burgundy" and Duke of Alamannia. The regal and ducal power had been bestowed upon him by the Empress Agnes, on the death of Henry III., whose son-in-law he was. Rudolf was from the manor of Rheinfelden, near Basel, and was a distant connection of the Burgundian royal family. He held vast estates on Geneva lake, and in Swabia, and thus met with no opposition on the part of the nobility of Burgundy. But this long period of peace was suddenly and sadly interrupted by a terrible catastrophe which fell upon the empire; the fierce antagonism which arose between Gregory VII. and Henry IV. The emperor was unwilling to submit to the excessive encroachments of the Church, or, rather the Pontiff, on his prerogatives, and like William I. of England, entirely repudiated the Pope's claims, and tried to check his encroachments. The "Conqueror" indeed had gained so much power that the Pope could not issue excommunications against English subjects except by William's permission, but Henry IV. fell a victim to the Interdict. Never was sovereign more humiliated by the Papal power, nor more humiliated himself to escape the terrible punishment, for interdicts were fearful weapons in the hands of the Pontiffs of the Middle Ages. The story of this long struggle—how the emperor failed to carry his point—his wanderings across the Alps in the depth of winter—his submission at Canossa—for all this, full of thrilling interest as it is, the reader must be referred to the history of Germany.

CATHEDRAL OF LAUSANNE.

On the deposition of Henry, our Rudolf of Rheinfelden was elected king by the opposing party, and was thence called the Popish king (Pfaffenkönig); thus Switzerland, it is almost needless to say, was drawn into the struggle and convulsed by intestine wars. The bishops of Lausanne, Geneva, and Basel; the seigneurs of Grandson and Neuchâtel, clung to the emperor; the counts of Geneva and Toggenburg, the houses of Habsburg, Kyburg, and Savoy, and the clergy of Alamannia and Chur-Rhætia sided with the new king. St. Gall rallied round its valiant abbot, Ulrich III., to uphold the cause of Henry. The wars were continued with alternate successes and reverses on each side, till the death of Rudolf in 1080 on the Grona, near Leipzig, it was said by the hand of Godefroi de Bouillon, the famous crusader, who fought on the side of Henry. The intensity of bitter feeling gradually abated. Henry even tried to establish his royal authority in Burgundy, but in Alamannia new quarrels broke out on the question of the succession to the duchy. Two native Swabian dukes contended for the duchy, Frederick von Staufen, grandfather of Frederick Barbarossa, the ancestor of the illustrious dynasty, and Duke Bertold von Zaeringen, brother-in-law and heir to the estates of the son of the late Rudolf of Rheinfelden, who died shortly after his father. The differences were settled by a diet at Mayence, in 1097, and Frederick von Staufen, son-in-law to Henry, who had staunchly upheld and fought for the imperial cause in the Popish quarrels, was invested with the Swabian duchy. Yet his power on the Swiss side of the

Rhine was more nominal than real, and it was exerted by Bertold II. of Zaeringen, who received in compensation for the loss of the duchy the ducal title, and the *Reichsvogtei Zürich* (a kind of prefecture), together with the royal prerogatives over the secular and religious institutions of the city. For Zurich was then the noblest and most conspicuous town in Swabia, as Bishop Otto von Freysingen, the most prominent historian of the Middle Ages, asserts. This severance of Swiss Alamannia, and particularly of the imperial prefecture of Zurich, from the empire tended greatly to bring about the gradual political separation. Under the Zaeringer came again a long period of comparative peace.

VIII.

THE REIGN OF THE HOUSE OF ZAERINGEN.

(1050–1218.)

THE rule of the Dukes of Zaeringen ushered in a long period of comparative peace (1100–1218), which improved the social and material condition of the people. Yet this time of peace was every now and again interrupted in the west by feuds with the Burgundian nobles. This Swabian family took their name from the ancestral manor of Zaeringen, near Freiburg, in the Breisgau (Black Forest). The vast estates they had derived from the House of Rheinfelden on its extinction reached from Lake Geneva to the rivers Aare and Emme, and gave them a dominant position in the country at the opening of the twelfth century.

Burgundy had been slowly falling away from the empire during its internal dissensions and its conflicts with the Papacy. But on the death of Count William IV., who was assassinated by his own people in 1127, the Emperor Lothair drew that province more closely to his realm, by bestowing the regency of it on his adherent, Conrad of Zaeringen. Conrad's position was, however, violently contested by Rainald III., a relative of the murdered count. The Burgundian nobles rallied round him, and made a desperate stand against German interference, and he maintained his independence in the Franche Comté, as the district was subsequently called. When Frederick Barbarossa married Beatrix, the daughter and heiress of Rainald, he claimed the Burgundian territory, and came into conflict with the Zaeringer. Berchtold IV. obtained the position of suzerain over the sees of Geneva, Lausanne, and Sion, and by this division Swiss Burgundy was being lopped off from its appendage beyond Mount Jura. The insubordinate prelates joined with secular princes to upset the German rule. To guard against these protracted struggles, and to increase their own influence in the country, the Zaeringer resorted to a means which does them great credit, and which won for them the affection of the people. They began to found towns, as they had done in Germany, or to raise settlements into fortified cities, and granted them extensive liberties. The lesser nobles and the common people found shelter in these walled towns against the overbearing amongst the high nobility; trade and industry began to thrive, and these city commonwealths rose to a flourishing condition, and became a source of wealth as well as a staunch support to their founders.

Bertold or Berchtold IV. (1152-1186) planned a whole strategical line of strongholds in the west, as a check on the nobles; and in 1177 he founded the free city of Freiburg on his own estates. The situation, on a high plateau above the Saane, was on the line of demarcation between the French and German tongues. To this new town he granted a charter of liberties similar to that granted to its sister foundation of the same name in the Breisgau.

Berchtold V. (1186-1218) followed in the steps of his father. He founded and fortified Burgdorf, Moudon, Yverdon, Laupen, Murten, Gümminen, Thun. These towns he founded to be not only places of military strength, but also centres of industry and trade, which should increase the prosperity of his people. But he had, however, to stand against the heavy opposition of the Burgundian nobles. As he was preparing to set out on a crusade with Frederick Barbarossa they rose in arms. Hastening back, he defeated the refractory rebels, both at Avenches and in the Grindelwald valley, in 1191, and immediately after his victories he resumed his strategical projects. On a promontory washed by the Aare, and on imperial crown lands, he raised a new citadel, to which he gave the name of Bern, in memory of Dietrich of Berne (Verona), a favourite hero of Alamannic mediæval poetry.[1] The lesser nobles of the neighbourhood, as well as the humbler people, poured into Bern for shelter, and, receiving a most liberal charter, these burgesses rapidly rose to wealth and power. Being built on imperial land, Bern took from the first a higher standing than the sister town, Freiburg.

[1] See Nibelungen.

These city foundations form a chief corner-stone in the fabric of Swiss liberties. Attaining political independence, the towns held their own against aggressors. To effect their deliverance from oppression, they united with kindred communities or with powerful princes, and thus began the system of offensive and defensive alliances.

A new enemy arose in the West, and Berchtold V. was defeated by Count Thomas of Savoy (1211), who encroached on Vaud, and seized Moudon. Yet the Zaeringer steadily and successfully strengthened their hold over the country, and obtained the most complete independence. And, indeed, the moment seemed drawing near when Switzerland was to be shaped into a durable monarchical state. However, she was spared that fate—from which no patriotic act of any national hero could probably have rescued her—by a natural, yet providential, event, the extinction of the ducal family. For in 1218 Berchtold V. died, leaving no issue.

This century is eminently an age of religious movements. And, although our space will not permit us to enter into full details, yet it is impossible to pass over the great religious revival which centred in the Crusades, that is, so far as that movement touches Switzerland.

On the 10th of December, in the year 1146, a most touching scene might have been witnessed in the minster of Schaffhausen. The Alamannic people were thronging the church to listen to a glowing sermon from a French Cistercian monk, Bernard de Clairvaux. Vividly depicting the distress of the Christians in Palestine, he invited his hearers to join the second crusade. France was ready, he said, but the House of Hohenstaufen was still wavering. His captivating manner, his noble earnestness, and the elegance and flow of his language—though it was but half understood by the masses—stirred the audience to bursts of enthusiasm. "Your land is fertile," were the concluding words of the monk, "and the world is filled with the reputation of your valour. Ye soldiers of Christ, arise! and hurl down the enemies of the Cross!" Laying his hands on the blind and lame, says the half-legendary story, he restored to them eyesight or the use of limbs, and, strewing crosses amongst the crowds, left the church. The people, in a state of ecstatic fervour, beat their breasts, and, shedding tears, broke into a shout of "Kyrie eleison, the saints are with us!"[1] On the 15th of the same month Bernard preached at Zurich, and on Christmas Day at Speyer, before Conrad III., whom he won for the crusade. His fervent exhortations seem to have found willing ears, too, in the country. Schaffhausen and Einsiedeln took an active share in the work. We hear of almost countless numbers of spiritual and secular princes, nobles, knights, and lesser people who joined in the crusade. The counts of Montfort, Kyburg, Habsburg, Zaeringen, and Neuchâtel, and bishops and abbots started for the East. Contemporary writers bewail the loss of so many of the best and bravest of South Germany who died in Palestine. The holy orders of the Knights of St. John, of the Teutonic order, and

[1] Prof. Bächtold, "Sermon Literature in Switzerland."

the Knights-Templars raised their aristocratic institutions in this country; new orders of monastic foundations sprang up, which we cannot here dwell upon. Amongst these new orders were that of Mendicant Friars, though it is worthy of note that these played no such part in Switzerland as they did in England.

Yet the Burgundian or western portion of the country plunged more deeply into the movement than did the eastern part. German enthusiasm was but slowly won by French religious ecstasy, which had to a great extent started the Crusades. Still the age was filled with religious and romantic frenzy. Not the mere practical aims of conquest or gain it was that stirred men's minds, but the mystical elements of the movement, and the grand, novel, and indeed fabulous sights that were to be witnessed; and the old love of wandering and adventure revived, and drove men to the East. By a happy coincidence the effect of Bernard's sermons was lessened to some extent in this country by the previous teachings of another enthusiast of a far different stamp. The intrepid Italian reformer, Arnold of Brescia, had for some time preached at Zurich and Constance, sowing the seeds of heresy. Boldly attacking the abuses of the Church, and advocating the return to the simplicity of the apostolic teaching, he invited people to no longer lavish wealth on Church institutions. Arnold fell a victim to his advanced religious and political views, but his teachings took hold of the people of the Alpine districts. To his influence may safely be attributed the staunch resistance to Papal aggressiveness shown in the thirteenth century by the people of Zurich and of the Forest Cantons.

IX.

THE HOUSES OF KYBURG, SAVOY, AND HABSBURG.

(1218-1273.)

WE are nearing the period of their history most dear to the Swiss, the period when the Eidgenossenschaft is forming, but before reaching it we have still to make our way as best we can through a short era of chaotic feudalism and political confusion generally, preceding the great struggle for Swiss independence. On the extinction of the House of Zaeringen Switzerland fell a prey to the designs of vassal princes who had started into eminence on her soil, and now contended for supremacy over her. The realm of the Zaeringen sovereigns fell to pieces, the Swiss portions with Freiburg, Burgdorf, Thun, going to a native prince, Ulrich, Count of Kyburg, brother-in-law of Berchtold V.; the Swabian portions to a German relative. Thus Switzerland was cut off from Swabia. The crown lands he had held in Swiss Burgundy, and likewise the royal prerogative, fell to the empire, and the Vice-regency, being vested by Frederick II. in his younger son, Henry, became

CHÂTEAU DE VUFFLENS, VAUD. (*Fourteenth Century.*)

gradually nominal and at length died out. In this way all vassal princes in the west, and all the territorial lordships and free cities, such as Bern, Solothurn, Morat, Laupen, Gümminen, which were built on crown lands, and had been subjected to the Zaerings, were now held directly from the emperor. Zurich was likewise restored to the empire. By this time most of these places had become virtually independent.

Switzerland reflects most faithfully the feudal and political condition of the empire at large. It was torn into an almost countless number of spiritual and secular territorial sovereignties. Taking advantage of the state of distraction prevailing throughout the realm, Church prelates, religious foundations, the greater and lesser nobles, and even the thriving burgesses of great city commonwealths, all strove to erect their lands into petty independent dominions. The bishops assumed temporal power in their own dioceses; the religious-houses, owing to their "rich immunities," enjoyed almost perfect freedom. The peasantry had dwindled into small bodies of men, and in the place of the Frankish county-officers (counts) a martial nobility had sprung up, and, grasping the public functions and dignities, had turned these offices into freeholds independent of the sovereign. Henceforward they assumed the names of the feudal manors they held, and began to raise *chateaux-forts* on commanding or picturesque spots. As many as two hundred territorial rulers held their feudal sway in Switzerland. To give even the names of these would be not only useless but absurd, yet they had their share in the political development of the country.

In the Low Valais the counts of Savoy had obtained a footing, and were moreover advancing into Vaud. Vaud was at that time governed by a host of more or less important nobles, such as the barons of Grandson, Cossonay, Blonay, &c., and was contended for by the bishops of Lausanne and Geneva, and the counts of the latter town, whilst the counts of Greyerz governed in the districts of the Saane, and those of Neuchâtel in the lake districts of the Jura. Little Burgundy, with Solothurn as capital fell to the counts of Buchegg. One of the wealthiest and most ancient of the native families was that of Lenzburg, whose counts held sway in Aargau, Zurichgau, and the Forest Cantons, and were governors of famous religious-houses. One of the counts of Lenzburg, Ulrich IX., was an intimate friend and a minister of Frederick Barbarossa, and on the extinction of the rule of these counts, their heritage fell to the Habsburgs, and gave that family a great lift in the early days of their rise. In the east we meet with the famous House of Kyburg, to which belonged young Werner, the friend of Ernest II. of Swabia. Their ancestral manor house near Winterthur is still in good condition. They had numerous vassals and followers. In Zurichgau the barons of Regensberg and others, and the counts of Rapperswyl were harassing the people. The most powerful nobles in the east were the abbots of St. Gall, who governed part of St. Gall and Appenzell, and the counts of Toggenburg, and in Chur-Rhætia and the Rhine districts the counts of Montfort and Werdenberg. This sufficiently shows how feudalism had grown apace in Switzerland, and what a hard struggle the people had to hold their own against the impositions of princes and nobles. How feudalism had arisen has been already shown in the previous chapter.

To find some explanation of this rapid growth and the distracted state that followed in its train we must turn for a moment to the empire. Owing no doubt to the loftiness of the imperial dignity—for the emperors were indisputably the greatest of the civilized monarchs—the vassal princes rose to far greater independence in the empire than in other countries. Yet the possession of the imperial crown was in the end the weakening of royalty. Henry III. had raised the empire to its pinnacle of greatness, and the imperial dignity increased the prestige of the German name, and surrounded the German monarch with a halo of glory and even reverence. But the engagements abroad, the campaigns in Italy, the struggles with the Pontiffs, and the close attention required to be paid to Italian affairs, kept the emperors away from duties and cares nearer home. The Italian claims and titles, in fact, proved in the long run injurious to German interests. Frederick I., Barbarossa, had indeed, by his just and powerful rule, forced his insubordinate vassals into submission, but it was far different with his grandson, the brilliant Frederick II. (1215–50). Born in Italy and brought up to love the land of his birth, Naples and Sicily, more than his fatherland, Frederick II. was more Southerner than Teuton. He gave Southern Italy a model administration, but allowed Germany to be weakened by a divided internal government. And though we

BRONZE FIGURES FROM THE MAXIMILIAN MONUMENT AT INNSBRUCK.

cannot but admire the unflinching spirit with which this "wonder of the world" carried on his unequal struggle with the Papacy, yet it is clear that the conflict which sealed the doom of his own family was equally ruinous to the empire.[1]

During the interregnum (1254-73) Germany was without an actual ruler, although two foreign princes had been elected as its sovereigns. One of these never even showed his face in Germany, and the other, Richard of Cornwall, could not make sure his ascendency in the country, notwithstanding all the money he lavished in the attempt. This was the unhappy time of the *Faustrecht*—the name indicates its character—when the right of the strong hand (fist) alone was of avail. The empire lost its prestige, and it slowly dissolved into a loose confederacy of some five thousand larger or smaller states and fragments of states, each struggling for independence.

Most eminent amongst the crowd of nobles on Swiss soil aiming at their personal exaltation were the counts of the great Houses of Kyburg, Savoy, and Habsburg. Taking advantage of the general state of misgovernment or want of government, they systematically planned the aggrandisement of their own families, whether by conquest, purchase, or unjust encroachment. Yet there was opposition from the city burgesses, who, seeing their liberties in danger, felt the love of freedom roused in their breasts.

The powerful Kyburger, the mightiest Swiss nobles, were the first to threaten the liberties of the

[1] For more complete account of the Hohenstaufen see Freeman's "Holy Roman Empire," Frederick I., II.

people. Count Ulrich was reckoned one of the wealthiest princes throughout Swabia. By clever policy he had arranged the union of his son Hartmann (the elder) with Margaretha of Savoy. Ulrich's daughter, too, was married to Albrecht of Habsburg, and became the mother of Rudolf, the German king. He upheld the cause of Frederick II., and his elder son, Werner, went with him on his crusade where he was carried off by the plague, leaving one son, Hartmann the Younger. Their territories, after they had inherited the Zaeringen estates, reached from Lake Constance to Swiss Burgundy. Both the elder and the younger Hartmann encroached without scruple on the crown lands adjoining their estates, whilst Frederick II. was engaged in his struggle with the Church. In this emergency Bern and Murten, whose independence was at stake, followed suit, and resorted to means which would be a precedent in the future struggles for Swiss freedom. They joined in an offensive and defensive union with the Kyburg city, Freiburg, with Lucerne and the Bishop of Sion (1243). Bern had always adhered closely to the Hohenstaufen, and when Hartmann ventured on an open attack in 1255, that city applied to the empire for help. Unable to obtain support, however, both Bern and Murten placed themselves under the patronage of Count Peter of Savoy, who was already at variance with Kyburg, and a peace was arranged.

Peter of Savoy, "the second Charlemagne" as he was styled, was a most remarkable man, and a striking figure amongst the Savoy princes. Being the fourth of seven brothers he had been placed in the Church by his father, Count Thomas. However, on the death of the father Peter doffed his priestly robes, married the heiress of Faucigny, and added that province and Chablais to his territories, and set up as guardian of his brothers. Like his father he had constantly his mind on Vaud, and the daily feuds amongst its leaderless swarm of nobles facilitated the conquest. Castles were erected to further his object; and Chillon, which to-day gives us an excellent idea of what a fine feudal castle was in mediæval days, became his princely residence, having indeed been, to a great extent, built by him. Invited to the Court of England by his niece Eleanor, he spent the greater part of his life abroad, gathering in the service of Henry III. men and money. These he used to achieve the acquisition of Vaud, to which he every now and then returned to overthrow his enemies. In England he occupied a high position in the Council, was knighted, and had titles and honours lavished on him; the palace of the Savoy in the Strand bears witness to his magnificence. Many of the nobles in his train, such as De la Porte, Grandson, Flechère, married Englishwomen, and hence arose the family names of Porter, Grandison, Fletcher. Possessing an iron will, and thoroughly versed in diplomacy, Peter of Savoy finally annexed Vaud, partly by conquest and partly by agreement. In truth, the whole nobility lay at his feet ready to do him homage and acknowledge him as lord paramount. The German government sanctioned his protectorate of Bern and Morat, and Richard of Cornwall his conquests in the Bernese Highlands. Thus West Switzerland became the portion of a Savoy prince, and in the place of the ancient kingdom of Upper Burgundy arose a feudal sovereignty. However, order, discipline, and wise organization were the fruits of Peter's rule. And his generous nature, his chivalrous spirit, and his love of justice and good government, won for him the affection of his people, and the title of Le Petit, or Le Second, Charlemagne.

Presently the Kyburg domains in Eastern Switzerland devolved on him, the male line having died out in 1264—the elder Hartmann leaving no children, and the younger but one daughter, Anna, a minor. But when Peter attempted to take possession of the inheritance in the name of his sister, Margaretha of Savoy, he found himself in conflict with a rival claimant of superior strength, Rudolf, of Habsburg. This prince confiscated the whole of the lands of Hartmann the Elder, regardless of the claims of the widow, Margaretha. There was no mistaking the meaning of this, and war broke out between Savoy and Habsburg. Rudolf invited the whole of the nobles of the west to rise against Count Peter. He was engaged in East Switzerland when the Burgundian lords proceeded to besiege Chillon, in 1266. Peter himself was at war in the Valais. He suddenly returned, and at dead of night fell upon the enemy. He found them asleep, and some eighty nobles, barons, counts, seigneurs, and followers fell into his hands. These he conducted into the castle of Chillon, but instead of treating them as prisoners, entertained them at a banquet. Thus Peter became once more master of the west. Bern by a " writ of submission "

ORIGIN OF THE HABSBURGS.

regained from the House of Savoy the freedom it had forfeited on a previous occasion.[1] Rudolf signed a peace at Morat, and obtained the Kyburg heritage with the exception of the lands settled on the Dowager Countess. On the death of the "Conqueror of Vaud," which occurred soon after, the sovereignty passed to his brother Philip, a man of far inferior stamp. French Switzerland, save Geneva, gradually became a loose confederation of petty states, and their languishing political life led to their gradual amalgamation with the Eastern Republics.

The most dangerous champion enters the lists when the great Habsburg prince seizes on the reins of government in Switzerland. In its early stages the rule of the Habsburger is closely linked with, and is indeed the incitement to, the national movement or rising, if such a word may be applied in the case of a people just forming. The famous Habsburg family was of right noble and ancient lineage. Whether they sprang from Swiss soil (Aargau), or had their origin in Alsacia, is not quite settled. As a matter of fact, they were a Swabian family who possessed vast estates in both those countries. Their estates, ("Eigen," allods or freeholds) with Windisch, Brugg Nurri, lay at the junction of the Aare and Reuss, in Aargau. Originally they dwelt in the castle of Altenburg, near Brugg, and subsequently in their

---

[1] The story runs that Peter allowed the town to ask a favour in return for past services, and the witty men of Bern at once begged for the restitution of their lost liberty. Henceforth Peter was regarded as the benefactor and second founder of the city.

THE OLD HABSBURG CASTLE (CANTON AARGAU).

manor of Habsburg, on the Wülpelsberg,[1] a little hill overlooking the ancient Vindonissa. Numerous other castles they held as time went on.

Rudolf der Alte (the Old) is the first of the ancestors of whom we know much. He accompanied Frederick II. on his campaigns, and that great emperor stood godfather to his son Rudolf, who was later on to wear his royal crown. On his death the dynasty split into two branches, Habsburg-Austria (senior), and Habsburg-Laufenburg Aargau (junior), the heads being respectively Albrecht the Wise and Rudolf the Silent, his sons. Each of these branches followed its own separate policy, the junior holding to the Papacy. Albrecht cleverly contrived to marry Heilwig of Kyburg, hoping thus to inherit the estates of her childless brother, Hartmann the elder. He died, it was rumoured, whilst engaged in one of the crusades, and his estates passed to his sons, of whom, however, but one survived, our Rudolf of Habsburg. This man within the space of thirty years made his family one of the mightiest in the empire. Rudolf inherited from his father the family estate on the Aare, with Habsburg Castle. Besides this, he succeeded to various titles and lands, to the lordship of several towns in the Aargau, to the prefecture (*Vogtei*) over the religious-houses of Säckingen and Muri, to the landgraviate of Alsacia, and so forth.

Though but one-and-twenty when his father died,

---

[1] Tradition says that one of their ancestors, Radbot, hunting in the Aargau, lost his favourite hawk, and found it sitting on the ridge of the Wülpelsberg. Being delighted with the view, Radbot built a castle there, and called it *Hawk Castle*, Habichtsburg, or Habsburg.

Rudolf at once displayed great energy, as well as firmness and caution. In the struggle with the Papacy he held to the Staufen. It mattered little to him that his estates were under an interdict, and himself excommunicated. He held faithfully to the illustrious dynasty, and accompanied its last representative, Conradin, across the Alps, to Verona, in 1267. On the death of Conradin on the scaffold at Naples, and the consequent extinction of the Staufen line, Rudolf veered gradually round to the side of the Pope.

Rudolf was highly popular with the peasantry, winning their hearts by his affability, simple habits, and kindly good-nature. His tall and slender person, thin face, and aquiline nose, were striking features, and not easily forgotten when once seen. He had been known to mend with his own hands, after a campaign, the old grey coat he usually wore, and this was but a typical act of his. And the proud opposition he offered to a plundering nobility quite won for him the confidence of the people. The great cities stood on good terms with him, and sought his friendship and aid. Thus did the Alsacian towns seek his help against the bishops of Strasburg; Zurich against the barons of Regensberg and Toggenburg. On many an occasion did he render remarkable service in this way, of which one instance must suffice. The barons of Regensberg had a castle on the Uto, a mountain towering above Zurich, and from thence often sent men to waylay and rob the citizens who chanced to pass that way. Rudolf hit on a crafty device. Riding up the Uetliberg with thirty men of

Zurich, he placed behind each man a companion, and so came to the gate of the castle. The garrison despising a band apparently so small, rushed out of the gates upon them. But great was their terror when suddenly the men riding behind appeared in sight, and, taking to flight, they left the castle at the mercy of the strange attacking party. The place was levelled with the ground. Rudolf was asked by a body of free men of Uri to be their umpire in a dispute, and he actually sat in judgment on the matter, under the linden at Altorf, a fact which bears witness to his popularity amongst the people. Yet, with many amiable qualities, Rudolf was covetous, ambitious, and violent. Bent on raising his family to greatness, he reveals a most mercenary spirit, and shows himself unscrupulous in the pursuit of gain. It has been shown above, how he had seized the Kyburg lands; he also made himself guardian of Anna of Kyburg, and when she came of age, united her to his cousin, Eberhard of Habsburg. Thus was founded the new House of Kyburg-Burgdorf. He obtained from them Anna's heritage in the Aargau, besides Zug, Art, Willisan, Sempach, &c., as well as lands in the Forest Cantons. He was one of those chieftains who profited immensely by the distraction during the interregnum.

Whilst engaged in storming Basel, whose bishop had encroached on the Alsacian territories, the news was brought to Rudolf (October 1, 1273) that he had been elected King of Germany, at Frankfort, and, raising the siege, he at once proceeded to his coronation at Aix-la-Chapelle.

Rudolf's influence greatly altered the policy of Germany. He made his peace with Gregory X. at Lausanne in 1275, and entered into a close alliance with him. Thus an end was put to the unfortunate quarrels with the Papal power, and the German king was set at liberty to follow his own ambitions, aims, and plans. He resigned all claim to Italy, and so far also to the imperial dignity, which had once been of such splendour, and had indeed been almost equivalent to the government of the whole world. Sober, cautious, and matter-of-fact as he was, Rudolf cared not for merely ideal greatness, and devoted himself to following more practical aims. The empire had been impoverished by the late crisis, and by the different calamities which had befallen it; and the German princes had risen to positions of defiant independence. Seeing beforehand that the authority of the crown must be founded on the wealth and hereditary possessions of the sovereign, Rudolf made the aggrandisement of his family the chief object of his career. Fortune's favourite he seemed indeed to be, and gained a great victory over his opponent to the throne, Ottokar of Bohemia (1278), and secured from him the Duchy of Austria, with Steyermark. This he vested as a new possession in his own family.

Notwithstanding the extension of his power eastward, he likewise continued his aggressive policy in Switzerland. He forced from Philip of Savoy the cession of Payerne, Murten, &c., and waged war with Bern, which held to Savoy, refusing to pay the royal taxes (1279). Making ample use of his exalted position and unlimited power, he lost no opportunity of buying up princes and religious-houses in pecuniary difficulties. He compelled the Abbots of St. Gall, Alrich of Güttingen, and William of Montfort, to cede to him lands and farms, forcing on them as steward a worthless fellow who was a devoted adherent of the Habsburgs. When the male line of Rapperswyl died out, the fiefs which should have passed to the Abbey of St. Gall, he gave to his own sons. And, taking advantage of the pecuniary straits of the monastery of Nurbach, he obtained by one means or another Lucerne, which belonged to the abbey, as well as numerous farms reaching into the Forest Cantons. The stewardship of Einsiedeln and Pfäffers likewise fell to his share. Many more instances might be given to show how Rudolf's clever and unscrupulous scheming extended his power all over the midlands and the eastern districts, and how grievously his heavy hand was felt throughout the country. Yet the famous Habsburgs, able, warlike, and energetic as they were, met with one obstacle to their progress which they were unable to remove, and against which all their plans came to nought— the love of freedom innate in the Swiss peoples.

X.

THE CONFEDERATION, OR EIDGENOSSENSCHAFT.

(1231–1291.)

IN the present chapter we have to attempt the task of separating truth from fiction, at all times, perhaps, a difficult, and often an impossible, undertaking, in matters of history. This chapter indeed splits itself naturally into *Wahrheit* and *Dichtung.* Fortunately, the stories of Tell and the three Eidgenossen are everywhere well known, and will need but little description at our hands.

A lake of exquisite beauty extends between the Forest Cantons, and, so to speak, links them together, the whole forming a singularly picturesque stretch of country. Separated from the sister cantons and from the outside world, each of these little states formed a world of its own. The lake was the common outlet, and the rallying-point for the peoples of the secluded valleys. The various armlets into which it branches, like the districts which lie about them, have each their peculiar charm. Of these cantons Unterwalden has a pastoral character, and attracts attention by its beautiful verdure—velvety slopes, green meads, clusters of nut-trees in the lower parts, orchards of fruit trees, the country dotted everywhere with sunburnt huts, forming a *tout ensemble* truly idyllic. Schwyz is a canton of similar natural appearance, with green pastures and somewhat gentler slopes, but broad terraces with their red cottages line the valley. Above the chief town of the same name, which nestles at the head of the dale it commands, shining, dazzlingly white with its snug whitewashed houses, rise to the sky the torn but imposing pyramids of the two Myten. Uri is *par excellence* the highland district amongst the three little states. Towering mountains and inaccessible rocks hem in a strip of water, and give that wondrous hue which makes the charm of Uri lake.

The inhabitants are of the Alpine mould. Sinewy, robust, quick, shrewd, they are persevering, fearless, bold, and self-reliant; they are yet simple in their habits, artless in manner, pious, and strongly conservative, each people having however its own characteristic points of difference. Ever exposed to danger, their struggles with nature for the supply of their daily wants have increased their strength of body, brought out their mettle, and quickened their natural intelligence. Thus it was not the love of innovation, or even of reform, that led them to form their "League of Perpetual Alliance," in 1291. They entered into the Confederation but to check the aggressions of the Habsburgers.

Such is the district and such the race from which arose the three famed Eidgenossen, Walter Fürst von

Attinghausen, Werner Staufacher, and Arnold von Melchthal, who, on the "Rütli," swore a solemn oath to save their country from rulers shameless as they were cruel.

Tradition reports that King Albrecht, son of Rudolf (1298-1308), greatly oppressed the three Waldstätten, doing his best to reduce the people to the condition of bondmen. To the various stewards or bailiffs whom he set over them, he gave strict orders to keep well in check the people of

THALER OF THREE CANTONS—URI, SCHWYZ, AND UNTERWALDEN
[SANCTUS MARTINUS EPISCOPUS].
(*By Dr. Imhoof.*)

the Forest Cantons. These overseers grew into covetous and cruel tyrants, who taxed, fined, imprisoned, and reviled the unfortunate inhabitants. To complain to the monarch was useless, as he refused to listen. One of these stewards, or lieutenant-governors, was Gessler, and a particularly haughty and spiteful governor he was. Passing on one occasion through Steinen (Schwyz), he was struck by the sight of a fine stone-built house, and filled with envy he inquired of Werner Staufacher, who happened to be the owner, whose it was. Fearing the governor's anger the wealthy proprietor replied cautiously, "The holding is the king's, your grace's, and mine." "Can we suffer the peasantry to live in such fine houses?" exclaimed Gessler, scornfully, as he rode away. Landenberg, another of these "unjust stewards," at Sarnen, being informed that a rich farmer in the Melchi (Unterwalden), had a fine pair of oxen, sent his man for them. Young Arnold, of Melchthal, the son of the farmer, was standing by when the animals were being unyoked, and, enraged at the sight, raised his stick, and struck the governor's servant a blow, breaking one of his fingers. But being afraid of the governor's wrath, young Arnold fled. So Landenberg seized the old father, brought him to his castle, and had his eyes put out.

Werner Staufacher was consumed by secret grief, and his wife, guessing what was on his mind, gave him such counsel that, nerving himself to action, he went over to Uri and Unterwalden to look for kindred spirits and fellow-sufferers. At the house of Walter Fürst, of Attinghausen (Uri), he met with the young man from the Melchi, to whom he was able to tell the sad news that the old father had been blinded by Landenberg. Here the three patriots unburdened to each other their sorrowing hearts, and vowed a vow to free their country from oppressors, and restore its ancient liberties. Gradually opening their plans to their kindred and friends, they arranged nightly meetings on the Rütli, a secluded Alpine mead above the Mytenstein, on Uri lake. Meeting in small bands so as not to excite suspicion, they deliberated as to how best their deliverance might be effected. On the night of the 17th of November, 1307, Walter Fürst, Arnold of Melchthal, and Werner Staufacher, met on the Rütli, each taking with him ten intimate associates. Their hearts swelling with love for their country and hatred against tyranny, these three-and-thirty men solemnly pledged their lives for each other and for their fatherland.

Raising their right hands towards heaven the three leaders took God and the saints to witness that their solemn alliance was made in the spirit—" One for all, and all for one." At that moment the sun shot his first rays across the mountain-tops, kindling in the hearts of these earnest men the hopes of success.

In the meantime a very remarkable event had happened at the town of Altorf in Uri. Gessler had placed a hat on a pole in the market-place, with strict orders that passers-by should do it reverence, for he wished to test their obedience. William Tell scorned this piece of over-bearing tyranny, and proudly marched past without making obeisance to the hat. He was seized, and Gessler riding up, demanded why he had disobeyed the order. "From thoughtlessness," he replied, "for if I were witty my name were not Tell." The governor, in a fury, ordered Tell to shoot an apple from the head of his son, for Gessler knew Tell to be a most skilful archer, and, moreover, to have fine children. Tell's entreaties that some other form of punishment should be substituted, for this were of no avail. Pierced to the heart the archer took two arrows, and, placing one in his quiver, took aim with the other, and cleft the apple. Foiled in his design, Gessler inquired the meaning of the second arrow. Tell hesitated, but on being assured that his life would be spared, instantly replied, " Had I injured my child, this second shaft should not have missed thy heart." " Good!" exclaimed the enraged governor, " I have promised thee thy life, but I will throw thee into a dungeon where neither sun nor moon shall shine on thee." Tell was chained, and placed in a barge, his bow and arrow being put at his back. As they rowed towards Axenstein, suddenly their arose a fearful storm, and the crew fearing they would be lost, suggested that Tell, an expert boatman, should save them. Gessler had him unbound, and he steered towards Axenberg, where there was a natural landing-stage formed by a flat rock—*Tellenplatte*. Seizing his bow and arrows he flung the boat against the rock, and leapt ashore, leaving its occupants to their fate. Woe betide him, however, should the governor escape death on the lake! Tell hurried on to Schwyz, and thence to the "hollow way" near Kusnach, through which Gessler must come if he returned to his castle. Hiding in the thicket lining the road, Tell waited, and presently seeing the tyrant riding past, took aim, and shot him through the heart. Gessler's last words were, " This is Tell's shaft."

Thus runs the old story. The question naturally arises, What of all this is truth, and what fiction? just as it will in the case of Winkelried and others. The question is easier to ask than to answer, at least in the very limited space at our disposal. The truth is, this question has been for half a century the subject of controversy always lively, often passionate and violent. Some authorities are for making a clean sweep of all traditional annals, and all semi-mythical national heroes. Others, no less able and conscientious, and no less learned, have re-admitted tradition to investigation, and have made it their special care to pick out the historical grain from the chaff of fiction. It is impossible within the limits of our space to discuss the merits of the numerous chronicles, and popular songs and plays, in which the traditions of the Tell period are preserved. Suffice it to say, that the "White Book of Sarnen" (1470), naïve and artless as is its tone, is the most trustworthy; that of the " Swiss Herodotus," the patriotic Tschudi (1570), the most fascinating and most skilfully penned. The work of the latter is mainly a series of gleanings from the "White Book," together with additional pictures from Tschudi's own pencil. He combined and supplied dates and minor details, and cast the whole in a mould apparently so historical that it became an authority for Joh von Müller, the great Swiss historian of the eighteenth century. And the immortal Schiller deeply stirred by the grand epic, produced his magnificent drama, "William Tell."

It hardly needs to be said in these days that whilst no one thinks of taking these beautiful old-world stories literally, yet few of us would care to toss them contemptuously and entirely on one side. Truly they have a meaning, if not exactly that which was once accepted. In the present instance they represent and illustrate a long epoch during which a high-spirited people were engaged in establishing a confederation, and maintaining it against a powerful enemy—one long effort to secure emancipation from Habsburg tyranny—an epoch which opened with the acquisition of a charter of liberties for Uri in 1231, and closed with the brilliant victory of Morgarten in 1315.

It remains now to show briefly what may be considered the authentic history of the period, that is, the history as found in authentic documents.

And first, it is clearly absurd to suppose that the three Forest Cantons sprang suddenly into existence as democracies. Feudalism had spread its net over the Waldstätten as elsewhere in Switzerland and Europe generally. But the inborn love of freedom amongst the "freemen" of the three cantons was intensified by two things, the secluded Alpine life and the tyranny and aggressiveness of the Habsburgs. The inhabitants of the Forest were Alamanni, who, in the seventh century, had moved into the higher Alpine regions, the immigration into those regions being greatly promoted by a decree of Charlemagne, that whoever should cultivate land there with his own hands should be the owner thereof. But besides these farmer freemen, land was taken up by religious-houses, and by the secular grandees, who claimed the soil cultivated by their serfs, bondsmen, and dependants of all kinds. By the bounty of Louis the German, the "Gotteshausleute" (God's-house-people), had become of great importance in Uri; in 853 that monarch had bestowed his royal lands in Uri, with everything appertaining thereto, on the Abbey of our

Lady at Zurich, an abbey founded for his daughters. Beneath the mild rule of these royal ladies the inhabitants had acquired great independence, and had shared with their mistress the high privilege of the "Reichsfreiheit," which saved their lands from being mortgaged, or from falling under the power of vassal princes. Besides the Lady Abbess, there were other proprietors in Uri—the Maison Dieu of Wettingen, the barons of Rapperswyl, and other high-born or noble families, and, lastly, a body of "freemen."

This scattered and various society was knit into one close boundary-association by the possession of the "Almend," a stretch of land common to all, according to the old German custom—to free and unfree, rich and poor, noble and serf, who were brought together in council for deliberation. These assemblies gave rise to the political gatherings of the "Landsgemeinde."

Now by a decree of the Emperor Frederick II., Uri was severed from the jurisdiction of Zurich Abbey in 1218, and placed under the control of Habsburg, who had succeeded to the governorship of Zurichgau, a district which then included the three Forest states. "Reichsfreiheit" was lost, and the inhabitants, fearing their state would fall into the hands of the Habsburgs, applied for protection from Henry, son of Frederick II., then at variance with the Habsburg family. He complied with their request, and on the 26th of May, 1231, granted them a charter of liberties, restored "Reichsfreiheit," and received them into the pale of the empire. Uri was now under the direct control of the monarch, and the local authority was vested in an *Ammann* chosen from the native families. An imperial representative appeared twice a year in the country to hold his half-yearly sessions, and to collect the imperial taxes. When Rudolf of Habsburg rose to the imperial throne, he recognized fully the validity of the Uri charter. However a charter was but little check on the monarchical tyranny, and we find the country exasperated by Rudolf's grinding taxation.

The inhabitants of Schwyz were no less bold, resolute, and energetic, than those of Uri, and no less averse to falling into the hands of the Habsburgs. Here the freemen predominated, and owned the largest portion of the country. There is not space to tell of their long quarrel with the monks of Einsiedeln respecting some forest lands. Suffice it to say that, after a stout stand for their rights, they were ordered to share the *corpus delicti*, the forest, with their opponents. During the quarrels between Rome and the Hohenstaufen, Schwyz staunchly upheld the cause of Frederick II., but the wavering policy of Rudolf of the junior line, Habsburg-Laufenburg, was a strong temptation to separate themselves from him (1239). They sent letters, messengers, and most likely auxiliaries, to Frederick, when he was besieging Faënza with the view of recovering the Lombard cities, and begged for the protection of the empire. Frederick expressed his gratification that the freemen of Schwyz should voluntarily place themselves under his protection, and sent them a charter similar to that of Uri (1240)—to "his faithful men"—by which they obtained the "Reichsfreiheit," and an assurance that they should not be severed from the empire.

A very few years later we hear of the first federal union of which we have any certain knowledge. The great quarrel between the emperor and the Pope, and the flight of the latter to Lyons, had set Europe on fire. Schwyz took up arms to defend the founder of its liberties, and entered into an alliance with Uri and Unterwalden—and even Lucerne—to throw off the yoke of the younger Habsburg line. War raged fiercely in the valleys of the Forest and by Lake Lucerne, till the Popish party was brought to bay, and the overseer driven from the Habsburg castle. We do not know the result of this insurrection; it closed no doubt with the death of Rudolf and Frederick in 1249–50.

It is to this period of the insurrection doubtless that the stories of Tell, the oath on the Rütli, &c., apply most clearly. They are reminiscences probably of some forgotten episodes of the campaigns. Had the annalists connected the stories with these times instead of with the reign of Albrecht, their validity could hardly have been contested.

When Rudolf III. of Habsburg-Austria became emperor, and had bought from the younger branch of his house the estates and titles in the Waldstätten, he drew Schwyz most closely to his family. He refused to confirm Frederick's charter on the plea that that monarch had been excommunicated. The magistrates were officers of his own; he gathered the taxes in his own name, and, in 1278, assigned them as dowry to the English bride of his favourite son, Hartmann. Schwyz did not feel comfortable under all this, and stood on its guard.

Unterwalden,[1] the lowland district of the Forest, was politically quite behind the times. It was exceedingly fertile, and was much in request, and in the thirteenth century was parcelled out amongst religious-houses, great nobles, and lesser freemen. The Habsburgs being not only the greatest proprietors, but also stewards of the religious-houses, naturally held sovereign sway. It was only by the aid of friendly neighbours indeed that Unterwalden could hold its own against such powerful masters, and of all its neighbours the men of Schwyz were not only the best organized, politically, but the most energetic and far-seeing. That the Schwyzers took the lead in the emancipation of the district is pretty clear from the name that was given to the newly-formed state by surrounding lands, and by the Austrians after the battle of Morgarten.

The death of Rudolf in 1291 was good news to the men of the Forest, and all their pent-up hopes of the recovery of their ancient rights once more burst forth. Yet dreading new dangers from new governors, they took measures of precaution. Within a fortnight of Rudolf's death the three districts of Uri, Schwyz, and Unterwalden had entered into a perpetual league of defensive alliance (*Ewiger Bund*), a renewal no doubt of a previous pact, probably that of 1246. They may have met on the Rütli to swear the solemn oath which was to bind them into a confederation, *à perpetuité*.

---

[1] Unterwalden is parted into two unequal halves by a mountain range running from the Titlis to the Buochser Horn, with the wood of Kerns in its centre. The districts on both sides have thence taken the names of Ob and Nidwalden, above and below the wood.

The various acts of agreement were drawn up in Latin, and the document—the Magna Charta of the Eidgenossenschaft—treasured up at Schwyz, is held in veneration by the whole Swiss nation. It bears an essentially conservative character, and witnesses to the thought and consideration given to the matter, no less than to the strong sense of equity and clear judgment of the contracting parties. Amongst other things it enjoins that every one shall obey and serve his master according to his standing; that no judge shall be appointed who has bought his office with gold, nor unless he be a native; that if quarrels shall arise between the Eidgenossen (*inter aliquos conspiratos*), the more sensible shall settle the differences, and if the one party does not submit, the opposition shall decide in the matter. To the document were affixed the seals of the three countries as a guarantee of its authenticity.

XI.

THE BATTLE OF MORGARTEN.

(1315.)

THE primary object of the Perpetual League was to secure for the three Waldstätten that safety which the empire, with its fluctuating fortunes and condition, failed to ensure. Rich and mighty cities in Germany and Italy had joined in alliance with similar intent, but whilst these alliances had come to nought, the simple peasants of the Forest, hardened by continual struggles, had developed into a power before which even the Habsburgs were of no avail; for, gifted with striking political understanding and far-sightedness, these born diplomatists knew how to turn the tide of events to their own advantage.

As an additional security, they entered within a few weeks into an alliance with Zurich and the Anti-Habsburg coalition that had sprung up in East Switzerland when Adolf of Nassau was chosen successor to King Rudolf in preference to his son Albert, whose absolutism was dreaded by all. The

Zurich forces attacked Winterthur, a Habsburg town, but owing to the absence of reinforcements sustained a severe defeat (1292). Taking advantage of their heavy losses, Duke Albert laid siege to the imperial city of Zurich. Great was his dismay, however, when from his camp he saw a formidable force drawn up in battle array on the Lindenhof, an eminence within the city. The armour-bearers, their helmets, shields, and lances glittering in the sun, appeared to the foe to indicate an overwhelming force, and Albert made his peace with the remarkable city. This was gladly accepted, as well it might be, for it is said that the dazzling array seen by Albert consisted of the Amazons of the place, to wit, the women of the town, who had lit on this stratagem to save their city

King Adolf guaranteed the "liberties" of Uri and Schwyz in 1297; but on his death in the following year, in battle against his rival, Albert of Habsburg, these were again at stake—for charters had to be submitted to the sovereign's pleasure at every new accession—and in fact were never acknowledged by the succeeding king. As the object of the Habsburgs was to join the Waldstätten to their Austrian possessions, their policy was naturally to oppose the freedom of the district. It was a fact highly favourable to Swiss interests that the German monarchy was elective; for the princes and prince-electors, with their personal and selfish aims, shut out the mighty Habsburg dynasty, whenever candidates presented themselves whom they considered more likely to favour their views. On such grounds Adolf of Nassau was elected, as was also Henry of Lützelburg later on.

Albrecht was not the cruel, taciturn, tyrant Swiss chroniclers and historians have pictured him. They have, in fact, confounded him with previous rulers, chiefly of the junior Habsburg line. Albrecht was bent on the aggrandizement of his house, but, if anything, less selfishly so than his father Rudolf III. He was, however, no friend of Swiss liberties, and, had he lived longer, would doubtless have checked any efforts on the part of the Swiss to gain greater freedom. But he was cut off in the very prime of life, by his nephew and ward, John of Swabia, who believed himself defrauded of his heritage. With John were other young Swiss nobles—Von Eschenbach, Von Balm, Von Wart, &c. ; and by these Albrecht was stabbed, within sight of his ancestral manor, Habsburg, as he was on a journey to meet his queen, Elizabeth. He sank to the ground, and expired in the lap of a poor woman (1308). The assassins got clear away, excepting Wart. A terrible vengeance was taken on him, and on the friends and connections of the fugitives, however innocent. A thousand victims perished, by order of the bloody Elizabeth. On the spot where her husband had fallen the queen built the Monastery of Königsfelden (King's Field), a place which afterwards attained great fame and splendour. The stained windows of the church still in existence, are masterpieces of Swiss work, showing all the exquisite finish of the fourteenth century, and testifying to the former magnificence of the abbey.

Once again the Habsburgs were passed over, and Henry VII. became King of Germany. To him Unterwalden owes its charter, which placed the three small states on an equal footing politically. However, he died in Italy when going to receive the imperial crown—it is thought by poison. On his decease the opposing parties elected two sovereigns, Louis of Bavaria, and Frederick the Handsome, of Austria, son of Albrecht. During a short interregnum, which occurred after the death of Henry VII., Schwyz began hostilities against the Abbey of Einsiedeln, of which the Habsburgs were stewards. This greatly vexed Frederick, and his annoyance was increased by finding that the Forest generally sided with his rival. Goaded beyond bearing, Frederick determined to deal a crushing blow against the rebellious Forest states, and, late in the autumn of 1315, hostile operations commenced. We are now in our story on the eve of the famous battle of Morgarten, which is justly regarded by the Swiss as one of the noblest of the many noble episodes in their stirring history. There is not a civilized nation in the world to which the name of Morgarten is not familiar.

Both parties prepared for war. The Wald Cantons fortified such parts of their district as offered no sufficient security, and placed troops at the entrance to the valley. Duke Leopold, a younger brother of the king, a great champion, and eager for combat, undertook the command of the campaign, with much dash and self-reliance. He gathered a considerable army together on the shortest notice, the Aargau towns, with Lucerne and Winterthur, and even Zurich, sending troops, whilst the nobility espoused his cause, and rallied to his standard at Zug. In order to divide the forces of the enemy the leader ordered a section of the army, under Count Otto of Strassberg, to break into Unterwalden by the Brünig Pass. Leopold himself commanded the main force, and directed his principal charge against Schwyz, which was particularly obnoxious to him. Of the two roads leading from Zug to Schwyz, he chose—probably from ignorance—the one which was the more difficult, and strategically the less promising. On the 15th of November, the day before the feast of St. Othmar, he brought his cavalry to Ægeri, and thence moved in a heedless fashion along the eastern bank of that lake, taking no care either to watch the enemy or to reconnoitre his ground Amongst his baggage was a cartload of ropes, with which he intended to fasten together the cattle he expected to seize. Hurried on by the nobles, and himself eager for the fray, he neglected even the most elementary measures of precaution, which, indeed, he deemed quite unnecessary when marching against mere peasants. His *cortège* resembled a hunting party rather than an army expecting serious warfare. Reaching the hamlet of Haselmatt, the troops began slowly to ascend the steep and frozen slopes of Morgarten, in the direction of Schornen. Soon they were hemmed in by lake and mountain, when, without a moment's warning, there came pouring down upon the dense masses of horsemen huge stones, pieces of rock, and trunks of trees.

Dire confusion followed at once. This unexpected avalanche had been hurled down upon them by a handful of men posted on the mountain ridge, and well informed respecting the movement of the Austrians. Presently the main body of the men from Schwyz and Uri appeared behind Schornen, and like a whirlwind rushed down the hill on the terrified and bewildered foe, who were caught in the narrow pass of Morgarten, as in a net. It was quite impossible to ward off such an attack as that. Then the Eidgenossen began to mow down the Austrians with their terrible weapon the halberd, an invention of their own.

A confused scramble and a terrified *melée* ensued, in which it was at once seen that the foe must succumb, utterly disorganized as they were, and well-nigh helpless through terror. Many in sheer despair rushed into the lake. Soon lay scattered over the wintry field the "flower of knighthood," amongst them the counts of Kyburg and Toggenburg, and other Swiss nobles. Leopold himself had a narrow escape, and hurried back to Winterthur, "looking," says Friar John of that place, an eye-witness, "like death, and quite distracted." Otto of Strassberg, hearing of the disaster, retreated with such rapidity that he died overcome by the physical efforts he had made. "Throughout the country the sounds of joy and glory were changed into wails of lamentation and woe." Such was the ever-memorable battle of Morgarten. As to the number of men who fell on that day, the accounts vary hopelessly, and we do not venture to give any figures. The infantry probably fled, and had no share in the encounter.

Such was the first proof the young Confederation gave of their mettle and skill in warfare. The battle has been called the Swiss Thermopylæ, but it was more fortunate in its results than that of the Greeks. It confirmed the national spirit of resistance to the house of Habsburg, and commenced a whole series of brilliant victories, which for two centuries increased the glory, as they improved the military skill of the Swiss nation. In humbleness and in a spirit of true devotion, the victors fell to thanking God on the battlefield for their rescue, and they instituted a day of thanksgiving to be observed as year after year it should come round.

On the 9th of December in the same year (1315) the Eidgenossen proceeded to Brunnen, to renew by oath, and enlarge by some additional paragraphs, the treaty or league of 1291, and this for nearly five hundred years remained the fundamental code of agreement between the three Waldstätten. The Forest Cantons, having grown into three independent republics, claimed each separate administration or autonomy. The idea of a federal union thus started by the Forest men gradually grew in favour with neighbouring commonwealths struggling for independence; and these, so attracted, slowly clustered round the Forest Cantons, to form a bulwark against a common foe.

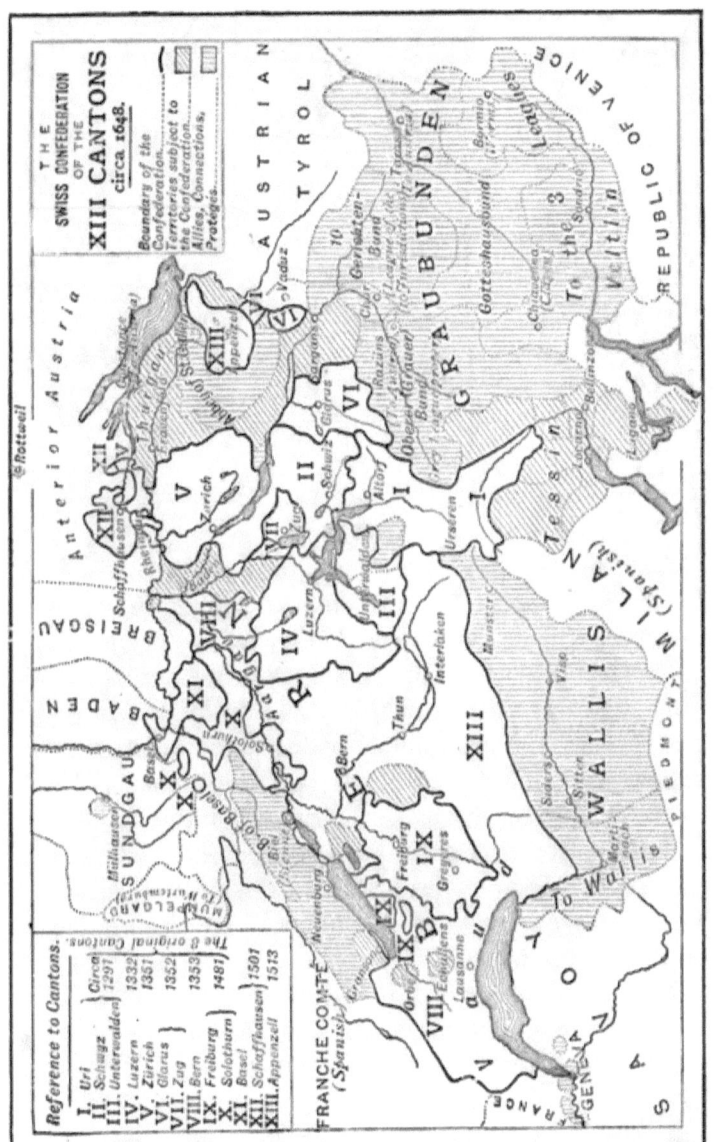

MAP OF OLD SWITZERLAND.

XII.

THE LEAGUE OF THE EIGHT STATES.

(1332-68.)

ONE by one the Swiss lands were reached by the breeze of freedom blowing from the Forest Cantons after the great victory of Morgarten. Yet it was only very gradually and in small groups that the other districts entered within the pale of the Eidgenossenschaft. Eight states made up the nucleus for some time; indeed, till after the Burgundian wars, in 1481, they jealously kept out all intruders. In fact, the confederate states looked on outsiders merely as "connections," or subjects, and associated with them on no other footing. It is a somewhat startling and unusual thing to find republics ruling over subject lands, yet in this case the result was to knit the whole more closely together in after centuries. In the fourteenth century the union was of the loosest kind; alliances wavered, and politics were swayed by separate ends. The other commonwealths, in joining themselves with the Forest states, had no notion of giving up their individual life, but were wishful to create a body powerful enough to secure independence against the aggressions of Austria; and at the price of continued struggle, and steady perseverance no less admirable, they achieved that object.

Attracted by common interests as a near neighbour, and being moreover the mart of the Forest Cantons, Lucerne was the first to be drawn into the union. This town had acquired great independence under the mild rule of the famous Murbach Abbey. But in 1291 the convent, having got into financial straits, had sold the town to the Habsburgs. Finding but little liberty under their new rulers, the men of Lucerne formed in 1332 with the Forest the union of the four Waldstätten,[1] with the view of shaking off the Austrian yoke. Lucerne was bound by treaty not to league herself with outsiders without the consent of the Forest Cantons.

In 1351 Zurich followed suit. Her clever and powerful burgomaster, Brun, was keenly desirous of raising her to greatness. He was less regardful of the interests of the Eidgenossen, and indeed had strong leanings towards Austria and the empire, as affording a wider scope for ambitious politics. Consequently he would not permit her superior position as an imperial free city, nor her foreign and commercial relations, to be injured by submission to the Forest control, and he carried a clause which left her free to join in any other alliances she choose, provided that with the Waldstätten was not broken. He also

[1] Compare *Vierwaldstättersee*, the German for Lake Lucerne.

bound the Forest states by treaty, to secure to Zurich its own constitution. The documents connected with this alliance show that the five states formed a power quite ready to cope with Austria. And well for them that they were so ready. Louis of Bavaria, the protector of the Forest Cantons, was dead, and his successor on the German throne was Charles IV., son of the famous blind King of Bohemia, who fell so bravely at Cressy. To maintain his authority Charles fell back on the friendship of Austria, and to win the favour of Albrecht (the "Wise," or "Lame"), he nullified all the measures which Louis had enacted against Austria, measures which had destroyed the power of that country in the Waldstätten. The destruction of Rapperswyl[1] (Zurich), and the union between Zurich and the other four states were regarded by the Habsburgs as a challenge, and gave rise to a long-protracted war, marked rather by feats of diplomacy on the part of Austria than by feats of arms. Albrecht was desirous of having a reckoning with the Eidgenossen generally, yet for the present he confined his attacks to Zurich, their strongest outpost. The assault by sixteen thousand men in 1351 was stoutly opposed, and collapsed suddenly by proffers of peace. Queen Agnes of Königsfelden, the duke's sister, was called in as umpire, and Brun temporizing with Austria to save his town, a verdict was passed so injurious to the people of the Forest, that they refused the mediation of this "wondrously shrewd and quick woman," who had for these thirty years swayed the Habsburg politics, and the quarrel broke out anew.

[1] See Chapter xiii.

The Zurcher now assumed the offensive, and defeated the Austrians at Tätwil, being led by Roger Manesse, the grandson of the amateur poet. They then marched on Glarus, and conquered that valley in November, 1351. Clarona, like Lucerne, had drifted from beneath the spiritual rule, and had fallen under that of the Habsburgs, much to her dislike. An old chronicler reports that "the Glarner were well disposed towards the Eidgenossen," and it is not difficult to believe that they consented willingly to be conquered, for in the spring of the next year they utterly defeated the Austrian forces under Count Stadion, who had returned with the intention of recovering the country if possible. The union of the Glarner with the Confederates was fixed by a treaty, on June 4, 1352, but, curious to relate, they were received as inferiors or *protégés* (Schutzort) and not as equals. The Confederates no doubt reasoned that the acquisition of the valley, with its open villages, offered no adequate advantages for the extra risks to which it exposed them.

Zug was the next to be brought into the union. The very situation of Zug, surrounded as it was by the federal territory, rendered it quite necessary that that state should be brought into the fold of the Eidgenossen. The country districts surrendered at the approach of the federal forces, but the town of Zug offered a stout resistance. However, the townsmen heard nothing from Albrecht, much less received any help from him, and yielded on June 27, 1352. Thanks to the greater security she offered, Zug was admitted as a full member.

In July, 1352, Albrecht renewed his attack on Zurich, with an army double the one first brought against her, Bern, Basel, Strasburg, Solothurn, and Constance, being bound by treaty, sending troops. But this second venture likewise miscarried, after stout opposition and much wasteful ravaging. This plan of storming an imperial city was unpopular amongst the neighbouring towns, and Eberhard " the Quarrelsome," who held the chief command in the place of the lame duke, displeased with the secret negotiations, left the camp, and the army was dissolved. Again the Austrians resorted to diplomatic machinations, and recovered by the pen what they had failed to keep by the sword. The treaty, or rather truce, of Brandenburg, so called from its author, reinstated the Habsburger in their Forest possessions. Glarus and Zug were compelled to give up their union with the Eidgenossen, and, like Lucerne, to return to the Habsburg rule. Nevertheless, though complying outwardly, the states still maintained their friendly *liaisons*. And the league of the five states remained intact, and was indeed strengthened by the alliance of Bern with the Waldstätten, with which she had been more closely connected ever since the great battle of Laupen, where the Forest men had proved such staunch and useful friends. The treaty is dated March 6, 1353.

Albrecht was dissatisfied with the results of the last truce, and renewed the hostilities in the spring of 1353. Prevailing on Charles IV. to intervene that monarch twice visited Zurich, and held interviews with her representatives, and those of the Wadstätten. Yet it was evident his purpose was to give every advantage to Austria. The citizens trusting that his mediation would be just, received him with "imposing pomp and great honours." But their high hopes were soon dashed. Influenced by the Austrian counsellors about him, Charles strongly upheld the old Habsburg claims, and on his second visit even denied the validity of the ancient charters of the Forest, and requested the Eidgenossen to dissolve their union. Naturally, the Confederates were unwilling to throw away the results of a century's hard struggling, and, insisting on their unchangeable and undeniable rights, they simply answered that his "views were incomprehensible to them." Charles at once returned to Nürnberg, and thence sent to Zurich his declaration of war.

Albrecht, who had bought and rebuilt Rapperswyl, assembled there his forces, and laid waste the borders of the lake. The king fixed his camp at Regensberg; and thence the two pushed forward and formed a junction at Küsnacht. Their united forces, estimated at fifty thousand, formed the most formidable and magnificent army seen that century. Ravaging the lovely vineyard slopes, laments a contemporary annalist, they marched on Zurich, and, in spite of the sallies of the Zurcher to avert such a fate, completely encircled the town. Entirely cut off from all supplies, the inhabitants had no hope of holding out for any length of time, especially against a foe ten times more numerous. But at the most critical moment the place was saved by a stratagem. For suddenly the imperial banner was seen floating over the citadel.

The burgesses (or their leader Brun) had hoisted it up as a declaration that they were the subjects of the Holy Roman Empire, and meant no disobedience to the king. The incident made a deep impression on the enemy, and Charles at once suspended the siege. Thus for the third time foiled Albrecht retired in high dudgeon to Baden, and thence began to indulge in mere petty warfare. As for the king, he betook himself to Prague, there to enrich the Domkirche with the numerous relics and antiquities he had delightedly amassed during his stay in Swiss lands. This king was the founder of Bohemia's greatness, and of the splendour of its capital.

On his return from Italy as Roman emperor he concluded a peace at Regensburg, in July, 1355, and the war came to an end. The result, as in the case of the previous war, had been injurious to the interests of the Confederation. Glarus and Zug remained excluded from the League, and the Habsburgs retained their lands in the Forest. The only thing left was the union of the six states. Zurich had borne the burden of the war for the last four years, and, unless she wished to forfeit her very existence, was compelled to have peace at any price. And as she was completely exhausted, and yet was made the surety for the Waldstätten, the Eidgenossen submitted to the harsh conditions imposed.

In 1358 Albrecht died, and was succeeded by his enterprising son, Rudolf IV. This ruler made it his special object to extend his power on the Upper Zurich lake. Rapperswyl was fortified and enlarged, and the famous wooden bridge across the lake was built—not for pilgrims wandering to Einsiedeln, as common report had it, but—to connect the territories he had conquered, or was expecting to conquer. Besides, he wished to cut off Zurich from the direct route to, and trade with, Italy, and from the Forest. But in 1360 died the all-powerful Brun, who had ever sympathised with Austria ; and, in 1364, the old Queen Agnes (the widowed queen of Hungary), who had resided for twenty years at Königsfelden. Rudolf likewise died about the same time, and with their decease the Austrian spell was broken, and the hold of the Habsburgs on Zurich for a while loosened. Charles, now unfriendly towards Austria, tried to win favour with the Eidgenossen. He heaped privileges on Zurich, and sanctioned the league of the six states. Zurich refused to renew the treaty of Regensburg by oath, and as persistently declined to punish the people of Schwyz for breaking it. A fresh outbreak of war seemed imminent, but was averted by the peace of Torberg, 1368, which established a better agreement between Austria and the Confederation. By this treaty Zug was permitted to be re-annexed to the league. Zug had been conquered by Schwyz in 1365, at a moment when the attention of Austria was withdrawn. Glarus did not return to the Confederation until it had, so to speak, qualified itself for re-admission, by gaining the most remarkable victory of Naefels, the story of which will be told later on.

XIII.

ZURICH AN EXAMPLE OF A SWISS TOWN IN THE MIDDLE AGES.

(853-1357.)

WE may perhaps do well to pause here awhile before proceeding to show how the various Swiss cantons were gathered into the fold of the Eidgenossenschaft—a long process, as a matter of fact—and devote a short chapter to a glance at an aristocratic city whose polity and development contrast with those of the Forest lands. Zurich presents a fair example of a city whose origin dates back to a remote age, and whose transition from the condition of a feudal territory into the position of an independent commonwealth can be clearly followed. That Turicum is a word of Celtic origin, and that the place was one of the lake settlements in prehistoric times, and a Roman toll-station later on, has been already shown.

The chief founders of this Alamannic, or Swabian, settlement, however, were the Carolinger. Louis the German had raised the Grand Abbey and Church of

Our Lady (Fraumunsterabtei) in 853, to provide his saintly daughters, Hildegarde and Bertha, with positions and incomes equal to their rank. His ancestors, Pepin the Short and Charlemagne, had founded or enlarged the minster, with its vast establishment of prebends, and the Carolinum, or clerical colleges. Both institutions were richly endowed with land, and granted many prerogatives, especially the *immunity*, most precious of all, viz., the severance from the county or local administration of Zurich. They thus came again under the immediate control of the empire, and there were developed, two distinct centres of feudal life. Yet a third nucleus was formed by the dependants of royalty, the *fiscalini*, and followers of the monarch and of the Swabian dukes. These were grouped around the imperial palace (Pfalz) on the Lindenhof, a fortified stronghold on the site of the Roman *castrum*, and a favourite residence of the German sovereigns, who were attracted thither by the natural beauty of the place. The houses of the Alamannic free peasantry were scattered over the slopes of Zurichberg, and reached down to the Limmat river. Gradually these four distinct settlements approached each other, and in the tenth century the inner core at the mouth of the lovely lake was girt with strong walls with towers, and the *tout ensemble* now looked like a picturesque mediæval city with its suburbs. The rights of high jurisdiction over the whole were exercised by a royal governor, or representative of the sovereign. This was the so-called *Reichsvogtei*, or Advocacia in imperio.

The noble counts of Lenzburg were imperial governors from about 970 to 1098, but when the Zaerings became the governors of the Swiss lands the Lenzburgs became their holders till their death. Then the *Reichsvogtei*, that is, the city and its vicinity, fell back into the hands of the Zaerings, and was held by them directly till the extinction of the dynasty, 1218. From that time the charge was entrusted to the city-board, as Vögte. In Zurich the Lady Abbess acknowledged as her superior none but the governing Zaeringen duke, and later on, that is, after the dynasty had come to an end, took the foremost position. Indeed Frederick and the Hohenstaufer created his *Reichsfürstin*, Princess Abbess, and thus the office became one of very special dignity, and was bestowed generally on ladies of noble birth. By the acquisition of territory—reaching into Alsacia and to the St. Gothard—by privileges acquired under successive monarchs, by monopolies (coinage, fees, and tolls on markets and fairs, &c.), the institution rose to an eminence and splendour truly royal. Dukes and counts visited the abbey to pay court to its illustrious abbess—*die Hohe Frau von Zurich*, as she was styled—and entrusted their daughters to her care. Yet it was for court life these high-born damsels were to be prepared rather than for the religious vows. The inner life of this great monastery, though highly interesting in itself, cannot enter into a short sketch like the present. Not only was the Abbess Lady Paramount over her clergy and vast abbatial household, with its staff of officers and its law-court, but she also bore sway over the city itself.

When the administration began to require increased attention she enlarged its council, and presided at its meetings. This curious state of things continued till the thirteenth century, which saw the rise of a general political emancipation in German cities. Though apparently under a thraldom, yet the citizens really grew beneath the mild and equitable female rule into a powerful and thriving body, and at length began to contest with their mistress for self-rule.

To Frederick II. they owed their emancipation. By him Zurich became a free imperial city, governed by its own council. Council and citizens gradually becoming alive to their own civic interests, step by step wrested the civil power from the hands of the Lady Abbess, and emerged into the condition of an independent commonwealth. By this time society within the city had arranged itself into three distinct classes. (1) The clergy, headed by the abbess and the provost. (2) The knights, owing military service to emperor and abbess, and the burghers, or chiefly free landowners, and important commercial men. This second order was the governing class, and out of it came the members of the council. (3) The craftsmen, who exercised their trades only with the permission of their masters, the governing class. The workers were excluded from all share in the government, and were even prohibited from forming guilds. The majority of the artisans and serfs lived without the gates, in the outer city or walled-in suburbs. These political inequalities at length met with violent opposition, and in 1336 there broke out a revolution.

The industry of the thrifty and energetic population increased the material wealth of the city, and commercial treaties were entered into with neighbouring countries, with Italy particularly, and Italian influence made itself felt ever since the twelfth century, through four hundred years, not only in trade, but also in architecture. Zurich became an emporium for silk, and the silk manufacture, introduced from Italy, became a speciality, and was found in no other German town.[1] The activity displayed in building churches and monasteries was simply astonishing. The present minster, in the Lombard style, on the type of San Michele at Pavia, was built in the twelfth century, and the abbey was restored by the noble ladies in the thirteenth. The frequent visits of kings and emperors, who held their diets here, naturally increased the importance of the city. Taking it altogether, Zurich must have been, even in the thirteenth century, a fine specimen of a mediæval town, for Barbarossa's biographer, Otto von Freysing, calls it the noblest city of Swabia ("Turegum nobilissimum Sueviae oppidum").[2] Her policy of entering into alliances with the Swabian and Rhenish towns, and with the vast South-German coalition, and the friendly political and commercial relations she maintained, show that she fully grasped the situation, and

[1] White silk veils in the guise of bonnets were exported to Vienna, and even as far as Poland. This silk-making, of course, increased the prosperity of the town. It declined, and was reintroduced in the sixteenth century in a far more advanced condition, by the persecuted Protestants from Locarno.

[2] He also reports that one of its gates bore the inscription, "*Nobile Turegum multarum copia rerum.*"

gave her that security which promoted her trade and industry, and allowed her to develop freely.

The thirteenth century spread enlightenment amongst the benighted people of the Middle Ages, and increased the growth of political freedom in the cities, thanks to the struggles between the Papacy and the Hohenstaufen. Zurich had early emancipated herself from the spiritual sway and influence of her abbess mistress. Already, in 1146, the people had listened with keen interest to the advanced religious teaching of Arnold of Brescia, and in the ensuing quarrels sided with the freethinking Frederick II. During the interdict of 1247-49 Frederick's staunch adherents boldly drove from the town those clergy who refused to perform their spiritual functions. On a second expulsion from the town the friars took sides with the citizens, and obeyed the order literally, for they went out by one gate of the town, and re-entered by another, and resumed their offices. That the Zurcher had grown strong and self-reliant is shown by their alliance with Rudolf of Habsburg, in the feuds against their common foes, the neighbouring nobles, whose raids they checked, and by openly resisting the heavy taxation imposed by the monarch on the city. On one occasion — it was at a drinking-bout — the chief magistrate denounced this oppressive policy most wrathfully in the very presence of the queen and her daughters.

The Staufen epoch, seething with social and political movements, was also full of the spirit of romanticism. The English and French met the Germans in the Crusades, and quickened in the

Fatherland the love of poetry and romance. Then the great religious wars themselves opened out a whole new world of thought and fancy. The glorification of the brilliant exploits of the Staufen sovereigns, themselves poets, inspired many a grand or lovely song, the highest flights producing the Nibelungen and the *Minnelieder*. In Swiss lands also minstrelsy flowed richly, and Zurich stands out as a "Poets' Corner" in the thirteenth century. At the hospitable manor of Roger Manesse, a famous knight and magistrate of the city, or at the great Abbey Hall, a brilliant company of singers clustered round the Princess Abbess Elizabeth, an eminent woman, and her relatives, the Prince Bishop of Constance, Henry of Klingenberg, and his brother Albrecht, the famous chevalier. Then the Prince Abbots of Einsiedeln, and the abbots of Petershausen (Constance), the counts of Toggenburg, the barons of Regensberg, of Eschenbach, and Von Wart, together with many other lords, spiritual and temporal, and many a fair and illustrious lady—all these thronged the courtly circle to listen to the recital of the *Minnelieder*, or perchance to produce their own. The famous Codex Manesse, lately at Paris, and now in Germany,[1] bears witness to the romantic character of the age. It contains the songs of some hundred and fifty German and Swiss minstrels, who sang between the years 1200 and 1350. Manesse and his son, a canon at the minster, undertook the collection out of pure enthusiasm. Their amanuensis

---

[1] It happened to be in the possession of the Elector of the Palatinate, and was carried off to France when Louis XIV. laid waste the province.

was a comely young fellow named Hadloub, the son of a freeman farmer from the Zurichberg. A pretty story is told how during his mechanical labour of copying there grew strong in him the love of poetry, and he became himself a poet. For he fell in love with a high-born lady at Manesse's court, who however noticed him not. Then he told his grief in love songs which Manesse added to his collection. Indeed these songs close the series of Swiss poems in the Codex Manesse. Gottfried Keller, of Zurich, one of the greatest German novelists of the present day, has treated of the period in his exquisite novel "Hadloub" (*Zurcher Novellen*). Space does not permit us to give any account of the story, and the reader must be referred to the fascinating tale as it stands. Hadloub was indeed the last Swiss minstrel belonging to that fertile age. The love and beauty of woman is the theme of his songs, and in depicting these he particularly excels—the real *Minnegesang*. Uhland, the great lyric poet says of him, "In the clear soul of this poet the parting minstrelsy has once more reflected its own lovely image."

But whilst poetry was rejoicing the hearts of the nobles, political clouds were fast gathering over the city, to break at length into a wild hurricane. As a matter of fact, a few distinguished families had established an oligarchy in the place of the city council in process of time. The craftsmen, excluded from any share in the administration, and moreover finding fault with the financial management of the state, and galled by the domineering conduct of the aristocracy, rose in fierce opposition. Rudolf Brun, an ambitious ruler, but a clever statesman, being at variance with his own patrician party, suddenly placed himself at the head of the malcontents. Overthrowing the government before it had time to bestir itself, Rudolf had himself elected burgomaster, an official in whom all power was to centre. In 1336 he presented a new constitution, making the whole assembly swear to it. To insure its validity this code (*Geschworne Brief*) was submitted to the sanction of the abbess and the provost, and was also approved by the emperor. This new constitution was quite in keeping with the political views of the age, and remained in its chief points the leading constitutional guide of the commonwealth down to the revolution of 1798. It was a curious blending of democratic with aristocratic and monarchical elements. The craftsmen, who up to the present had counted for nothing in politics, were now formed into thirteen corporations, each selecting its own guildmaster, who represented its members in the governing council. The nobility and the wealthy burghers who practised no profession, or the Geschlechter (patricians), and rentiers formed a highly aristocratic body known as the Constafel (Constables), and were likewise represented in the state council by thirteen members, six of whom Brun named himself. The position of the burgomaster was the most striking of all, and was, in fact, that of a Roman dictator of old, or resembling the Italian tyrannies of the Visconti or Medici. Elected for life, vested with absolute power, the burgomaster was responsible to none, whilst to him fealty was to be sworn by all on pain of losing the rights of citizenship.

The idol of the people to whom he had granted political power, Brun was regarded as the true pilot and saviour in stormy times. The fallen councillors brooded revenge, and being banished the town, resorted to Rapperswyl, the Zurich *extra muros*, and at the other end of the lake. There they made *chose commune* with Count John of that place, who was desirous of evading payment of the debts he had contracted in Zurich. Feuds and encounters followed, and John was slain in battle in 1337. The emperor tried to restore peace, but the exiled councillors were bent on bringing back the old state of things, and on regaining their seats. They plotted against Brun's life, and those of his associates, and fixed upon the 23rd of February, 1350, for making an attack by night on the city, with the intention of seizing it by a single *coup-de-main*. They relied on the help of sympathisers within the town. The burgomaster, being apprized of the plot, summoned his faithful burghers to arms by the ringing of the tocsin. A bloody hand-to-hand fight in the streets took place, thence called the *Zurcher Mordnacht*. The conspiracy was crushed by the majority, and Count John of Rapperswyl, son of the above-mentioned count, was thrown into the tower of Wellenberg, a famous state prison. There he passed his time in the composition of *Minnelieder*.

Brun made a bad use of his victory. His cruelties to the prisoners and to Rapperswyl, which he burnt, are unjustifiable, and seem inexplicable in so far-sighted a statesman. He was ambitious, and desired not only his own advancement, but also that of his native city. He had depended on Austria, hoping to rise through her alliance and aid, but, suddenly forgetting all moderation, and disregarding all traditional *liaisons* with her, he laid waste the territory of the counts of Rapperswyl, cousins to the Habsburgs. This of course entangled Zurich in a war with Austria, who threatened to level her with the ground. Having estranged the neighbouring states by her cruel proceedings, or rather by those of Brun, Zurich stood alone, and was compelled to look around for aid and countenance. Though by no means friendly towards the bold Forest men, the dictator Brun concluded an alliance with them. The Waldstätten were quite ready to receive into their league a commonwealth so powerful and well-organized as Zurich, a state likely to be at once their bulwark and their emporium. They therefore willingly agreed to Brun's stipulations (May 1, 1351), and, further acquiesced in the proviso that Zurich should be allowed to conclude separate treaties. These treaties or alliances were very common at that time, and changeable as they were, they nevertheless gave additional security for the time being.

But though Brun had introduced a *régime* of force, he yet made concessions to the masses, giving them a share of political power. And his constitutional system answered the wants of the city, to a great degree, for some four centuries and a half.

XIV.

BERN CRUSHES THE NOBILITY: GREAT VICTORY OF LAUPEN, 1339.

THE alliance of Bern was a great acquisition to the federal league. She formed the corner-stone of the Burgundian states, and brought them into connection with, and finally into the pale of, the Swiss Confederation. Her early history has been touched upon in previous chapters. True to her original position as a check on the nobility, and forming a natural stronghold, this proud Zaeringen town shows a singularly martial, and indeed dominant spirit, and runs a military and political career of importance. Bern had effectively resisted the encroachments of the old house of Kyburg (1243-55), and stoutly opposed the oppressive tax of 40 per cent. imposed by Rudolf of Habsburg. And, though she had suffered a severe defeat at Schosshalde, in 1289, the disaster was more than compensated by a great victory at Dornbühl, in 1298, and she had carried over her rival, Freiburg and the nobles of the highlands, partners of the latter. It was always a most usual thing in the fourteenth century for states to enter into leagues, with the view of better safeguarding themselves against neighbouring and powerful foes. And thus Bern gathered all the kindred elements of West Switzerland into a Burgundian Confederation—the free imperial valley Hasle, the rich monastery of Interlaken, the house of Savoy, the new house of Kyburg-Burgdorf, the bishops of Sion, the cities of Bienne, Solothurn, Freiburg,—all these were at one time or another in union with Bern. The friendship with Freiburg, however, was often disturbed by feelings of jealousy that at times grew into feuds, but that for Solothurn was lasting. It was, in fact, based on similarity of political views and aims, both agreeing in refusing to acknowledge the rival kings, Louis of Bavaria and Frederick the Handsome. In consequence of their obstinacy, Leopold, who had been defeated at Morgarten, and wished to reassert the authority of his brother, laid siege to Solothurn in 1318. The Bernese came to the help of the sister city. A memorable scene was witnessed during the course of the assault. The river Aare was much swollen at the time, and a bridge that the beleaguering forces had thrown across was carried away by the flood, and their men were being drowned in numbers. Then the Solothurner, forgetting all injuries, rushed out with boats to save their enemies. Leopold was so touched by such magnanimity that he at once raised the siege, and presented the town with a beautiful banner.

Bern's strong bent for territorial extension was quite a match for the encroaching tendencies of the Habsburgs. To get a footing in the canton the latter

UPPER FALL OF THE REICHENBACH (MEYRINGEN).

made use of a crime committed amongst the Kyburger. That illustrious house, well-nigh ruined morally and financially, had been compelled by its adverse fortunes to place in the Church a younger son, Eberhard. The young man submitted with great reluctance. Happening to fall to a quarrel with Hartmann, at the castle of Thun, high words arose and were succeeded by blows, and Hartmann was slain. This was in 1332. On the plea of avenging the murder, the Habsburgs set up a claim to the Kyburg property. Bern however confirmed the count in his possessions, and purchasing Thun from him, returned it as a fief, requiring him to give an undertaking that Burgdorf should never be mortgaged without her knowledge and consent. But Eberhard gradually forgot the services Bern had rendered his house, and, fearing her power, veered round to Freiburg, and became a citizen of that town. The differences then swelled into an outbreak, which had been for some time impending. Bern, it is to be noted, had in many ways got the start of the sister city; for instance, she had become an imperial free city in the year 1218, on the extinction of the Zaeringer, and this had given her a considerable lift. Then, in 1324, Bern had secured the mortgage of Laupen, an excellent stronghold on the Saane, and had driven the Freiburger from the district. And in 1331, after the house of Kyburg had joined its fortunes with those of Freiburg, the strong fortress of Gümminen had been demolished, as well as many Kyburg castles. Gümminen belonged to her rival, and was a place of singular strategical importance.

But these were mere preliminary episodes, and more serious warfare followed. Many of the surrounding nobles had outlived their time of prosperity and greatness, and yet clung to the prerogatives of their class without possessing any longer the means to maintain them. Bern took advantage of all this to secure her own aggrandisement, and gain for herself more territory, for originally she had possessed no lands beyond her walls. The Bernese Oberland was the first district on which she set her eyes. Here the counts of Greyerz,[1] the dynasts of Turn (Valisian nobles), and the barons of Weipenburg, held the chief territorial lordships, and formed a strong Alpine coalition with Austrian sympathies, as against the rising city of Bern. With the last mentioned Bern strove for the supremacy, and stormed their stronghold, Wimmis, in the Simmenthal, both town and castle, and demolished the *Letzinen*,[2] or fortifications in the valley. The old baron and his nephew had no means to fight out the quarrel, and were compelled to accept the terms dictated by the victors. They were bound to render military service, and were required to pledge their castles for their submission, and so forth. But what most nearly touched them was the loss of Hasle. That beautiful valley, stretching from Brienz lake to the Grimsel pass, with romantic Meiringen as its central place, has had a strange history. The inhabitants were at first free Alamannic farmers, owing

[1] Von Greyerz still occurs amongst the Bernese aristocracy.
[2] Letzinen are walls constructed across a valley, and are peculiar to Switzerland.

allegiance to no sovereign, or lord, except the German monarch, and they chose their Ammann from amongst themselves, or had him chosen by the king. They had allied themselves as equals with Bern, in 1275, but in 1310 their subjection was sealed. Henry VII. wanting money for his coronation at Rome, mortgaged Hasle to the barons of Weipenburg, for 340 marks. In 1334 Bern bought up the mortgage, and the valley thus came under Bernese rule. Bern now appeared likely enough to stretch her power even up to the snow-clad mountain lands, and laid the foundation of her future pre-eminence amongst the western cantons. But she stirred up fierce opposition, especially on the part of the Burgundian nobles. Fearing for their very existence, the counts of Greyerz, Valangin, Aarberg, Nidan, Neuchâtel, Vaud, Kyburg, headed by Freiburg, encouraged, though not actually assisted, by Louis of Bavaria, rose in arms. Bern called for help from Hasle, Weipenburg, and the Forest Cantons, but found it a difficult matter to get together the scattered forces. On the 10th of June, 1339, an army of fifteen thousand foot and three thousand horse marched against Laupen, whose defence devolved upon some four hundred Bernese. On the 21st of the same month there arrived at the town the forces of the Eidgenossen, amounting to barely six thousand men. They wore a white cross of cloth, and marched to the relief of the beleaguered city animated by the stirring words of Theobald, a priest of the Teutonic order. The battle actually took place, however, on a plateau a little more than two miles east of the town. During the day the besiegers had amused themselves with various sports, mocking the preparations of their opponents, and it was not till vespers that Count Valangin commenced hostilities. It was a desperate struggle that followed—a second Morgarten. The Waldstätter had begged to be allowed to engage the cavalry, and a hard task they found it. Yet within two hours the enemy was completely routed, and took to flight. No fewer than fifteen hundred men lay dead upon the field, and amongst them the counts of Valangin, Greyerz, Nidan, the last count of Vaud, and others. Seventy full suits of armour, and twenty-seven banners had been taken. Their hearts overflowing with joy and thankfulness the victors sank on their knees at nightfall, when all was over, and thanked God for His mercy. It would be uninteresting to a foreign reader to give an account of the discussions which have taken place as to the leadership of the Bernese force. But it may be mentioned that two distinguished generals, Rudolf von Erlach and Hans von Bubenberg, have by different authorities been credited with the honour.

The war was not yet concluded, but degenerated into one of simple devastation. The Freiburg forces were defeated at the very gates of their town by Rudolf von Erlach, according to some records, which would seem to show at any rate that he is no mere fictitious personage. Bern added victory to victory, and the saying ran that, "God Himself had turned citizen of that town to fight for her just cause." In July, 1340, a truce was agreed upon, and Bern

PORCH OF BERN MINSTER, WITH STATUE OF RUDOLF VON ERLACH.

resumed her old alliances with Kyburg, the Forest, Vaud, and even Geneva. The diplomatic Lady of Königsfelden, Agnes, anxious to secure so staunch an ally, drew Bern into a league with Austria, which lasted for ten years, and strongly influenced the politics of the town. It was not till after the expiration of this league, and after the peace of Brandenburg, that she could enter into an alliance with the league of the seven states. This closed the list of the eight Orte, and the league proved to be perpetual. Though Bern was a great check on the feudal nobility, she yet herself possessed a thoroughly aristrocratic form of government, in which the lesser people and craftsmen had no share whatever.

The mad schemes of Rudolf of Kyburg, who hoped to mend his fortunes by conquering Solothurn and other towns, gave rise to protracted warfare, in which Burgdorf and Thun fell to the share of Bern, by purchase, in 1384. To dwell on this is impossible, within the limits of our space, but it may be mentioned that a first siege proved a failure. Retaliation was made by the siege of Burgdorf, which likewise miscarried, through the intervention of Leopold. The doom of the house of Kyburg was, however, sealed, and it fell beneath the sway of Bern. The treachery of the Habsburgs in breaking their promise to the Eidgenossen was one of the chief causes leading to the battle of Sempach, the most famous of all Swiss battles.

XV.

THE BATTLES OF SEMPACH, 1386, AND NAEFELS, 1388.

SELDOM, if ever, has Switzerland seen a more eventful month than that of July, 1386, for in that month she fought and won the ever-memorable battle of Sempach. To set down all the petty details as to the causes which led to this engagement would be tedious indeed. It is sufficient to point out—what is but a truism—that there is seldom much love lost between oppressor and oppressed, and Austria and the Swiss Confederation had for some time held that relation to each other. A ten years' peace had indeed been concluded between the two powers, but it was a sham peace, and the interval had been used by both to prepare for new conflicts.

Austria was secretly assisting the impoverished house of Kyburg in her ravishing expeditions against the towns of the Confederation. Ruthlessness was met by ruthlessness; Zurich laid siege to Rapperswyl with the intent to destroy the odious Austrian toll-house; Lucerne levelled with the ground the Austrian fort Rothenburg, and entered into alliances with Entlebuch and Sempach to overthrow the Austrian supremacy. This was equal to a declaration of war, and war was indeed imminent.

Duke Leopold III., of Austria, was most anxious to bring the quarrel to an issue, and to chastise the insolent Swiss citizens and peasantry. The Swiss cities had joined in league with the Southern German towns, which like themselves professed the policy of resisting the encroaching tendencies of princes and nobles. Mutual help in case of need had been pledged amongst themselves by this league of cities, but the burghers of the German towns were mere puppets in the hand of Austria. She, dreading the rising of wealthy towns, cajoled them by fine promises, and they pleaded for submission, and sought to compose the differences between the Swiss and the Austrians. Of very different mettle, however, were the towns on this side the Rhine; they objected to the weak and wavering policy of their more northerly neighbours, and determined on fighting, if necessary, alone and unaided.

Leopold III., a descendant of that Leopold so disastrously defeated at Morgarten, possessed most of the virtues held of account in his day. He was manly, chivalrous, dauntless; he was possessed of dexterity and adroitness in both sports and the more serious business of war. His indomitable spirit and personal daring knew no bounds. He had once, clad in full armour, forded the Rhine at flood-time, and in the sight of the enemy, to escape being made prisoner. Like Rudolf of Habsburg he was vastly ambitious, and bent on securing wealth and greatness for the house of Austria. A clever manager of his estates and a generous master, he was yet neither politician nor tactician; as a man of action, and filled with hatred of the refractory towns, he spared no pains to check their struggles for independence. No wonder then that the nobles of Southern Germany rallied round the gallant swordsman, and made him their leader in the expeditions against the *bourgeoisie* and peasantry. And no sooner had the truce expired (June, 1386), than they directed their first attack on the bold Confederation; no fewer than one hundred and fifty nobles sending letters of refusal (= a challenge) to the summons to war sent out by the Swiss Government.

Leopold's plan was to make Lucerne the centre of his military operations, but in order to draw away attention from his real object, he sent a division of five thousand men to Zurich to simulate an attack on that town. Whilst the unsuspecting Confederates lay idle within the walls of Zurich, he gathered reinforcements from Burgundy, Swabia, and the Austro-Helvetian Cantons, the total force being variously estimated at from twelve thousand to twenty-four thousand men. He marched his army in the direction of Lucerne, but by a round-about way, and seized upon Willisan, which he set on fire, intending to punish Sempach *en passant* for her desertion. But the Confederates getting knowledge of his stratagem left Zurich to defend herself, and struck straight across the country in pursuit of the enemy. Climbing the heights of Sempach on the side of Hiltisrieden, overlooking the town and lake of that name, they encamped at Meyersholz, a wood fringing the hilltop. The Austrians leaving Sursee, for want of some more practicable road towards Sempach, made their way slowly and painfully along the path which leads from Sursee to the heights, and then turns suddenly down upon Sempach. Great was their surprise and consternation when at the junction of the Sursee and Hiltisrieden roads they came suddenly upon the Swiss force, which they had imagined to be idling away the time at Zurich. The steep hillsides crossed by brooks and hedges looked a battlefield impracticable enough for cavalry evolutions, yet the young nobles in high glee at the prospect of winning their spurs in such a spot pleaded for the place against the better reason of all men.

The Swiss, confident of success, and trusting in the help of God and the saints, as of old, drew up in battle order, their force taking a kind of wedge-shaped mass   /‾‾\   the shorter edge foremost, and the bravest men occupying the front positions. The Austrians, on the other hand, relying proudly on the superiority of their high-born knights and nobles, looked disdainfully on what they believed to be a mere rabble of herdsmen. And, in truth, the handful of fifteen hundred men, inadequately armed with short weapons or clubs, battle-axes or halberds, seemed but a sorry match for that steel-clad army of six thousand well-trained lancers, cavalry, and foot. But the possession of cavalry in such a spot could not in itself give any advantage to the Austrians, and their knights dismounted and handed their horses to the care of attendants. To avoid getting their feet entangled in the long grass of a meadow close by the noble cavaliers cut off the beaks or points of their shoes—then the fashion—and the spot is to this day called the "beak-meadow" (Schnabelweide). Claiming for themselves the right to win honour that day, they ordered their infantry to the rear. According to another account, however, their infantry were still at Sursee, the noble horsemen declining their aid. After ancient custom, the Austrians formed themselves into a compact phalanx, the noblest occupying the front ranks, the preparations being necessarily hurriedly and somewhat indefinitely made.

The onset was furious, and the Austrian Hotspurs, each eager to outstrip his fellows in the race for honour, rushed on the Swiss, drove them back a little, and then tried to encompass them and crush them in their midst. The Swiss quickly fell back, but some sixty of their men were cut down before the Austrians lost a single soldier. The banner of Lucerne was captured; the Austrian phalanx was as yet unbroken, and all the fortune of the battle seemed against the Swiss, for their short weapons could not reach a foe guarded by long lances. But suddenly the scene changed. "A good and pious man," says the old chronicler, deeply mortified by the misfortune of his country, stepped forward from the ranks of the Swiss—*Arnold von Winkelried!*

Shouting to his comrades in arms, "I will cut a road for you; take care of my wife and children!" he dashed on the enemy, and, catching hold of as many spears as his arms could encompass, he bore them to the ground with the whole weight of his body. His comrades rushed over his corpse, burst through the gap made in the Austrian ranks, and began a fierce hand-to-hand encounter. Fearful havoc was made by the Swiss clubs and battle-axes in the wavering ranks of the panic-stricken enemy, whose heavy armour and long lances indeed greatly impeded their movements. Nevertheless the Austrians made a brave stand, and Leopold, who had been watching the issue, now rushed into the *mêlée*, and fell one of the bravest in the desperate struggle. The nobles and knights, calling for their horses, found that the attendants had fled with them. Seeing that all was lost, the knights became panic-stricken, and rushed hither and thither in the greatest disorder. There still remained the infantry, however, and these attempted to stay the flight of the hapless cavaliers, and restore order, but it was all in vain. A fearful carnage followed, in which no mercy was shown, and there fell of the common soldiers two thousand men, and no fewer than seven hundred of the nobility. The Swiss lost but one hundred and twenty men. Rich spoils—arms, jewellery, and eighteen banners—fell into the hands of the victors.

This defeat of a brilliant army of horse and foot, of knights and noblemen, all well-trained, by a mere handful of irregulars—citizen and peasant soldiers—was a brilliant military achievement, and attracted the attention and admiration of the civilized world. It brought to the front the *bourgeoisie* and peasantry and their interests, and struck terror into the hearts of their oppressors. This great victory gained by the Swiss not only widened and established more firmly the career of military glory commenced at Morgarten, but it gave to the Confederation independence, and far greater military and political eminence. What Platæa had been of old to the Greeks, that Sempach was to the Swiss; it struck a deadly blow against an ancient and relentless foe. Austria, her rule on this side of the Rhine thus rudely shaken, was compelled to waive all rights of supremacy over the Confederation. Not that she relinquished those rights readily; it needed an equal disaster to her forces at Naefels, in 1388, before she would really and avowedly renounce her pretensions to rule the Swiss.

The story of Winkelried's heroic action has given rise to much fruitless but interesting discussion. The truth of the tale, in fact, can neither be confirmed nor denied, in the absence of any sufficient proof. But Winkelried is no *myth*, whatever may be the case with the other great Swiss hero, Tell. There is proof that a family of the name of Winkelried lived at Unterwalden at the time of the battle. But no Swiss annals referring to the encounter at Sempach were written till nearly a century later. The Austrian chronicle gives no account of Winkelried's exploit, and for good reason, say the Swiss: all the men of the Austrian front ranks, who alone could have witnessed the exploit, were killed, and the rear ranks

WINKELRIED'S MONUMENT AT STANZ   (*From photograph by Appenzeller, Zurich.*)

fled at the very first signs of disaster in front of them. A fifteenth-century chronicle of Zurich, and the numerous songs and annals of the sixteenth century, are full of praise of Winkelried and his deeds. But whatever may be the real truth of the matter it is certain that the grand old story of Winkelried and his splendid self-sacrifice is indelibly written on grateful Swiss hearts. Whether it was a single man or a whole body of men that offered up life itself for their country, it clearly proves a dauntless spirit of independence, a hatred of wrong and tyranny to have been innate in the breasts of the old Switzers, and to have led to the deliverance of their country from foreign oppression. And in spite of the many and often bitter controversies of the past twenty years the memory of Winkelried will ever remain an inspiration and a rallying-point whenever the little fatherland and its liberties are threatened.

The victory of Naefels forms a worthy pendant to that of Sempach, and as such cannot be passed over in silence. The Austrians, having recovered their spirits after the terrible disaster, and the "foul peace" (*faule Friede*) hastily arranged having expired, they carried the game to its conclusion. Despite all prohibitions, Glarus had kept up its friendship with the Eidgenossen, and in conjunction with them had, in 1386, captured Wesen, the key to the district. To Glarus, therefore, Albrecht III. now gave his whole attention. But Glarus itself, feeling much more free after Sempach, assembled its inhabitants, in the spring of 1387, for the first time as a Landsgemeinde, and drew up for itself a constitution. Wesen on

176 THE BATTLES OF SEMPACH AND NAEFELS.

Walensee was recaptured by the Austrians on their way to Glarus. This happened through the treachery of the inhabitants of the town, who, siding with their old masters, opened their gates. The federal garrison was surprised as they slept, and put to the sword (February, 1388). The Austrians assembled at Wesen a force of six thousand horse and foot, and on the 9th of April set out in two divisions. Count Hans von Werdenberg, the chief mover in the enterprise, climbed the opposite heights, with the intention of forming a junction at Mollis, whilst Count Donat von Toggenburg and other nobles led the main force along the river Lint. Reaching Naefels, at the entrance of the Glarus valley they found their passage barred by an Alpine fortification—a *Letzi*, as it is called—consisting of rampart and ditch. This, however, was stormed without difficulty, as the guard was insufficient for its defence. In truth, the Glarner were unaware of the Austrian movements, and though Ambühl and his two hundred men fought with the utmost bravery, they were no match for the far superior numbers against them. Like a torrent the Austrians rushed into the open and defenceless valley, and, fancying no doubt there was no further opposition or danger to fear, dispersed in all directions, pillaging property, firing houses, driving cattle. Plunder and destruction seemed indeed to be now their sole aim; but meanwhile the tocsin was sounding through the valley to call the villagers to arms in defence of their country. Fast they flocked to the standard of Ambühl, who had posted himself with his troops on the steep declivity of Rautiberg, waving high the banner of St. Fridolin to attract his friends. Here, six hundred men all told, including a handful of men from Schwyz, awaited the foe. At last, in straggling and disorderly fashion, the Austrians appeared in sight, many lingering behind for the sake of plunder. Their attempt to ascend the eminence occupied by the foe was met by a shower of stones, which threw the horses into confusion. With true Alpine agility the mountaineers now dashed down the slopes and fell on the cavalry. A fierce encounter followed, and then a terrible chase, during which the Austrians are said to have ten times stopped in their flight and attempted to hurl back their Swiss pursuers, but ten times were compelled to give way again before the terrible strokes which met them. Darkness set in, and with it came on fog, and a sudden fall of snow. A superstitious panic seized on the Austrians, and they fled in the utmost confusion to Naefels, and thence sought to regain their faithful Wesen. But here a fresh catastrophe awaited them. Thronging the bridge spanning the outlet of the lake their weight broke down the structure, and hundreds of fugitives dragged down by their heavy armour sank with it, and were drowned. Count Werdenburg, who was watching the disaster from his eminence, fled as fast as he could. This disaster explains the loss by the Austrians of so disproportionate a number of men, viz., seventeen hundred, as against the fifty-four who fell of the Glarus force. The latter fell chiefly in defence of the Letzi.

Year after year the people of Glarus, rich and poor

alike, Protestant and Catholic, still commemorate this great victory. On the first Thursday in April, in solemn procession, they revisit the battlefield, and on the spot the Landammann tells the fine old story of their deliverance from foreign rule, whilst priest and minister offer thanksgiving. The 5th of April, 1888, was a memorable date in the annals of the canton, being the five-hundredth anniversary of the day on which the people achieved freedom. From all parts of Switzerland people flocked to Naefels to participate in the patriotic and religious ceremonies. A right stirring scene it was when the Landammann presented to the vast assembly the banner of St. Fridolin—the same which Ambühl had raised high—and thousands of voices joined in the national anthem, *Rufst du mein Vaterland*, which, by the way, has the same melody as *God save the Queen*. If the Switzer has no monarch to love and revere, he has still his national heroes and his glorious ancestors, who sealed the freedom of their country with their blood.

In 1389 a seven years' peace was arranged, and Glarus returned to the Confederation. This peace was first prolonged for twenty years, and afterwards, in 1412, for fifty years. Finally, after a strife of more than one hundred years, Austria renounced her claims to rule over the Forest, and all her rights in Zug, Lucerne, and Glarus. In process of time the various dues were paid off in ordinary form.

XVI.

HOW SWITZERLAND CAME TO HAVE SUBJECT LANDS.

(1400–1450.)

IN the fourteenth century the Eidgenossen established a *ménage politique* of their own, and fixed its independence; in the fifteenth they raised it to power and eminence, and obtained for it an important military position in Europe. Yet though their family hearth was established, all was not done. The allied states could not stop there. They were still surrounded by lands ruled by Austria, by Italy, by Savoy; lands which could and did threaten the independence of the little infant republic. In fact, at a very early stage, the acquisition of additional territory became a vital question. This was to be done by means of new alliances, or by purchase or conquest. Zurich, for instance, had already, between 1358 and 1408, spent some two million francs in the buying of land. The struggles for independence had kindled a like desire for emancipation amongst the neighbouring Alpine states. But the efforts resulting were not all equally successful. Some of the states drifted from monarchical subjection to that of the federation or canton as subject lands (*Unterthanen laender*); others became "connections" (*Zugewandte*), or allies of inferior rank; others, again, took the position of *Schirmverwandte*, or *protégés*. One might indeed go thus through a whole graduated scale of relationships developed amongst the crowd of candidates seeking admission into the league. And though as yet kept outside they received a helping hand from the Eidgenossen. But it is not till the opening of the nineteenth century that we find the list of twenty-two cantons made up. Thanks to the mediation of Napoleon Bonaparte (1803), St. Gall, Thurgau, Grisons, Aargau, Vaud, and Ticino were added to the confederation of states. And by the Congress of Vienna, in 1814-15, were also added Valais, Geneva, and Neuchâtel. The latter, however, still continued under the sway of Prussia, although partly a free state, till 1857. The reader will clearly see into what a complicated fabric of unions the league is growing, and that the Swiss fatherland did not spring at once into life as a *fait accompli*. Each canton had its separate birth to freedom, as was the case with the free states of ancient Greece, which joined into confederations for a similar end—protection against a common foe. Each little state has its own separate history, even before it amalgamates with the general league. We shall, however, notice only the leading features.

Appenzell opens the series of *Zugewandte*, or "connections." The shepherds and peasants scattered around the foot of Mount Säntis, oppressed by the abbots of St. Gall, began a rising that partook of a revolutionary character. A succession of heroic feats followed—the battle of Vogelinseck in 1403, that of Am Stoss in 1405, and others [1]—and the prelate and his ally, Frederick IV. of Austria ("Empty Pocket"), were completely defeated. Somewhat curiously we find Graf Rudolf von Werdenberg throwing in his lot with that of the humble peasants, and stooping to the humiliating terms they insisted upon. He had been robbed of his lands by the Habsburgs, and hoped to recover them by the help of the Alpestrians, and actually did so. But the peasantry were somewhat diffident concerning him, and would not entrust him with command. So the noble knight of St. George put aside his fine armour and his magnificent horse, and donned the peasant's garb to be admitted into their ranks. Elated by their succession of triumphs the hardy Appenzeller rushed on to new victories. Bursting their bounds, like an impetuous mountain torrent, they spread into neighbouring lands, and even penetrated to the distant Tyrol. Serf and bondsman hailed them as deliverers, and whole towns and valleys along the Upper Rhine and the Inn came into alliance with them—*Bund ob dem See*, above Lake Constance —that was to be a safeguard in the East. At last the Swabian knighthood plucked up courage enough to oppose this mountain hurricane. At the siege of Bregenz in 1407, they were, through carelessness, put

---

[1] It is related that Uli Rotach kept at bay with his halbert twelve Austrians, giving way only when the hut against which he leant was set on fire.

to flight. The Bund collapsed, and its prestige departed, but the men had secured their object, viz., independence from control by the Abbey of St. Gall. By and by they bought off some of the taxes, and they met at their Landsgemeinde to consult respecting the weal of their country. Down to our own days this institution remains famous. Their application in 1411 for admission into the league was granted, but quite conditionally. Bern kept aloof from them, and Zurich found it necessary to checkmate their revolutionary tendencies, and they were received as *Zugewandte*, or allies of second rank. It was not till 1513 that the new-comer rose to the position of full member of the league. St. Gall, too, became " a connection " —and no more—in 1412.

The emancipation of the Valais (Wallis) is but one succession of feuds between the native nobility and Savoy, the owner of Low Valais, on the one hand, and the bishops of Sion and the people, on the other. In was, in fact, a contest between the Romance and the German populations, the latter of whom the French had driven into a corner. The dynasts Von Turn had Bishop Tavelli seized in his castle and hurled from its very windows down a precipice. This foul murder was avenged in the great battle of Visp, where Savoy is said to have left four thousand dead (1388). The barons of Raron sustained a defeat at Ulrichen, in 1414, though assisted by Bern (of which town they were citizens) and Savoy. These powerful nobles left the country, and the Valisians gradually secured autonomy, and, being helped in their quarrels by the Forest men, they finally drew nearer to the Confederation, as *Zugewandte* (1488).

We must not pass over a singular custom which prevailed amongst the Valais folk. It was a custom observed as a preliminary to serious warfare. If a tyrant was to fall, he was attainted and doomed by the Mazze. This was a huge club on which was carved a distressed-looking face as a symbol of oppression, the club being wound round with bramble. It was carried from village to village, and hamlet to hamlet, even to the remotest spots, and set up at public places to attract the attention of the people. One of the malcontents would then step forward and denounce the oppressor to the figure, and promise help. It was said that when the name of Raron was pronounced the figure bowed deeply in token of assent, and the insurgents drove nails into the face as a declaration of hostility, and the instrument was deposited at the gate of the baron's castle.

Graubünden (Grisons), the land of ancient and mediæval memories, of crumbling and picturesque castles, was, on account of its rugged surface and its almost countless dales, split up into numberless territorial lordships. Here in this rocky seclusion held sway the Belmonts, the Montforts, the Aspermonts, the Sax-Misox, and many others whose sonorous names tell of their origin. Here also were found the families of Haldenstein, Werdenberg, Toggenburg, and many more — Italian, Romansch, and German mingling closely. Yet the lord-paramount of them all was the Bishop of Chur, who had attained the rank of *Reichsfürst* or duke, who had a suite of nobles attached to his quasi-royal household, and who held lands even in Italy. Quite contrary to the usual rule, noble and peasant in general lived amicably together. The political freedom of the state was due rather to remarkable coalitions than to acts of war or insurrection. In the fourteenth century, when the bishops of Chur revealed a strong leaning towards Austria-Tyrol, the Gotteshausbund sprang into existence as a check on the alien tendencies of the prince-bishops. This league was formed in 1367 by the *Domstift* (chapter of clergy), the nobles, and the common people. The bishops themselves ruled over people of three different nationalities. A glance at the place-names on the map of Bünden shows how the old Latin race (Romansch), the Italians, and the migrated German race, were mixed up pell-mell in the district. Yet the Walchen Romansch (Welsh) were slowly retreating before the Valser, or Germans of the Valais, who had a strong bent for colonization and culture. In 1397 the *Graue Bund* (Grey League) was started in the valleys of the Vorder-Rhine by the Abbot of Disentis, some of the nobles, and the people at large. On the death of the last of the Toggenburgs in 1436 his various domains of Malans, Davos, Prättigau, &c., dreading Austrian interference, united into a league known as the ten *Gerichte Bund* (Jurisdictions), so called because each of the districts had its own place of execution. Gradually the three leagues formed a federal union (1471), and held their diets at one centre, Vazerol. Thus Bünden, developing after the manner of the Forest Cantons, grew into a triple and yet federal democracy which, threatened by the

Austrian invasion during the Swabian wars, turned to the Eidgenossen for help, and joined with them in 1497 as "connections."

In 1414 met the famous Council convoked by the Emperor Sigismund to remedy the evils which galled the Church, that Council which by a strange irony of fate sentenced to death by fire John Huss, the staunch opponent of the very abuses which the Council was called to redress. The Council proved fatal to the Habsburg interests in Swiss lands. Frederick IV. of Austria—the enemy of Appenzell—refused his homage to the German monarch, and for material reasons espoused the cause of John XXIII., one of the three deposed popes. John gave a tournament to cover his departure, and during the spectacle fled in a shabby postillion's dress to the Austrian town, Schaffhausen, whither Frederick followed. Excommunicated and outlawed—within a few days no fewer than four hundred nobles sent challenges to him—Duke Friedel, as he was familiarly called by his faithful Tyrolese peasantry, who alone stood by him, was driven from his lands and from his people. On all sides German contingents fell upon his provinces. Sigismund called on the Eidgenossen in the name of the empire to march on Aargau, his ancestral land, promising them the province for themselves. As they had just renewed their peace with Austria, the Eidgenossen were unwilling to break it, but it was urged by the emperor that their promise to Frederick was not binding. Bern, ever bent on self-aggrandisement, and determined to secure the lion's share if possible, threw away her scruples, and within seventeen days took as many towns and castles.[1] Zurich, consulting with the Eidgenossen, followed suit and seized Knonau. Lucerne took some fragment, and the Forest did likewise. Aargau, the retreat of the Habsburg nobles, offered no serious resistance; but Baden, which was seized by the Eidgenossen conjointly, the castle of Stein, the royal residence of the Habsburgs, was being stormed, when Sigismund tried to stop the siege; for Frederick in despair had in the meantime made an abject submission, and most of the confiscated lands were restored to him. However, the Eidgenossen were unwilling, because of the emperor's wavering policy, to relinquish so good a chance of adding to their territory. Matters were settled by their paying over a sum of money to Sigismund, who was ever in financial straits. Henceforth Friedel was nicknamed "With-the-empty-pocket."[2] Aargau was divided amongst the Eidgenossen as subject land, what they had seized separately becoming cantonal, and what conjointly federal, property. Baden and some other places became federal domains (*gemeine Herrschaften*), over which each of the eight states in turn set a governor for two years. With this precedent we enter upon the curious period in which the Swiss cantons split into two sets, the governing and the governed.

Whilst the republics vied with each other in ex-

[1] To Bern fell the classic spots Habsburg and Königsfelden.

[2] As a retort to those who thus nicknamed him this extravagant prince built a balcony at Innsbruck whose roof was covered with gold, at the cost of thirty thousand florins—it would be twenty times more money now. Every visitor to that romantic city will be struck by the quaint *Haus zum goldenen Dachere* (House with the golden roof).

tending their borders, two, Uri and Unterwalden, were unable to increase their territory, being hemmed in by lofty mountains. They turned their eyes towards the sunny south, beyond St. Gothard, where they might find additional lands. Like the Rhætians of old they had often descended into the Lombard plains, though for far more peaceful ends. When the St. Gothard pass was thrown open in the thirteenth century, there was a lively interchange of traffic between the two peoples—the cismontanes and the transmontanes. The men of the Forest sold their cheese, butter, cattle, and other Alpine produce at the marts in the Lombardian towns, and got from thence their supply of corn and other necessaries. And they of the Forest acted as guides across the mountains, as they did down to the railway era. Their youths, too, enlisted amongst the Italians soldiers, induced either by the prospect of gaining a living, or by a mere desire for amusement. Thus the Swiss associated on friendly terms with the southerners. But all this pleasant social intercourse was suddenly cut off. Whilst the Eidgenossen under the ægis of a weakened empire secured independence, the mighty Lombard cities, which had objected to imperial fetters, however light, by a singular contrast sank beneath the tyrannies of ambitious native dynasts, and under the Visconti the duchy of Milan sprang up from these free Italian towns. Quarrels that broke out between the Milanese and the people of the Forest prepared the way for the acquisition of Ticino by the Swiss. In 1403 Uri and Unterwalden were robbed of their herds of cattle at the mart of Varese by the officials

of the Visconti, on what pretext is not clear. Failing
to get redress, they at once decided on resorting to
force. They seized the Livinenthal or Leventina,
which willingly accepted the new masters. Fresh
robberies in 1410 were revenged by the annexation
of the Eschenthal, with Domo d'Ossola, which greatly
preferred Swiss supremacy to that of the Duke of
Milan. This is not much to be wondered at, seeing
that Gian Maria Visconti was a second Nero for
cruelty. The human beings who fell victims to his
suspicion or revenge he had torn to pieces by huge
dogs, which were fed on human blood. To strengthen
their Italian acquisitions the Eidgenossen bought
Bellinzona (1418) from the barons of Sax-Misox or
Misocco of Graubünden. But the Milanese dukes
would not brook the loss of these lands, and a long-
protracted war ensued with varying success. Most
of the more distant cantons being opposed to these
Italian conquests declined to send help, but hearing
that Bellinzona had been captured by the Visconti,
some three thousand Eidgenossen marched to its
relief in 1422. They were, however, no match for
the twenty-four thousand troops gathered by the
famous general Carmagnola. Lying in ambush for
the Swiss he succeeded in completely shutting them
in at Arbedo, with the exception of six hundred who
had escaped into the valley of Misox. For six hours
the small Swiss band fought to the utmost, refusing
to give way, though opposed by a force of ten times
their number, and well trained. Suddenly their
brethren came to their relief, or they would have been
crushed. The Swiss loss was two hundred, that of

the enemy nine hundred. But the conquests were forfeited for the present. Yet the Swiss pushed on to new war to redeem their misfortunes under the Sforza. A brilliant victory was that of Giornico (Leventina), 1478, where six hundred Swiss under Theiling from Lucerne defeated a force of fifteen thousand Milanese soldiers. This tended greatly to spread Swiss military fame in Italy.

ARMS OF URI.

XVII.

WAR BETWEEN ZURICH AND SCHWYZ.

(1436-1450.)

A GLOOMY picture in Swiss history do these civil wars present, marking as they do the chasm separating the Confederates, who were each swayed by a spirit of jealous antagonism. Yet it was clear that the town and the country commonwealths—citizens and peasants—formed such strong contrasts that they would not always pull together. Indeed, the smouldering discontent was suddenly fanned into flame by questions respecting hereditary succession that threatened to consume the whole Confederation. Feudalism was tottering to its fall in Switzerland, but it seemed as if the famous counts of Toggenburg were for a while to stay its ruin in the eastern portion of the country. Frederick III. (1400-1436) possessed what would come up to the present canton of St. Gall, the Ten Gerichte, a large portion of Graubünden, Voralberg (which he had wrenched from Friedel "of the Empty Pocket"), and other districts. Despite the popular struggles for freedom he managed to maintain his authority by adroit and designing policy and by alliance with Zurich and Schwyz, which stood by him against foes domestic and foreign. Having no children Frederick promised that on his death the two cantons should receive his domains south of Zurich lake, which acquisition would round off their territory. He died in 1436, but left no will —intentionally, as was thought by some, with the view of entangling the Confederates in quarrels— "tying their tails together," as the expressive but not very polished phrase had it. Be that as it may, the apple of discord was soon in the midst, and there set up as claimants numerous seigneurs of Graubünden, barons from the Valais, near relatives, as well as Austria and the empire. Zurich and Schwyz also contended for the promised stretch of land. To penetrate into the maze of petty conflicts which followed would be ridiculous as it would be impossible. In accordance with her more aristocratic inclinations Zurich paid court to the dowager countess whilst Schwyz humoured rather the subjects as the future masters, and the three latter proved in the end to have had the better judgment. The strife, indeed, fell into one of emulation between the two most energetic and talented statesmen of the two commonwealths. One of these leading men was burgomaster Stüssi, of Zurich, and the other was Ital von Reding, from Schwyz, both highly gifted and energetic men. Even from their youth they had been rivals, incited by the Emperor Sigismund whose favour they enjoyed.

Save the battle of St. Jacques on the Birse, the

war brought forth no great military exploits, and as it effected no material changes it may be very briefly passed over. It splits naturally into three periods. The first of these (1436-1442) is simply a series of wasteful feuds waged by the Confederates alone. Schwyz had taken for itself the whole heritage in question, with the exception of one fragmentary portion left to its rival. Zurich, thus deprived of her portion, and disappointed in her scheme of planning a direct commercial road to Italy through Graubünden, retaliated by shutting her market against Schwyz and Glarus, causing a famine in the two districts. The Confederates did not act with impartiality in the matter, but, laying all blame on Zurich, drove her to arms. She was, however, again a loser, for her territory to the east of the lake, which was the theatre of war, was terribly wasted. This portion of the land Schwyz wished to annex, but was prevented by order of the federal Diet. Nevertheless Zurich lost to Schwyz and Glarus three villages on the upper lake, and the island Ufenau which she had governed for half a century, and she was compelled to re-open her roads and market.

Deeply wounded by the position of the Confederates in the opposition ranks, and still more by the humiliation inflicted on her by the rustics of Schwyz, the proud, free city of Zurich thirsted for revenge. Thus the second period of conflict began, and in June, 1442, Zurich sought a foreign alliance. Stüssi, or his secretary, who was his right hand, taking advantage of her old leanings towards Austria, conceived the Machiavelian plan of joining in union with the deadly foe of the Confederates. Despite the firm opposition of a strong party of noble and eminent patriots, the coalition was arranged. The plea was put forward that the "imperial city," by virtue of her exceptional position, and the treaty concluded under the auspices of Brun, in 1351, was allowed to make any alliances she chose. Disloyalty was thus coloured by a show of truth. The Emperor Frederick III. and his brother, Albrecht of Austria, proceeded to Zurich to receive the homage and allegiance of the enthusiastic population. The Confederates guessing the meaning of this move tried to convince the renegade member of her perfidy. But their efforts failing, all, Bern included—though she took no prominent or active part, being chiefly occupied by her Burgundian politics—sent their challenge to Austria and Zurich. The war, though fiercer and bloodier than the first, was just as luckless, owing to dissensions arising amongst the allies, the men of Zurich being unwilling to submit to a many-headed Austrian lordship. The struggle was carried on by fits and starts, the Confederates returning home on one occasion for the annual haymaking. Having laid waste the Zurich territory the Confederates proceeded to attack the capital itself. During a sally to St. Jacques on the Sihl, Stüssi fell in defence of the bridge over that river, whilst endeavouring to keep back the foe and stay the flight of the fugitives. His heroic death makes one almost forget his ambitious and misguided policy. At last the Zurich forces drew up their guns on the Lindenhof, an eminence within the town. A single ball worked wonders, for, piercing the walls of a barn, it upset the table at which were sitting a party of Glarner, and carried off the head of the topmost man at the table. Greatly impressed by this result the besiegers rushed from the premises, stopped the siege, and began negotiations for a truce. But the Austrians objected to the truce, fearing a reconciliation between Zurich and the Confederates, and they incited the mob to make a set against the patriotic councillors who were believed to be the prime movers in the peace negotiations. A state of terrorism set in, five of the leading men were demanded by the populace, and were publicly beheaded; and ten more suffered the same fate. Thus powerless had Zurich grown in the hands of Austria. The truce being thus prevented the Eidgenossen proceeded to besiege Greifensee, a strong fortress in the Zurich midlands. For four weeks the garrison of eighty men held out, but, being at last betrayed by a peasant, were compelled to surrender at discretion. Sentence of death was passed on the brave defenders by a majority of the Confederates, and the cruel sentence was carried out in a meadow at hand. Ital von Reding stood by to see that the imperial custom of passing over every tenth man should not be followed in this case. However when sixty had fallen he turned away, and the rest were spared. Strange stories attach to that bloody spot, and indeed Nemesis soon avenged the cruel deed. A second siege of the capital was undertaken by the Confederates, but proved a failure like the first. The men of Zurich, in fact, made light of the siege, and a band of young men even sallied forth and captured wine and other provisions.

Wishful to bring matters to an issue, Austria turned to France for assistance, well knowing that she herself was no match for the Eidgenossen in open field. She was, besides, tired of the profitless and resultless kind of war which had hitherto been carried on. Charles VII. was anxious to get rid of his mercenary troops, the savage Armagnacs, which he had led against England, and was glad to launch them on Swiss lands. This combination of Austrian and French arms—the Zurcher remained at home to defend their still beleaguered city—introduces the third and last portion of the war. The Dauphin (Louis XI.), with an army of thirty thousand men, marched against Basel, and the Eidgenossen, unacquainted with the numbers of the enemy, set out to meet them. When they came within sight of the foe, they crossed the river Birse in the most exuberant spirits. Soon, however, they were split into two divisions by the heavy fire of the French, and one of these being surrounded on an island in the river was completely annihilated by the overwhelming numbers, though fighting with marvellous bravery. The other division took up a position behind the garden walls of the infirmary of St. Jacques, on the river (August 26, 1444). Here for six hours a small body of some five or six hundred men held their ground. Twice they withstood the assault of a foe twenty or thirty times their number, and twice themselves rushed on in attack. But at last the walls gave way, pierced through and through, and the foe rushed through the breach. A hand-to-hand fight followed, till the hospital being fired the Swiss were compelled to

succumb. Yet, though failing, each man died a hero. Some drew arrows from their wounds, and hurled them at the enemy; others who had lost one hand swung their halberts with the other. The Armagnacs, who had fought in many a bloody battle, confessed that never before had they met with a foe so dauntless, so regardless of death. The Austrians, however, denied the Swiss such testimony. On the day following the battle a German knight was riding over the field wading in blood, and boasted to his comrades, "To-day we seem to be bathing in roses." "There, eat thy roses!" yelled a dying Uri soldier, flinging at his head a large stone which struck him dead from his horse. Louis, who had lost some four thousand men in the fight, was greatly impressed by such show of bravery on the part of the Swiss, and concluded an honourable peace with them at Ensisheim, on the 28th of October, 1444. St. Jacques is a second Swiss Thermopylæ, and sheds immortal honour on the combatants. Though beaten the Confederates were not dishonoured. Like the brave Spartans under Leonidas they preferred death to servitude and dishonour. This battle was also the turning-point of the federal war; it rendered the Confederates more pliant. And though desultory feuds still showed themselves, peace was at last concluded, in 1450, by which Zurich was forced to give up her Austrian alliance. The federal league was knit more closely together than ever before; old injuries were soon forgotten, and the Eidgenossen accepted an invitation to Zurich to join in the carnival festivities got up to celebrate the reconciliation, 1454. A deplorable incident took place during the festivities, the seizure by the Eidgenossen, at the minster, of the famous savant, Felix Malleolus, a canon of the Church. Born of an ancient family at Zurich, he was educated first at the Carolinum in his native city, and afterwards at the university of Bologna, which was the glory of the Middle Ages. Bold, and of an unbending will, early acquainted with the corruptions of the Church and clergy, he hurled bitter invectives against the guilty, and raised for himself a host of enemies amongst the priesthood. And during the early years of the war

ARMS OF SCHWYZ.

he had likewise attacked the Eidgenossen as enemies of his native town, and called them an illiterate, uncouth, and belligerent race. His own chapter had objected to so stern a man as provost, and he had consequently contented himself with the position of canon, a position which left him ample time for study, and the composition of learned pamphlets. When the Eidgenossen seized him he was bending over his beloved books. He was hurried to Constance, and was there, by the bishop, thrown into the same prison as that occupied by the martyr Huss. The higher clergy as a rule connived at the deed, and, though promised release, he was handed over a prisoner to the monks at Lucerne. Here the lofty words of Cellano, "*Dies irae, dies illa,*" so well known from their use in Mozart's Requiem Mass, seem to have been a great consolation to the unfortunate canon. It is not known exactly when he died.

XVIII.

BURGUNDIAN WARS.

(1474-1477.)

THESE wars raised to its height the military glory of the Eidgenossen, and instead of the limited sphere occupied by most of the previous wars, we find ourselves now watching a scene of world-wide interest and importance. Three Great Powers — France, Germany, and Austria—if such a term is applicable in the fifteenth century, are striving for the downfall of a fourth great realm, Burgundy, in some respects the mightiest of them all. The Swiss League, no less interested in the issue, is made the instrument for bringing about that tragical ending which strikes Burgundy for ever from the list of future kingdoms.

Charles the Bold aimed at the re-establishment of the ancient kingdom of Lorraine, such as it was created by the treaty of Verdun in 843.[1] This was to be a middle kingdom between French and German territory—a kingdom which, stretching from

[1] See Chap. VI.

ELIZABETH, WIFE OF ALBERT II.; MARIA OF BURGUNDY; ELEANOR OF PORTUGAL; KUNIGUNDE, SISTER OF MAXIMILIAN.
(*From Maximilian Monument at Innsbruck.*)

the North Sea through to the Mediterranean, would absorb the Swiss Confederation, and what of other territory we cannot tell. A striking scheme, and one which, if it had succeeded, would have greatly changed the face of modern politics. Charles's deadliest foe was Louis of France, who was unswervingly bent on his destruction. Politically, the two men were the very antipodes of each other. The romantic duke is the embodiment of mediæval chivalry; the sober Louis that of modern absolutism. His reign seals the fate of dying feudalism. Louis is like an immovable rock against which the effete Middle Ages dash themselves in vain. He stands, indeed, between two great historical epochs. Charles is doomed to fall; for pitilessly Louis crushes his unruly vassals, and feudatory France is by his power welded into a mighty and absolute monarchy. The ambitious hotspur, the warlike duke, believes himself a second Alexander. And, indeed, in all Christendom there is no court so splendid as his, no treasury so vast. His magnificence is more than royal, more even than imperial, and he grapples with numberless intricate problems. To carry out his plans he stakes realm and life, but lacking patience and sound political judgment he fails in his chief enterprises.[1]

The preliminary steps leading to the war are a

[1] One curious instance of his failures may be given. The Burgundian crown was ready for him, and he proceeded to Trier (1473) to have it placed on his brow by the (Roman) emperor, and push his imperial claims. However, Frederick III., becoming alarmed at the presumption of the future Welsh-German sovereign, broke off negotiations, and fled at night with his son Max, who was to have married the daughter of Charles.

diplomatic maze, revealing the double-dealing of the actors, and likewise showing the uncertain position held by the Swiss League in the empire. The destruction of this league, and the overthrow of Charles the Bold were chiefly aimed at. The maze of intrigue is, indeed, well-nigh impenetrable; yet, because the preliminaries are far less known than the wars which followed, and the actual facts have been often distorted, they will, no doubt, command general interest, and we shall try to disentangle the skeins as best we can. The battle of St. Jacques had secured for the Confederates, not only the sympathies of Louis, but also the alliance of his father, Philip the Good, of Burgundy, the Sforzas of Milan, and others. Since those times of prowess the young republic had been growing into a prosperous and powerful nation, not without its influence on continental military affairs. Admired, envied, and feared, by turns, its friendship was greatly appreciated, and it lent protection to all who sought it. So strong was its love of warfare, that it was at all times ready to avenge any wrong or fancied wrong done to itself or its friends. Thus, Zurich, in 1456, laid waste the lands of the Austrian knight-robbers who had plundered some Strasburg merchants on a Swiss round. Despite the distance between them, the two towns of Strasburg and Zurich were on terms of close friendship.[1] At the bidding of Pius II., the elegant Latin writer commonly known as Æneas

---

[1] A pleasant story is related to the effect that, on one occasion, some young Zurich men started off in a boat by way of the Limmat and the Rhine, taking a dish of hot lentils with them. Reaching Strasburg in the evening they placed the dish, still hot, on the mayor's dinner table. A famous poem, "Glückhaft Schiff," describes the event.

Sylvius, who had fallen out with his literary friend, Duke Sigmund of Austria, the Eidgenossen conquered Thurgau, which had remained still an Austrian province, and placed it amongst their subject lands. The quarrels of Mulhausen and Schaffhausen with Austria entangled their friends of the league into a war with Sigmund (1468), who, to secure peace, agreed to pay over the sum of ten thousand florins, guaranteeing them their recent conquests. This feud of Waldshut (Black Forest) led to the Burgundian wars.

Extravagant but poor, Sigmund failed to find even that modest sum, and applied to Louis of France for help, but was by him referred to Charles of Burgundy. The astute Louis saw that a quarrel between the dukes would be injurious and possibly fatal to Charles, who, all unaware of the pitfall prepared for him, readily fell in with the proposals of Sigmund. He was anxious to join together Alsace, Breisgau, the Aargau towns on the Rhine, &c., and advanced fifty thousand florins as mortgage on the dominions of Sigmund, expecting they would soon fall to him entirely. By the treaty of St Omer, in 1469, their mutual terms of agreement were thus fixed:—Charles to give help in case of need against the Swiss, and Sigmund to promote the long-planned marriage between the son of his cousin and Maria of Burgundy. Rejoicing at this turn of fortune, the emperor at once disannulled the treaty of Waldshut, and the new lands were by Charles the Bold entrusted to the management of his favourite, Peter von Hagenbach.[1] A tyrant and a libertine, his acts of violence, and those of his foreign

---

[1] Well known from Scott's "Anne of Geierstein."

soldiery, exasperated the German populations of Alsace, Basel, Bern, and Solothurn. Their merchants being robbed on the Rhine, their envoys imprisoned —one Bernese man was killed in a fray—they complained to the duke, but without result for the cruelties and oppression continued.

Artful and ever on the watch, Louis found that the Eidgenossen, disgusted by the grasping tendencies of Charles, were fast drifting away from their good understanding with Burgundy, and strove to draw them to his own side. Anxious to secure a friend, the Swiss lent willing ears to the flattery and insinuations of the crafty Louis. He actually succeeded in effecting a reconciliation between the Eidgenossen and Austria. It was a cleverly calculated bit of diplomacy, that secured for the Swiss their recent conquests, isolated Charles, and strengthened the opposition against him. Louis fixed a pension on Sigmund, and urged him to pay off the mortgage on his lands, whilst the Alsacian towns likewise leagued themselves with the Swiss, and actually advanced Sigmund the sum of money required. Charles, however, disappointed in his plans, refused to receive the money. A popular rising took place at Breisach, and Hagenbach was seized, imprisoned, and brought before a tribunal, at which some of the Eidgenossen assisted. He was condemned to death, and publicly beheaded, as a sort of popular judgment. Enraged beyond measure though he was, yet Charles deferred vengeance for the death of his favourite, being, indeed, at the time, otherwise engaged. Taking advantage of this delay, Louis won over to his side Frederick, also lavishing flatteries on the Swiss, and pensions on Nicolas von Diesbach and his followers. This Nicolas was a Bernese nobleman and a skilled politician, and was a fit instrument in the hands of a king who calculated his schemes rather on men's *mauvaises passions* than on their virtues. Louis hastened on the outbreak of war, and on October 9, 1474, Frederick called on the Eidgenossen to take their part in the attack on Charles. They hesitated, but the pensioner and creature of France, Diesbach, notwithstanding the resistance offered by Adrian von Bubenberg, a Bernese noble of far loftier character, in hot haste declared war against Charles in the name of the empire, and with the consent of the Confederation. But war once actually afoot the Swiss were made a mere catspaw by their partners, and left to their own devices.

In a short story like this it is impossible to discuss the merits or demerits of the various factions, or those of Hagenbach or Diesbach,[1] yet we must dwell for a moment on the federal policy, and more especially on that of Bern. The position of the Swiss League at the outbreak of the war was very similar to that of "Sweden, under Gustavus Adolphus, in the Thirty Years' War." Threatened by the preponderating power of Austria, she would not take up arms till France, equally interested in the downfall of Habsburg, under Richelieu, drove her to war by sending subsidies. But French gold was by no means the actual and moving cause of the war. Many things

---

[1] For these matters the reader is directed to Freeman's admirable essay on Charles the Bold.

concurred to give rise to it, not the least being Bern's extraordinary bent for aggrandisement and conquest. Her aggressiveness and her farsightedness were quite remarkable for that age, and her policy was conceived on so large a scale that she has been not inaptly compared to ancient Rome. Bordering on Swiss Burgundy, Bern had strong western leanings, if one may so speak, and very early set her eyes on Vaud and Geneva. She considered Mount Jura as the true western boundary, for French Switzerland still lay without the pale of the Confederation, and belonged for the most part to Savoy, or the vassals of Savoy. However selfish the policy of Bern may appear at this distance of time, yet she has the unquestionable merit of having brought Swiss Burgundy into the federation, thus connecting the French with the German portions of Helvetia. The political views of Bern are clearly evidenced by her foreign relations at the time. Her nobility sent their sons to foreign courts to be educated and trained for a military or a diplomatic career—Bubenberg, for instance, spent his youth at the Court of Burgundy. Her leading men were well-trained military officers or skilled politicians, and the aristocracy which formed the governing body of the town clung obstinately to the prerogatives still left them in those moribund Middle Ages.

The country cantons were less interested in Burgundian troubles, well knowing that Bern would take the lion's share of any conquests. Bern and Zurich were rivals, and, like Athens and Sparta of old, followed each its separate ends. Yet when the safety of either, or that of the fatherland, was at stake, private aims and private animosities were dropped, and the Confederates rallied to the common standard, displaying that wonderful heroism which strong love of fatherland seems ever to inspire.

The first event of the war was the siege of Héricourt, near Belfort, at the bidding of Frederick III. This was in November, 1474, and there followed wasteful inroads into Vaud, by Bern, Freiburg, and Solothurn, on the pretext of punishing Savoy for siding with Charles (1475). Place after place fell to the victors, and with the help of Bern, Lower Valais was wrenched from Savoy, and restored to Upper Valais. But when once the Swiss were fairly launched on the war all their partners withdrew from the stage, and made their peace with Charles. The Burgundian prince thus having his hands more free pushed on alone his expedition against Duke René, the minstrel poet of Lorraine, in November, 1475. In the January of the following year he opened his campaign against the Swiss.

With an enormous army of fifty thousand of the best-trained soldiers in Europe, besides heavy artillery, he started in high spirits across the Jura, resolved on crushing the Swiss peasants, and levelling Bern with the ground. Count Romont was sent on in advance, with instructions to reconquer Vaud. This he effected within a fortnight, the district being inefficiently garrisoned. Charles then marched on Grandson, whither the main Bernese force had retired. The odds were desperate, five hundred men against so vast an army, and, after a resistance of ten days, the garrison was allured into a surrender by vain promises of safety, and by impudent forgeries. The fate of Dinant (Belgium) awaited the body of 412 men who surrendered. They were bound with ropes and drowned in the lake, or hanged from the trees lining the roads (February 28, 1476). In great straits Bern summoned the assistance of the other cantons, and, on March 2nd, the federal army of eighteen thousand horse and foot, well trained and equipped, assembled at Neuchâtel, and Charles went to meet this force. A large division of the Swiss having gone on in front suddenly noticed from the vineyard slopes the Burgundian troops in the plain beneath. As was their wont in warfare — they were very religious, almost superstitiously so, at that time—the Swiss knelt down, and extended their hands in prayer. To the enemy it seemed as if they were begging for mercy, and Charles exclaimed, "These cowards are ours!" and ordered his men to fire. His artillery swept down whole files, but, though their ranks were broken, the Swiss stoutly held their ground against the oncoming foe. Suddenly Charles ordered his forces to fall back, with the double intention of getting more room, and of alluring his foe into descending from the higher ground. But his men unapprised of their leader's intentions mistook the movement for an actual flight, and their ranks began to show signs of falling into disorder. At this most critical moment the chief body of the Swiss appeared on the heights, their armour glittering in the sun. The deafening noise of their war-cries and war-horns (Uristier of Uri, Harsthörner of Lucerne) "struck such terror into the Burgundians," reports an old

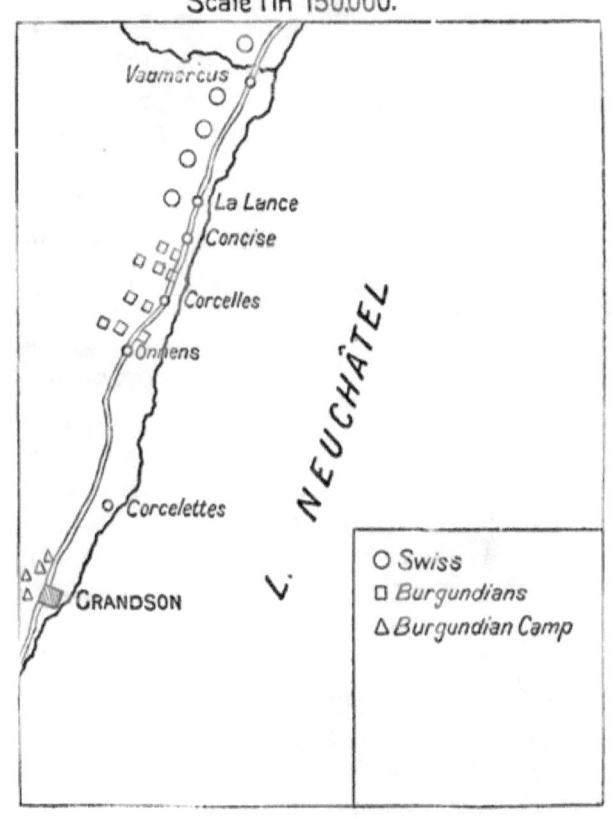

MAP OF GRANDSON DISTRICT.

chronicler of Neuchâtel, "that they took to their heels, and disappeared from sight, as if a whirlwind had swept them from the earth." Not far, however, did the Eidgenossen pursue, for, "with indescribable joy," they dropped on their knees to render thanks for the great victory. When they neared the camp of Charles the terrible sight they saw stirred up still more their desire for revenge. Their brethren were still suspended by dozens from the trees by the wayside.

The battle of Grandson is remarkable for the immense quantity of spoil that fell to the victors. For Charles and his nobles were wont to carry the splendour of their court even into their camps. Four hundred silk tents came into the hands of the Swiss, as well as the arras carpets, and Charles's sets of gold plate and dishes, the admiration of the sovereigns of the time. His Flemish lace and fine linen were cut up like homespun, and divided amongst the rough soldiers; his money dealt out in helmets; his artillery, his beautiful swords and hand-guns; and, most precious of all, his jewellery, were shared amongst the victorious Swiss. Of his three famous diamonds the finest passed finally to Pope Julius II., another to Henry VIII., of England, and thence to Philip of Spain, and the third to the kings of Portugal. It would require pages to give even a bare list of the spoils.[1]

[1] The suits of armour, guns, and banners—the suit belonging to Charles's court jester who fell at Morat, is at Soleure—are stored up in the museums of various capitals. The golden seal of Burgundy is at Lucerne, whilst the town library of Zurich possesses the seal of the Great Bastard, brother of Charles.

Despite this great disaster, Charles did not lose heart, and within a fortnight began to reassemble his scattered forces. His movements were closely watched by the Bernese, who strongly fortified Morat, their strongest outpost, sending Adrian von Bubenberg with fifteen hundred men to hold it against the duke. On the 9th of June, 1476, Charles appeared before the town with twenty-five thousand men, and his artillery soon made terrible havoc amongst the weak fortifications. Von Bubenberg, however, vowed that he would not surrender so long as a drop of living blood remained in his veins. The Eidgenossen forces, which had returned home after the last engagement, did not reach Morat till the 21st of June, but determined to give battle on the 22nd, that day being the anniversary of the ever-memorable Laupen. Charles had drawn up his troops on the plateaux of Munchwiler, Courlevon, and Cressier, opposite Morat, and had strengthened his front with a ditch and a barricade of trees, having also lined the hedges with his artillery, and flanked it with his horse. It was raining in torrents; to weary the foe the Swiss spent the morning in dubbing knights; Duke René of Lorraine, who had joined the Swiss ranks as simple spearman, and Hans Waldmann having that honour bestowed upon them. Towards noon the sun unexpectedly broke forth, and Hans von Hallwyl, a Bernese nobleman, brandishing his sword, exclaimed, "Onward! brave men. God lights up our path. Do not leave your wives and children to the stranger!" Leading his van in a wide circle to avoid the hedge he fell on the right wing of Charles. Seeing him thus engaged

Hans Waldmann of Zurich, with his ten thousand troops occupying a central position in the field, marched up, sprang on the intrenchment, and trampled down the hedge. Carrying their guns across their shoulders, they rushed on the artillery, who were keeping up a deadly fire, and, thrusting back the enemy, soon silenced their guns. Then the Swiss force advanced in a close phalanx to the hostile centre, where stood Charles with the Prince of Orange, and other distinguished officers, and where, too, were placed the English archers under Somerset. A murderous engagement ensued, Charles fought like a lion, and soon fifteen hundred nobles lay at his feet. Suddenly Bubenberg sallied forth with his force, and attacked the Burgundian left wing, stationed between Munchwiler and Morat, whilst Hertenstein of Lucerne attacked Charles's centre in the rear. A terrible panic seized Charles, and his army became suddenly disorganized, and fled in wild haste, the Swiss closely following in pursuit. For the whole distance from Morat to Avenches there were terrible hand-to-hand conflicts, for the Burgundians resisted stoutly, and the Swiss gave no quarter. Countless numbers were driven into the lake, and altogether twelve thousand of the foe fell that day, the Swiss themselves losing three thousand men. Charles escaped with a few horsemen to Morges, but quite dazed with despair, and the Eidgenossen turned homewards laden with rich spoils. All over the country the bells were set ringing to welcome the heroic men who had saved Switzerland from becoming a subject-province of Burgundy. The great battle of Murten, a purely

OLD WEAPONS AND ARMOUR PRESERVED IN THE ARSENAL, ZURICH.

defensive engagement so far as the Swiss were concerned, still exerts on them the same spell as Morgarten and Sempach.

Luckless Duke Charles had shut himself up in his castle near Pontarlier, a prey to a morbid despair, but hearing that René was reconquering Lorraine, he was spurred into taking up arms once more, and started for Nancy with a new force. René went back to Switzerland, and even with tears implored the Federal Diet to help him. The Diet would not themselves organize a new army, but permitted men to enlist of their own will under René's banner. Some eight thousand soldiers enlisted, and, under Hans Waldmann, retook Nancy, on January 15, 1477. The fate of the unhappy Charles is well known; his corpse was found in a bog embedded in ice and snow. A popular rhyme thus characterizes Charles's triple misfortune :—

"Zü Grandson das Gut,
Zü Murten den Mut,
Zü Nancy das Blut."

The acquisition of the victors were in no way adequate to the labour expended. Franche Comté, to which the Eidgenossen had a title, and which the cities wished to annex, was sold to Louis for a sum of money, which he never paid, however. The Swiss merely retained the protectorate over the province, whose envoys had begged on their knees that they might be admitted to the Swiss Federation, to prevent their falling into the hands of France or Austria, a fate which was, however, to be theirs. Grandson

Murten, Bex, &c., remained with Bern and Freiburg, but the greater part of Vaud fell back to Savoy, for a ransom of fifty thousand florins. Geneva had to pay half that sum as a war contribution; yet the way was paved for the annexation of Vaud. Freiburg and Low-Valais were entirely rescued from the grasp of Savoy.

XIX.

MEETING AT STANZ, 1481, &c.

GRANDSON, Morat, and Nancy stamped the Eidgenossen as the *enfants gâtés* of Europe, and as a nation of the highest military standing on the Continent, nay, even as an umpire in continental politics, and a guardian of the peace. Everybody lavished flattering praises on the prowess of the Swiss. Nation after nation made overtures to them—France foremost, Italy, the Pontiff, the Emperor, distant Hungary, and even England, this last desirous of breaking the French alliance. The meetings of the Federal Diet often became brilliant congresses, lasting for weeks, where princes and ambassadors vied with each other in bestowing bounties and favours on the Swiss leaders, in order to secure their aid, deeming themselves invincible if the Swiss fought on their side. The period 1476-1512—from Morat to Marignano—a noble victory and a scarcely less noble defeat, adds another glorious page to the military history of the Swiss League, but the *revers de la médaille* shows bitter contention and moral decline. In truth, the Burgundian wars closed a glorious epoch, but brought about a baleful change in the face of more noble warfare, for Nancy is linked with that period of mercenary service and foreign pay which became the curse of Switzerland, and which could not be checked even by the grand efforts of the Reformation period.

Leaving the foreign wars for the moment let us cast a glance at home matters. It is not necessary to dwell at length on the excesses indulged in by the disbanded soldiers, unoccupied and unaccustomed to regular labour after the Burgundian wars. These things nearly always result from long-continued struggles.

More serious danger threatened the League, through the cropping up again of the old antagonism between the country commonwealths and the city states. Disputes arose concerning the distribution of the Burgundian conquests, and the admission of Freiburg and Solothurn, which had solicited the favour, into the federal fold. In the fifteenth century the balance of political power was gradually inclining towards the cities. Zurich, Bern, and Lucerne, had far outstripped the "Länder" in population, wealth, influence, and culture, and in 1481 their forces amounted to 35,000 as against the 15,500 of the other five cantons. They advocated the division of the spoil in proportion to their soldiery, and the reception of their two helpmates in the previous wars by way of reward. But the three Forest States, presuming on their prestige as the primary stock and foundation of the league, and anxious to maintain their position, resisted measures that would throw the weight of power entirely on the opposite side. Their narrow and selfish views and their obstinacy placed the Confederation in jeopardy. Meetings, held to settle differences, only deepened the bitterness. A final Diet was fixed for the 18th of December, 1481, at Stanz (Unterwalden), and the foremost men met to arrange, if possible, a compromise. But high words were exchanged, and when the excitement had reached its height, the pastor of that place, Im Grund, stole away, and proceeded at dead of night to the cave Zum Ranft, in a wilderness near Sachseln. Here he took counsel with Nicholas von der Flüe, the famous hermit, who had dwelt there for the space of twenty years. Mild words and deep thoughts proceeded from the good man, whose love for his country had always been of the strongest. In his earlier days he had served as a soldier and a magistrate, had married, and had had several children born to him. But always given to meditation, he was at the age of fifty-one suddenly filled with religious enthusiasm, and, unable to appease his yearning soul, took leave of his family, and retired into deep seclusion. His commune built him a cell and chapel—still to be seen near Sachseln—on a rock called die Flüe, hence his name. A few planks formed his bed, and his pillow was a log of wood. Stores he needed not, for he lived on roots and wild berries, and the saying went abroad amongst the country folk that he was sustained by the bread of the holy sacrament alone, and ate no other food. The peasants regarded his person with wonder and awe, and though he was seen at times worshipping at Einsiedeln, no man ever saw him on his way to or from that place. The fame of his wisdom spread

INNER COURT OF THE ABBEY OF OUR LADY. LUTH CHAPTER OF ZURICH.

beyond the boundaries of his own land, and many were the high personages who came to consult his oracle—from all parts of the empire and Italy, envoys from Sigmund and Frederick. But into subtle discussions he never entered, leaving them rather to his priests. "Pure water does not flow through golden pipes, but through pipes of lead," he used to say to those who complained of the dissolute and degenerate lives of the clergy. To this man, then, the good pastor unburdened his mind, and from him received solace and wise words. Then he toiled back to Stanz, December 22nd. Finding the Diet broken up, and the envoys on the point of leaving for their respective homes, he ran to the various hostelries, and with tearful eyes begged the men to return once more. All opposition melted at the name of Bruder Klaus, the envoys reassembled, and listened with thrilled hearts to the profound truths uttered by him. Their jars and differences were settled within the hour, and Freiburg and Solothurn were unanimously admitted into the league. Blessing the memory of the "Peacemaker," the delegates returned home, and the glad tidings of the establishment of concord were everywhere celebrated by the ringing of bells.

Another feature of this memorable day was the signing of the Covenant of Stanz, a series of measures prepared beforehand, but in which Nicholas had no hand. They were levelled chiefly against the excesses and tumultuous risings that were continually taking place in the country cantons, their object being to re-establish order and prevent a repetition of the insubordination, and to set bounds to "the too much freedom in the Länder." Despite the resistance of Schwyz the agreement was ratified, and gradually became part and parcel of the judicial enactments of the Confederation. Breathing as they do the vigorous spirit of Hans Waldmann, the most influential Swiss statesman of his time, these measures were, though wrongly, attributed to him.

This Waldmann is indeed the most conspicuous figure in Switzerland in the fifteenth century, and forms a singular contrast to the humble recluse Zum Ranft, for he shared in all the vicissitudes of his times. Full of vital energy, teeming with lofty schemes, his life is a bright picture, darkened however, here and there, by deep shadows thrown by that stirring, luxurious, fast-living epoch, an epoch itself coloured by the Burgundian wars. The career of this remarkable man is a piece of moral, social, and political history, quite worthy of a few moments' notice.

A poor peasant boy Waldmann had raised himself to the highest position in the country, that of Burgomaster of Zurich, and head, or king, as he pleased to call it, of the Eidgenossen. The mobile and passionate Zurcher, more than any other members of the league, lend themselves to infatuations, and never do things by halves, whether for good or for evil, to-day hurl down their idol of yesterday, and hand him over to the executioner, so it has been said. A strange career was that of Waldmann. Born in the canton of Zug, about 1436, he wandered in early youth to Zurich to seek his fortune, and at the age of sixteen bought the citizenship there. Apprenticed in various callings he turned at length to the iron trade, but his restless mind being unalterably bent on the battlefield he enlisted as a soldier at the first beat of the drums, and plunged into the impending struggles as captain of the Zurich men, and condottière of German princes. In the intervals of peace he turned again to business, giving himself up at the same time to the pleasures of the town. Young, fiery, handsome, with an intelligent face and winsome manners, he fascinated the women, whilst his eloquence and joviality made him a general favourite with the men, and especially with the masses. Many stories were current as to his adventurous life, and the excesses in which he indulged in company with other young men of the town caused him to be lodged in the Wellenberg, a state prison built in the lake. Yet in that age of dissoluteness such failings did not detract from his personal charm and credit. He married a gay and handsome young widow of good family, and called himself the squire of Dübelstein, from the manor he acquired. This union raised his position in society, and with the help of the Constafel, the body of aristocracy with which he became connected, he hoped to get a position in the Government. But the Junker, or young nobles, treated with disdain the pretensions of a man who had once been a tanner, and accordingly he turned his attention to the craftsmen and guilds, and was returned as councillor by them in 1473. Beneath his exuberant spirits and brawling temper lay the superior gifts of the general and the politician, gifts which the Burgundian wars were to exhibit to the world. From first to last he shared in the campaigns. At Morat we have seen him knighted, and leading the principal charge against Charles the Bold; the recovery of Nancy was chiefly his doing, for he it was who advocated the continuation of the war and the appeal to arms by René of Lorraine, at the Federal Diet. At the council-board and in the federal assemblies he rose to eminence by his political and diplomatic talents, and showed himself to be an astute ambassador. Sent to the French Court to negotiate with Louis XI. respecting Franche Comté, he lent himself to French influences, for his moral principles were by no means equal to his intellectual gifts. He became a pensioner of that same king, who was thus the first to corrupt the Swiss leaders with his gold. In his own city of Zurich, Waldmann filled a series of public offices; as edile he built the fine Wasserkirche, the Pantheon for war trophies, &c. In 1480 we find him occupying a high position as tribune, and head of the guilds, and, three years later, he was chosen Burgomaster. To obtain this last position, however, he had ousted the powerful Chevalier Goldein. He ruled Zurich as a veritable sovereign, head of the republic, and swayed also the foreign policy of the Federation. He dictated terms of peace; to him foreign princes applied for alliance or troops; and on him they showered their favours. He was made Hofrath of Milan, and, becoming a pensioner of Austria, began to lean more towards that country than to France, and rightly so, perhaps. Waldmann rapidly became, in fact, the most influential statesman, and, notwithstanding his extravagant habits, and boundless generosity, the wealthiest of the Eidgenossen. Thanks to his great ascendency Zurich was restored to that pre-eminence in the state which she had forfeited in the civil strife, and which Bern had gained in the time of the Burgundian troubles.

Ambitious, and readily bribed, Waldmann still professed lofty views in his home policy and in his administration, and these views he proposed to put into practice by the help of a political club he had founded. This club he placed under the care of twelve influential citizens, who followed his guidance. There was, in truth, a singular charm about his person, and his intellectual gifts commanded the admiration of his whole circle. He intended making some sweeping reforms that were to change the face of the Zurich republic. And he addressed himself first to the nobility, of whom he was no friend.

Hitherto the aristocracy and the craftsmen had been equally represented in the government (Kleiner Rath, see Zurich), each having twelve seats (one having dropped away). Waldmann, however, did away with half that number, and supplied their places by men from the Zünfte, or Guilds, who were almost to a man on his side. This not only strengthened his power as dictator, but increased the importance of the democracy generally, whilst it lessened that of the nobility. Nor did he spare the clergy. In 1486 he issued a series of orders against abuses, and compelled Innocent VIII. to give his sanction to them. Waldmann would at times good-humouredly style himself pope and emperor at Zurich. In one of his writs he laments the evil consequences of the Burgundian wars, and of the Reislaufen, mercenary service. Foreign influence was indeed spreading fast;

the rich contracted expensive foreign tastes, French and Spanish dress became fashionable, public amusements increased in number, and magnificent family feasts — weddings, baptisms, and the like — grew general among the people of Zurich. Waldmann began to take steps to regulate these extravagant tastes, although he himself did not practise what he preached—going so far as to fix the number of guests to be invited, and the cost of the presents to be given. Public amusements were checked or suppressed, even when of an altogether innocent character. Reding of Schwyz advocated Reislaufen in full.

The indefatigable Waldmann extended his writs and orders to the country districts, and, anticipating the views of the sixteenth century, strove for the centralization of power. This was with the hope of strengthening his government, and bringing the detached portions of the country under one general code of laws. For each village had so far its own distinct judicature. Regensberg, for instance, jealously maintained its curious right of indulging in car-boxing at the cost of five shillings in each case, whereas the same doubtful amusement cost elsewhere double and treble the money. The city Waldmann considered to be the head of the republic, whilst the country parts he looked upon as the less honourable or subject portion of the body politic. The trade and manufacturing industry he monopolized for the town, limiting the country districts to agriculture and the cultivation of the vine. Numberless were the measures of improvement which the bold reformer showered on his country, but many of them were inadvisedly introduced, and the severity with which he carried out his plans alienated all classes, and none more than the nobles. Consequently a conspiracy was formed by the Junker (the Göldli, the Escher, the Meyer von Knonau, &c.), against the Burgomaster, whose manifest opulence gave the lie to his affectation of republican simplicity. But blinded by the flatteries of the crowd and by his own power Waldmann did not see the storm which was rising fast.

The ill-advised execution of Theiling of Lucerne, the hero of Giornio, by the orders of Waldmann, whom and whose banner he had insulted in that campaign, turned the tide of popular favour against the ruler of Zurich, although Lucerne, overawed by the powerful Burgomaster did not dare to accuse him. But a more absurd if less iniquitous order was issued by him, and at length caused the tempest to burst forth against him. He seems however to have been urged on by his enemies, who wished to hasten his ruin, and he issued the order most reluctantly. It was to the effect that the country folk were to kill all their large dogs, his plea being that the animals did injury to the vineyards and hunting grounds. The consternation was as great as if Charles the Bold had once more come to life. Some obeyed, but at Knonau five hundred peasants met, and resisted the messengers who had been sent to effect the slaughter. With this example the whole district rose in arms, and, marching on Zurich, demanded admittance, March 4, 1489. It would occupy too much space to give the story of this outbreak; it was stopped for a time, but broke out again on April 1st. Waldmann bent on amusement had actually returned to Baden, a gay watering-place near Zurich, and the rendezvous of the *grand-monde* of various nations, but he at once rode back to the town with his troop of horses, hoping to check the revolt by his personal influence. But the majority was too strong for him, and surrendering, he was with his adherents rowed off to the Wellenberg tower, where he was placed on the rack, however without anything worthy of death being discovered. Meanwhile the burgesses held a town's meeting in the Wasserkirche; passed sentence of death on him, and hurriedly instituted a government to confirm the verdict. In his last hours Waldmann revealed his nobleness of soul; no bitter accusation against his enemies ever passed his lips; and he never lost heart, for he knew within himself that he had ever aimed at promoting the greatness of the town, and at that only. Had he appealed to the crowds he might have been saved, but he had promised to his confessor that he would make no such appeal, and on his way to the block he merely begged the thousands who had flocked to the bloody spectacle to forgive him and pray with him. The people were moved to tears, but just then a false alarm was spread that an Austrian army was coming to his rescue. This hurried on his doom. He was executed in a meadow on an eminence outside the walls, so that the armed men might be kept out of the town, April 6, 1489. "May God protect thee, my beloved Zurich, and keep thee from all evil!" were the last words of the dying man, as he turned his eyes towards his loved city for a moment before the fatal blow fell. The new government, called the "Horned Council," on account of its incapacity, was for a while unable to stop the revolts, and more executions followed. The "Compromise of Waldmann" (*Waldmann's Spruch*) secured to the city the supremacy over the country districts, whilst it restored to the city itself its old liberties. To ask to be represented on the council had as yet not entered the mind of the country folk. It may perhaps be added that the question is frequently being ventilated in Zurich whether or no a monument shall be erected to Waldmann's memory. Opinion is divided on the subject.

ARMS OF UNTERWALDEN.

XX.

THE LEAGUE OF THE THIRTEEN CANTONS COMPLETED.

(1513.)

No traveller visiting the picturesque town of Innsbruck should miss turning into the Hofkirche to inspect one of the most remarkable master-pieces of German art, the imposing monument erected by Maximilian, of Austria to himself. Amongst the numerous magnificent bronze effigies adorning this monument, we find those of Rudolf of Habsburg, Leopold III., who fell at Sempach, Charles the Bold, and many others whose names are familiar to the reader of the "Story of Switzerland." But the grandest figure there is that of Maximilian himself, a personage hardly less interesting to the Switzer, from the part played by that ruler in the separation of Switzerland from the empire.[1]

---

[1] Maximilian, however, lies buried at Wiener (Vienna) Neustadt. The monument at Innsbruck was planned by the emperor himself, though it took some generations to execute the work (1509-83). Twenty of the relievi were the work of Colin of Mecheln, and excited

MAXIMILIAN'S MONUMENT AT INNSBRUCK, MARBLE RELIEVI.
(*From a Photograph of the Original.*)

Maximilian, the son of Frederick III., is the first of a long series of monarchs who regarded their high vocation as a serious trust, and earnestly desired the well-being of the people whom they ruled; and of an empire sadly torn by the dissensions amongst the various factions of prelates, princes, and cities, each of which followed its own special ends, regardless of the welfare of the empire as a whole. Desirous of drawing more closely together the various members of his kingdom, he sought to lighten his hold over the Swiss Confederation, the bonds between which and the empire lapse of time had loosened. He was at the same time hopeful that he might win Switzerland over for his Italian schemes. He first invited, and then ordered the Eidgenossen to acquiesce in the new constitution (1495), and to join the Swabian Bund, a league formed by the nobility and the great cities, under the ægis of Austria. But this sacrifice of their freedom and independence did not at all suit the Swiss, and they flatly refused. They quite realized by this time that their own federal union was a much better guarantee of safety for them than the dubious assistance of party-torn Germany. Moreover they felt that the Reichstag, composed only of aristocratic elements, would ever fail to really represent and promote their republican and democratic interests. And besides, their strongest feelings were arrayed against Austria. The imperial crown had

---

the admiration of Thorwaldsen even. The whole monument is highly interesting from both an artistic and an historical point of view. Among the bronze figures that of King Arthur is the most exquisite, and is by the famous Peter Vischer.

become almost hereditary in the Habsburg family, and to submit to imperial rule meant to the Swiss the loss of all the political freedom and advantages they had gained. Last, but not least, after the double-dealing of Frederick III. in the Burgundian wars, the Swiss could have but little confidence in imperial rulers. The position of the Eidgenossen was indeed much like that of the Americans three hundred years later. They refused allegiance to a government which placed burdens upon them, but in which they had little or no share. Maximilian threatened the Swiss with invasion, whilst his chancellor proposed to bring his pen to bear upon them. But a Swiss envoy replied to the monarch that he would be very ill-advised to start on such a venture, whilst to the chancellor he said, "Why, sir, should we fear your goose quills? We are known not to have feared your Austrian lances." For the first time, perhaps, the Swiss truly realized that they were in a singularly independent position, and needed no foreign support for their protection. The truant child had grown strong and self-reliant, and would certainly decline to give up his dearly-bought and much-cherished freedom.

This stout refusal, the great friendship of the Swiss for France—for since the days of St. Jacques they had been slowly drifting to the French side—and their independent bearing, nettled beyond measure their Swabian neighbours. Mutual recriminations and accusations followed, and the desire of both sides for war was intensified by vexatious lawsuits, and by serious troubles in the Grisons. At last the flame burst forth. That "Rocky Island" where three Swiss nationalities mingle peacefully together, afraid of falling beneath the Habsburg sway —for the Austrian and Rhætian lands were still inextricably mixed together—sought shelter with the Eidgenossen as Zugewandte connections (1497 and 1498), the Zehngerichte excepted. The Tyrolese Government, seizing on this occurrence as a pretext, summoned the Swabian League to its aid, and sent troops into the Münsterthal in the absence of the monarch. The Bündner replied by calling in the Confederates, and war was soon raging along the whole line of the Rhine, from Basel to the borders of Voralberg and the Grisons. The deliverance of Rhætia (Graubünden) thus went step by step with the separation of the Swiss League from the empire. This war, called the Swabian war, from the people who took the most prominent part in it, glorious though it was in many ways, cannot be described in detail here. Maximilian was drawn into the struggle, but his troops never entered into the spirit of the enterprise, and were completely routed. No Swiss war has been more fruitful in glorious deeds and acts of self-sacrifice. As an example we may just allude to the noble courage of Benedict Fontana, the chieftain of the Gotteshausbund. He led the charge on the strong fortress deemed impregnable in the narrow valley, An der Calven (Chialavaina), on the Tyrolean frontier. Lacerated by a bullet he nevertheless covered his wounds with one hand, fighting with the other till he fell exhausted, calling to his troops, "Onward, comrades! I count but for

CITY WALLS OF MURTEN.

one man; to-day we are Rhætians and allies, or nevermore!" Fired by his example, Von Planta and other noble leaders sacrificed themselves; the fort was taken, and the two leagues were rescued from the Austrian grip. The Swabian war had lasted for six months, the Swabians themselves had suffered reverses on ten occasions, whilst in only two cases had the Swiss been repulsed; the German territory beyond the Rhine had been wasted; two thousand villages and castles having been reduced, and twenty thousand of their soldiery killed. No wonder both the contending parties longed for peace, and this was secured by a treaty at Basel, September 22, 1499. The effect was the separation of the Swiss League from the empire, but this was understood rather than officially expressed. The Eidgenossen were released by the emperor from the Reichskamergericht, a step tantamount to acknowledging their independence. One hundred and fifty years later this independence was formally declared at the Peace of Westphalia. For a time, however, many curious anomalies continued; the Swiss still submitted their charters for the sovereign's approval, accepted patents of nobility, and so forth. But the late wars had again won for them the respect and admiration of many of their neighbours.

Admission into the league was now requested by Basel and Schaffhausen, and their request was granted in 1501. Basel ranked as the ninth link of the federal chain, and thus took precedence of Freiburg and Solothurn, in acknowledgment of its high position and great merits. Basel had indeed advanced greatly in prosperity. She had opened her University in 1460; her importance as an emporium was great; and she formed a fitting corner-stone in the West. She gloried in her union with the league and the protection it afforded her; and to show the perfect trust she felt, she dismissed all the guards at her gates, and placed in their stead an old woman with a distaff, who, much to the annoyance of the neighbours, used to receive the tolls. Henceforward the Swabians and the Swiss were looked upon as distinct nationalities. Wurtemburg and Bavaria joined in union with the Swiss the very next year, and even Maximilian himself renewed his friendship with the Swiss states. "Could there be a greater compliment paid to the excellence of the Swiss Union," says a German historian, Uhlmann, "than this mark of confidence on the part of Maximilian?" After various refusals, and only after having qualified itself for taking its position, Appenzell was admitted into the federal fold December, 1513, despite the resistance of the Prince Abbot of St. Gall, as a member on equal terms, and the list of the XIII. Orte, or cantons, was complete, and remained closed for three centuries.

The Italian wars which follow bear more or less the stamp of mercenary wars, and are interesting chiefly from a military point of view, only the essential points of their story will therefore be touched upon here. It has been shown how the league got a footing in Ticino under the Visconti;[1] and later on the Swiss not only strove to increase their acquisitions in Italy, but played a prominent part in the wars waged by

[1] See p. 187.

foreign princes and powers which set up pretensions to Naples, Milan, &c.

The period of the French invasion of Italy opened in 1494 when the Swiss assisted Charles VIII. of France in the conquest of Naples, which he claimed from the house of Aragon. His successor, Louis XII., took Milan from Ludovico Sforza, surnamed Il Moro, with the aid of the Swiss, promising to cede Bellinzona to the Swiss as a reward for their services. Of the numerous enemies he raised up against himself the bitterest was Pope Julius II., who counted on the help of the Eidgenossen in the task of driving the French from Italy, and the more so as he discovered amongst them a fit instrument for carrying out his schemes. Matthæus Schinner, a priest, was a most remarkable man. Born of the poorest of parents, in the Upper Valais, he had in early life sung in the streets for bread. From this humble origin he had raised himself to the position of Cardinal, and had become an intimate friend of the Pontiff. Having money, indulgences, and power liberally at command, he brought about a five years' alliance between the Papal See and Switzerland. The Swiss readily entered into this agreement, as they had been slighted by Louis, and, moreover, their contract with France had expired in 1510. Spain, England, and other powers, had likewise entered into league with Pope Julius, but his chief supporters were the Swiss. In their march through Lombardy, against the French (1512), Pavia surrendered, and Milan also fell to the victors. Zwingli, the reformer, who had been present in the campaign as camp-preacher, reports that it was curious to see the ambassadors of great powers appearing at the Tagsatzung held at Baden to decide on the fate of Milan, and pleading with the Eidgenossen for a greater or less share of the duchy.[1] Despite all flatteries, the Swiss envoys reinstated Maximilian Sforza in his heritage, and in return for this they received Lugano, Locarno, &c.

The attempt of Louis to re-conquer Milan miscarried. His fine army, commanded by the greatest generals of the age, Trémouille and Trivulzio, was defeated at Novara in 1513. This siege surpassed all the Swiss had yet gone through, yet they left open the gates, and in derision hung linen before the breaches. Foreign historians compared this battle with the greatest victories of the Greeks and Romans. The historian, Machiavelli, prophesied that the Swiss would one day acquire the leadership of Italy, but that was not to be, however.

On the accession of Francis I., that youthful and ambitious prince wished to signalize the opening of his reign by the recovery of Milan. Anxious to have Switzerland neutral he made overtures, which were rejected. But intrigues amongst the Swiss and dissensions among their allies worked in his favour, and Bern, Freiburg, and Solothurn, accepted a peace against the interests of Switzerland, and their men returned home. Cardinal Schinner, strongly averse to the French, by a false report that the enemy was

[1] "Here you might observe men's disposition," he writes, "caution, and cunning. They strive to puzzle one another with the view of drawing advantage from the confusion. They pretend to one thing, but hope to get another."

at the gate, brought up in wild haste the Eidgenossen, who had been wavering hitherto. The Swiss followed their leader who was mounted on his horse, his purple cloak streaming in the wind, and came up with the enemy at Marignano (the modern Malegnano) September 13, 1515. A terrific struggle ensued, abating only when the moon went down at midnight. Trivulzio had cut his way through the force with his sword. Bayard, the "Chevalier *sans peur et sans reproche*," for

FREIBURG CUSTOM-HOUSE.

the first time in his life fled. At dawn the Swiss renewed to the attack. Their fortunes fluctuated till noon, when the cries of "San Marco!" announced the approach of the Venetians. These appeared to be about to cut off retreat, and the plain on which the Swiss stood being now under water—for the French had broken down the dykes of the Lambro—the Eidgenossen were compelled to retire. This they did in perfect order, carrying with them their wounded, and retaining their guns and banners. They were, indeed, rather foiled than defeated, and Francis, full of admiration for the Swiss, forbade his troops to pursue. Trivulzio declared that the eighteen battles he had previously witnessed were but child's play to that of Marignano.

In the November of the following year (1516) an "eternal peace" was concluded between France and the Swiss, and this drew Switzerland closer to her powerful neighbour. The material results of the war were the acquisition of Ticino (which was admitted a canton in 1805), and of Valtellina and Chiavenna. This defeat was a turning-point in Swiss history, establishing as it did the supremacy of France. The part they had hitherto played in European politics had come to an end, and the ascendency they had so long maintained as a leading military power had been strangely shattered. A decline was clearly inevitable.

A few words may be given here respecting the famous monastery of St. Gall. The cloisters of St. Gall shed a bright lustre on Swabian lands during its best period, from 800 to 1050 A.D. This famous religious-house was a centre of art and high culture, and was a blessing to the whole country. We can but allude to some of its famous monks, such as the Notkers, Ekkehard, Rabbert, and so forth; many famous as poets, musicians, savants, historians, and teachers of the very highest rank. In the noted school attached to the monastery there resided and were educated some three hundred sons of the German and Helvetic nobility. The discipline kept up was most severe. A story runs that King Conrad I., on a visit to the institution, wished to put this to the test, and caused to be scattered under the school benches a basketful of fine apples. Not a single scholar touched the fruit, and, to reward them for this very remarkable self-restraint, Conrad gave the youths three holidays. But the number of anecdotes attaching to this magnificent institution is endless.

XXI.

THE GREAT COUNCILS; THE LANDSGEMEINDE AND TAGSATZUNG, OR DIET; LITERATURE IN THE HEROIC AGE.

PERHAPS no better place than this can be found for discussing the constitutional affairs of the enlarged Bund. A description of the *rouage administratif* of each of the thirteen republics would be far too tedious to the reader, and we shall therefore treat them collectively as far as possible. The cantons naturally split into two divisions, those *à Grand Conseil*, and the cantons *à Landsgemeinde*, the latter including the country republics, the three Waldstätten, Glarus, Appenzell, and Zug.

We have seen in the case of Zurich how her council sprang into existence and became the chief cornerstone of her constitutional freedom, after she had been for generations dependent on an abbey. In this latter respect Zurich but resembles Lucerne, Solothurn, Geneva, and others, which went through similar phases of development. Bern, however, received the stamp of independence at her very birth—in the very charter of

SARNEN, BERN.

liberties involved in her foundation—and her history ran more smoothly. Her government at once took an aristocratic tinge, a close corporation of dominant families ruling; and in this respect she resembled somewhat mighty Venice. In the eighteenth century these ruling families numbered 360, and kept at arm's length, as it were, the craftsmen, who, however, were not entirely excluded from a share in the government. Vast personal property and additional domains acquired by conquest formed the chief source of the power of Bern, and brought in a great income to the patricians. Rule, domination, statecraft, became the chief concern of the Bernese aristocracy, whilst in Lucerne, Solothurn, and Freiburg, the government was, if possible, still more aristocratic than that of Bern, and in all these cases was presided over by a Schultheiss, or Mayor. In the Zurich republic a more democratic spirit was found, and the inhabitants were given to industrial and intellectual pursuits rather than to rule and conquest. Her trade was considerable, and her constitution had done away with the prerogatives of the nobility. Owing to these things the way was opened for her burghers into the government, and there sprang up an ambition among the craftsmen to rise in the social scale. Zurich is the prototype of the Geneva of the eighteenth century, the two cities greatly resembling each other in their tendencies and movements, religious and political. At Geneva the craftsmen, occupying the *bas de la ville*, by their energy struggled to the *haut de la ville*, or quarter of the privileged classes. All authority was vested in the two councils—the "Grosse Rath," a sort

CITY WALLS OF LUCERNE.

of legislative body numbering one hundred or two hundred members; and the "Kleine Rath," a select committee of the former, consisting of from twenty-five to thirty-six members, in whom rested the executive and judicial power. In the liberal cantons the Burgomaster presided. The Council, however, encroached upon the rights of the people at large, and deprived them of direct influence in the management of affairs. Basel and Schaffhausen followed in the track of Zurich. Genuine democracies represent the cantons *à Landsgemeinde*. The government embodied the will of a sovereign people, and from its very antiquity commands our veneration and deserves special attention. To time immemorial the ancient custom goes back. It was known amongst the Greeks, and we meet with it in the "Volksversammlung" of the early German tribes—the gathering of a whole people around their king to administer justice or decide issues of peace or war. These assemblies sprang up again in the thirteenth century, in the Forest Cantons, but now became political meetings, from the necessity of guarding against a common foe. The rule by Landsgemeinde was adopted by eleven Alpine districts, of which two, Gersau and Urseren, were almost microscopical. Five of these were swept away, Schwyz amongst the number. Of these we shall not speak. Yet the hoary and patriarchal custom still lingers on in some of the secluded Alpine nooks, favoured by the isolation of the place, and the *génie conservateur* innate in the Alpine folk. Unable, however, to clearly understand the ancient Landsgemeinde except by reference to the present age, we prefer to draw the reader's attention to the living spring, the sacred spot where he can "look face to face on freedom in its purest and most ancient form"—to quote Freeman's fine words—a heart-stirring sight to witness.

The last Sunday in April is the date usually fixed for the holding of the Landsgemeinde. The gatherings all bear a general resemblance to each other, yet each shows the influence of the locality, the religion, or the industrial pursuits of the people. But whether we see the meeting in Protestant and manufacturing Glarus, in Catholic and conservative Unterwalden, or in picturesque Sarnen, the scene is one never to be forgotten. Dressed in their Sunday best, and wearing the sword, the badge of freedom—so orders the ancient ritual—the ardent burghers flock to the national ring, or forum, to discharge their civic duties. After early morning service, and a grand parade of Landammann and staff, halberdiers, troops, and bands of music, the Landsgemeinde opens at eleven with a religious ceremony. At Trogen the hymn, "All life flows from Thee," is sung by ten thousand voices, and, at the call of the Landammann, the vast crowd falls down in silent prayer. The effect is grand and solemn. An address by the Landammann follows, and then the business of the day is entered upon. The inspection of the yearly accounts, the election of magistrates and officials, amendment of existing laws and the promulgation of new ones, are the chief items on the agenda list. All the officers, from the Landammann himself down to the humblest public servant, are subject to yearly election, though in the case of the chief man re-election usually takes place for many years. There are indeed regular dynasties of Landammanns, so to speak, for the office may remain in the same family for many generations. Assent to a proposal is given by holding up the right hand, and this the crowd does with great eagerness. The list of candidates is drawn up by the Landsgemeinde, but, strange to say, free discussion on proposed reforms and new laws is permitted only at Glarus. The question is discussed beforehand by the Landrath, a legislative body elected by the parish. "De minoribus rebus principes consultant, de majoribus omnes," writes Tacitus of the German Volksgemeinde, and the words apply almost equally well here. The Landsgemeinde is, in fact, the supreme court, which approves or annuls. So recently as the spring of 1888, for instance, Urseren was deprived of its autonomy and joined to the Canton of Uri, by order of the Landsgemeinde. And at Sarnen the revision of the constitution was agreed to at the open and general meeting. The election of the Waibel, or Summoner, gives rise to much amusement, for in him the chief requisite is strength of lungs, he being the mouthpiece of the Landammann. The installation of the Landammann himself is the closing scene, and the most impressive one. Slowly and solemnly he takes the oath of fidelity to the constitution, and the people in return pledge themselves to stand by the leader. With hands uplifted the vast crowd repeats the phrases word by word as they are spoken by the Landammann. This mutual engagement between leader and people—their hearts filled with the sacredness of the moment, and their voices swelling into one grand roll—is almost overwhelming in its touching simplicity and fervour. That the custom has maintained itself with but minor changes through so many centuries answers for the admirable stability of the people, and the suitableness of the *régime* itself.

The common tie that bound together the thirteen autonomous states into one was the Diet or Tagsatzung. It met at one or other of the chief towns— Zurich, Lucerne, Bern, Baden, and so forth. Each canton was, as a rule, allowed one representative, and any one of the cantons could summon a meeting, though this was generally done by the Vorort or *canton directeur*—a position usually held by Zurich —whose member likewise presided. The various cantons joined in the discussions according to their rank and the order of their admission to the league. This will be made clearer by the accompanying list. The Boten, or envoys, not being plenipotentiaries, would post to and fro between their governments and the Diet, to report progress and receive instructions. As the proceedings were in later times committed to writing, we have extant a most valuable series of records called Abschiede (=leave or *congé*). Held at first but once a year, the Diet occasionally met as many as fifty times in the course of the twelvemonth. whilst a single session would last sometimes for several weeks. At one period the meetings became international congresses, at which the most important questions were deliberated. But, in truth, the Diet, down to its extinction in 1848, never again during its long existence exerted the vast influence it had in its brilliant fifteenth-century period. Yet despite its many defects, and its slow and roundabout way of doing business, the Tagsatzung worked successfully—far more so indeed than did the German Government.

A short sketch of the intellectual and literary life of the heroic period may here be given. It is clear at the outset that an epoch so largely given over to warfare and political progress would not be likely to produce much meditative or reflective poetry. "The clash of arms frightens the Muses," says an old proverb. (An exception must, however, be usually made in the case of the peaceful and sheltered cloister.) Yet this active and stirring period brought forth much national literature. Throughout we find singers who in verse or prose chant the national glory, and no episode of importance is without its poetic chronicle or interpretation; the national enthusiasm vents itself in war-song, in satire, in mock-heroics, or in rhyming chronicle. Wandering poets living on the scanty proceeds of their *lieder;* craftsmen who have taken up the sword; soldiers by profession—these are the bards of the time. Rugged and unpolished sometimes are their verses, for the Middle German is in a transition state, and poetry has long since left courts and descended among the people. In Germany, as everybody knows, had formed the body of the *Meistersinger*. The historical "Folk songs" (*Volkslieder*) are the overflowing of a nation's heart stirred to its depths by the thrilling scenes around it, and they are the true expression of the temper of the time. We need only allude to the songs inspired by Sempach and Naefels, and the fiery song of Morat by Veit Weber, an Alsacian, who fought in the Swiss ranks filled with patriotic enthusiasm. Lucerne, too, has brought forth many poets—Auer, Wick, Viol, Birkes, and others—who sang the glory of the great wars. A song and a play dealing with Tell appeared about this time.

Along with the poet the chronicler springs up, and numerous instances of this class are met with. At Bern we find Justinger (1420), the first to draw historical knowledge from the *Volkslieder*, Diebold Schilling (1484), and Anshelm; at Schwyz, John Fründ; at Lucerne, Melchior Russ, Diebold Schilling, the chaplain, whose account of the meeting at Stanz is most trustworthy, Petermann Etterlin, and Nicolas Schradin; at Zurich, Gerold Edlibach, the noble knights Strettlinger of Bern, who wrote the chronicles bearing their name, and the author of the "White Book of Sarnen," complete the list. The "White Book" is much referred to by modern writers. The most brilliant annalist perhaps is Tschudi, of whom mention was made in the chapter on the foundation of the league. Biassed as the writers often are—nothing else can be expected from the times—their records bear witness to the national spirit of the Swiss, and to the intellectual revival taking place. The first Helvetian typography was produced by Albert von Bonnstetten, a Zurich nobleman, and Dean of Einsiedeln, and one of the chief scholars of his age. He gave a trustworthy account of Nicolas von der Flüe, and the Burgundian wars. Another great scholar was his friend Nicolas von Wyl, a nobleman of Aargau.

The revival of letters introduced into the subtle scholasticism of the time a world of new thoughts, learning, and refined literary tastes—*humanismus* as the Germans so expressively call it. Nicolas von Wyl is one of the oldest German-Swiss humanists. He extended the Italian Renaissance to his native soil by his masterly translations of Petrarch, Boccaccio, Poggio, and others. Æneas Sylvius, the elegant poet, novelist, and orator, who rose to the Papal dignity as Pius II., would have had the world forget his fascinating but worldly writings. "Rejicite Æneam, suscipite Pium," was his request. For twenty years Æneas had laboured to bring classical culture to barbarian Germany. His earliest pupil, Von Wyl,[1] became a great favourite at the German courts, and with the literary circle which the highly-cultivated Duchess of Wurtemberg gathered around her. Von Wyl translated some of the Latin works of Felix Malleolus, his friend and benefactor; for instance, his biting satire on the idle Lollards and "Beghards." He died at Zurich.

But if the courts and the nobles promoted the growth of the New Learning, the universities were its chief support. That of Basel was opened in 1460, under the auspices of Pius II. (Æneas Sylvius), who granted its foundation charter. It rapidly gathered within its walls some of the brightest minds of the day, amongst whom we need only mention the world-famed Erasmus and Zwingli the reformer.

[1] Prof. Bächtold's "Swiss-German Literature."

XXII.

THE REFORMATION IN GERMAN SWITZERLAND.

(1484-1531.)

THE age of the Renaissance ushered in a century of intellectual revolution, and wrought remarkable changes in art, in science, in literature, in religion, and in every department of human life and energy. The space at our disposal will permit us to touch only on one of these developments, the religious. But the varying history of religious movement well-nigh fills up the sixteenth century. The revival of learning quickened the spirit of the Reformation, though most of the savants disapproved of the movement, as in the case of Erasmus and Glarean, a famous Swiss scholar. But whilst Luther's training was monastic rather than scholarly, and whilst he was, if anything, opposed to the New Learning, the great Swiss reformer was a scholar of the first order, who drew his profound and liberal ideas from his study of the classics. And it is a curious and noteworthy fact that with the spread of letters in Switzerland, there started up on its soil a host of men of parts[1] who, forming a school of disciples, as it were, espoused the cause of their great leader, Zwingli, and promoted it, each in his own canton. This is one peculiarity of the Swiss Reformation.

The degeneracy of the Church passed all belief, and was, as every one knows, the primary and chief cause of the Reformation on the Continent; but in Switzerland there was yet another cause, quite as important, which gave an impulse to the movement—the calamitous consequences of the mercenary wars, touched upon in previous chapters. Foreign pay had irresistible attractions for captain and man alike, and the country was constantly being drained of its stoutest arms and bravest hearts. It was difficult to over-estimate the baneful effects of this practice on the national welfare, and, of all the noble men who deplored these results, none felt it like Ulrich Zwingli. An enthusiastic scholar, a gifted preacher, a zealous patriot, and a remarkably able politician, he devoted his life to the work of rescuing his people and country from their moral decline. This he proposed to effect by the working of the Divine Word. Luther left the knotty skein of politics to his princely friends to unravel, but Zwingli, on the contrary, shrank from no political difficulties, encumbrances, or complications. To his clear and far-seeing mind social and political reform was inseparably bound up with religious change and pro-

---

[1] A mere list of names must suffice:—Lupulus, Wittenbach, Œcolompad, Vadian, Œconomius, Collin, Myconius, Pellikan Platter, Glarean (the poet laureate crowned with the wreath by the Emperor Max). The savants at that time were wont to latinize their names in their enthusiasm for the classics.

ULRICH ZWINGLI.
(*After Asper.*)

gress. The one would be of but little avail without the other, and the great object of his life became the total regeneration of the commonwealth—church and state both.

Ulrich Zwingli was born at Wildhaus, amongt the song-loving Toggenburger, in the canton of St. Gall, January 1, 1484. The talented youth was destined for the Church by his father, a highly-respected magistrate, and was sent to school at Basel, and afterwards studied at Bern. Here sprang up his enthusiasm for classical studies under the famous Lupulus, whilst the friars were so struck with his musical talents that they tried hard to keep him in the cloisters. However, in 1500 he left for the University of Vienna, and two years later we find him established as Latin teacher at Basel and a student of the university there. Steeped in the New Learning his attention was now drawn to scriptural studies by the enlightened Wittenbach. At Basel, too, he formed a friendship with the famed Erasmus. Obtaining the degree of *magister philosophiæ*, in 1506, he was nominated pastor at Glarus, and with regret tore himself away from that seat of learning. During his ten years' ministry at Glarus (a Landsgemeinde canton) his natural taste and talent for politics were brought into play. And though he founded a Latin school for clever youths, and pursued his own studies vigorously, and kept up a vast correspondence with Erasmus, Glarean, and other noted scholars, he was no mere pedant or bookworm, but took a profound interest in the political life of that stirring age. Twice he accompanied the men of Glarus on their Italian expedition as field chaplain, but though he naturally rejoiced at the glory their arms acquired, yet his eyes became fully opened to the disastrous results of the mercenary wars. His direct and unsparing attacks on the *Reislaufen* and foreign pension system roused such a storm against him that he was forced to take refuge at Einsiedeln, 1516. His two years' quiet retreat in the famous abbey afforded him a glimpse of the flagrant abuses rife in the Church. At first he appealed to the dignitaries of the Church to remedy the evils, but at length, driven no doubt by the sight of the superstitions around him, he introduced those sweeping measures of reform which did away with every vestige of Romanism that remained in the evangelical church. Preaching to the thousands who flocked to the wonder-working image of the Virgin, his sermons, full of force, novelty, and pithy eloquence, rapidly spread abroad his fame. He became friendly with other scholars and religious reformers. Rome made him tempting offers with the view of drawing him away from Switzerland and his life-work, but resisting all her persuasion, he accepted a call to Zurich, as *plebanus* at the Minster, December, 1518. Zurich was the foremost town of the Confederation, but was justly reputed a dissolute city, not unlike the then Geneva. Its enlightened Council saw in Zwingli a spirited leader.

His opening sermon, on New Year's Day, 1519, stirred his hearers in a marvellous way, and at once stamped him as an evangelical reformer of no common type. He briefly sketched out the plan by which he proposed to be guided in his future sermons. His subjects would be drawn from the Bible only,[1] especially from the New Testament, and he would follow the guidance of the Holy Spirit, and not human direction. So profound was the impression made by his impassioned and eloquent words that some of the listeners declared him to be a "new Moses who had arisen to save his people from spiritual bondage." The learned Platter writes that during the sermon he "felt himself lifted off the ground by his hair." The very first year of Zwingli's ministry at Zurich, two thousand souls were "saved by the milk of the Holy Gospel." And his practical goodness of heart was attested by his assiduous attention to the sick during the plague of 1519, in which he was himself stricken and brought very near to death. Three hymns composed during this trying time reveal his entire resignation and calm trust in God. Although he fiercely opposed the sale of indulgences there were no thunderings against him from the Vatican, such as were hurled against Luther.[2] The Eidgenossen, being useful to the Papal See, was rather indulged; it was even intimated to the Diet that they should send back from Bern Friar Bernhard Samson, who was preaching with great effect there, should he prove obnoxious. With unflagging zeal and courage Zwingli followed his ideal in politics, viz., to rear a republic on the type of the Greek free states of old, with perfect national independence. Thanks to

---

[1] It is necessary to bear in mind that at that time the Bible was well-nigh an unknown book to the common people. There were even to be found priests who neither possessed a copy of the Scriptures nor could have read it if they had.

[2] On such good terms with the Pontiff was Zwingli that one of the Papal Legates sent his own doctor to attend him.

his influence Zurich in 1521 abolished *Reislaufen*, and the system of foreign pay. This step, however, brought down on the head of Zurich the wrath of the twelve sister republics, which had just signed a military contract with Francis I. Zwingli addressed to Schwyz a "Holy Exhortation" to serve neither Pope nor Emperor; his exhortation, however, served only to increase the number of his political foes.[1] Relying rather on reason than on force, he prepared the way for his reforms with singular moderation and forbearance.

It was only in 1522 that he began to launch pamphlets against the abuses in the Church-fasting, celibacy of the clergy, and the like. On the 29th of January, 1523, Zwingli obtained from the Council of Zurich the opening of a public religious discussion in presence of the whole of the clergy of the canton, and representatives of the Bishop of Constance, whose assistance in the debate the Council had invited. In sixty-seven theses remarkable for their penetration and clearness he sketched out his confession of faith and plan of reform, and utterly confounded all objections of his opponents by showing the conformity of his theses with the Holy Scriptures. On the 25th of October, 1523, a second discussion initiated the practical consequences of the reformed doctrine —the abrogation of the mass and image worship. Zwingli's system was virtually that of Calvin, but was

---

[1] "It is meet that cardinals should wear red cloaks and hats," to quote one passage from the Exhortation; "if you shake them they drop crowns and ducats, but if you wring them there flows forth the blood of your fathers, your sons, and your brothers."

conceived in a broader spirit, and carried out later on in a far milder manner by Bullinger. To enter into a full comparison of the two systems would, however, be out of place here. The Council gave the fullest approval to the Reformation.

In 1524 Zwingli married Anne Reinhard, the widow of a Zurich nobleman (Meyer von Knonau), and so discarded the practice of celibacy obtaining amongst priests. She made him an excellent wife and helpmate, and bore him four children. The reformer's skill in music was often brought to bear on his children when they were inclined to be unruly; he would soothe them into peace and quietness by his performances on the lute or other instrument. To his stepson Gerald Meyer he was an excellent father. Tall, with grave but winning features, with a kind and generous heart and winning manner, Zwingli's personality was most fascinating. A scholar but no pedant, a plain but vigorous speaker, of sound and practical judgment, with vast stores of learning, and an unusual elevation of mind, he was also broadminded and compassionate. It may be mentioned that he provided on Ufenau Island in Zurich lake a last asylum for Ulrich von Hutten, who had been rejected by Erasmus and driven from Germany.

In 1524 Zwingli began to effect the most sweeping changes with the view of overthrowing the whole fabric of mediæval superstition. In the direction of reform he went far beyond Luther, who had retained oral confession, altar pictures, &c. The introduction of his reforms in Zurich called forth but little opposition. True, there were the risings of the Anabaptists but these were the same everywhere, and the revolt of the peasants was a general feature of the time.[1] Pictures and images were removed from the churches, under government direction, and nothing was left to distract men's attention, for Zwingli aimed at the re-establishment of the primitive Christianity in its pure, simple, and biblical form. The Holy Scriptures, expounded by the elect ministers of God, were to be men's highest guide and support. At the Landgemeinden,[2] called for the purpose, the people gave an enthusiastic assent to his doctrines, and declared themselves ready "to die for the gospel truth." Thus a national Church was established, severed from the diocese of Constance, and placed under the control of the Council of Zurich and a clerical synod. The convents were turned into schools, hospitals, and poorhouses. The famous Chorherrenstift, founded by the Carolingians, was turned into a University College, continuing to be called the Carolinum. This lasted till 1832, when it was formed into the University and Gymnasium of our own days. Zwingli was elected rector, and lectured on theology. He was also devoted to the study of Greek, and on New Year's Day, 1531, had a splendid performance of one of the plays of Aristophanes, for which he himself wrote the accompanying music, grave statesmen joining the professors and students in the representation. Zwingli was now, indeed, the idol of the people, and wielded the sceptre

---

[1] In Germany similar revolts took place, but Luther took no pains to appease the peasantry.

[2] Landgemeinden or gatherings of the parishes, a mode of appealing to the people which became the prototype of the modern Referendum.

in his little state. Under him Zurich became a centre of learning and religious enlightenment, and its influence spread over other Swiss lands, South Germany and elsewhere.

The reformed faith penetrated, but only gradually, into the northern and eastern cantons. Bern was reached in 1528, after a brilliant disputation held in that city. Basel and Schaffhausen followed in 1529, and then St. Gall, Appenzell, Graubünden, and Solothurn, though some of them had serious struggles within themselves and fell in only partly with the reforms. But in the Central or Forest Cantons it was that the fiercest opposition was encountered. Many things combined to produce this result. In the first place, the district was a very stronghold of Catholic and Conservative feeling, and religion was entwined with the fond memories of a glorious past. From the very simplicity of their lives the people ignored the degeneracy of the priesthood, and amongst these pastoral peoples the priests were of simpler manners and more moral life than those in the cities; they disliked learning and enlightenment.

Then there was the old feeling of antipathy to the cities, coupled with a strong dislike for the reforms which had abolished *Reislaufen*, that standing source of income to the cantons. Lucerne, bought with French gold, struggled with Zurich for the lead. So far was the opposition carried that the Catholic districts by a majority of votes insisted (at the Diet) on a measure for suppressing heresy in Zurich, whilst some were for expelling that canton from the league. The Forest Cantons issued orders that Zwingli should be seized should he be found within their territories; consequently he kept away from the great convocation at Baden, 1526. Serious collisions arose, but it is impossible to dwell on them here.

Wider and wider grew the chasm between the two religious parties, and Zwingli at length formed a "Christian League" between the Swiss Protestants and some of the German cities and the Elector of Hesse. On the other hand, the Catholics entered into an alliance with Ferdinand of Austria, a determined enemy to the reformed religion. At last the Protestant party was exasperated beyond bearing, and Zurich declared war on the Forest Cantons, Zwingli himself joining in the vicissitudes of the campaign. His camp presented the "picture of a well-organized, God-fearing army of a truly Puritan stamp." The encounter at Kappel, in June, 1529, however, took a peaceful turn, thanks to the mediation of Landammann Aebli, of Glarus, greatly to the disgust of Zwingli, who prophetically exclaimed that some day the Catholics would be the stronger party, and then they would not show so much moderation. All ill-feeling, indeed, subsided when the two armies came within sight of each other. The curious and touching episode known as the *Kappeler Milchsuppe* took place here. A band of jolly Catholics had got hold of a large bowl of milk, but lacking bread they placed it on the boundary line between Zug and Zurich. At once a group of Zurich men turned up with some loaves, and presently the whole party fell to eating the *Milchsuppe* right merrily. A peace was concluded on the 29th of June, 1529, by which the

Austrian League was dissolved, and freedom of worship granted to all.

Zwingli's closing years were devoted to vast schemes of European policy. With the view of forming a strong alliance of the Swiss Protestants with foreign powers favouring the reformed faith, and in opposition to the emperor Charles V., he entered into negotiations with France, with some of the German states, with the Venetian republic, and others. His plans were too bold and sweeping to be practical, and came to nought. His relations with Luther claim special attention, however. By his treatise, "De verâ et falsâ religione" (1525), Zwingli had, though unwillingly, thrown the gauntlet into the Wittenberg camp. The work was intended to be a scientific refutation of the Catholic doctrine of transubstantiation, and a war of words arose. The contest was by each disputant carried on *suo more* by Luther with his usual authoritative and tempestuous vehemence, by Zwingli in his own cool reasoning, dignified, and courteous style and republican frankness. Presently there came a strong desire for a union between the German *Protestants*, and the Swiss *Reformers*—the two were thus distinguished—the impulse to it being given by Charles V.'s "Protest" against the Protestants. Landgrave Philip of Hesse, the political leader of the German reformers, invited Luther and Zwingli to meet at his castle of Marburg, with the view of reconciling the two sections. The religious *colloquium* was attended by many savants, princes, nobles, and all the chief leaders of the Reformation, and might have done great things, but came to grief through the obstinacy of Luther, as is well known, or rather through his determination to approve of no man's views except they should agree exactly with his own. Luther insisted on a literal interpretation of the words "This is my body," whilst Zwingli saw in them only a metaphorical or symbolical signification. Zwingli's logic and cool, clear reasoning were acknowledged to be superior to those of his opponent, but Luther demanded complete submission. The conference, in short, resulted in nothing, and nearly ended in an open rupture between the two leaders. Zwingli extended his hand in token of friendship and goodwill, but Luther refused it. The truth was the two men looked at the matter from quite different points of view. With Luther religion was almost wholly a thing of a mystic basis, a creed of the heart—of feeling—whilst Zwingli, required his reason to be satisfied. The one wrestled in agony of soul with the spirits of darkness; the other looked to the Divine, all-embracing love under which all creation rests in trust and happiness, and under which all men are brothers, children of one all-kind Father.

To return for a moment to home politics. The peace of 1529 was a short-lived one. Zwingli anxious only to spread the reformed faith over the whole republic did not realize clearly the hatred of the Forest district against the new creed. Then there were faults on both sides—the Zwinglian party and the Waldstätten — but the history of them is too long and too trifling to be given here. Not the least of the mistakes, however, was made by Zwingli himself, in claiming well-nigh absolute power for the two chief reformed cities, Zurich and Bern. Again, the refusal of the Waldstätten to assist Graubünden against an Italian invasion was looked upon with grave suspicion, and caused much ill-feeling against them. War was imminent, and was indeed eagerly desired on *both* sides. Bern, finding that war was likely to be injurious to her private ends insisted on a stoppage of mercantile traffic between the opposing districts,[1] but Zwingli scorned to use such a means to hunger the enemy and so bring them to submit. However Zurich was outvoted in the Christian League (May 16th), and the Forest was excluded from the markets of that city and Bern. The rest may be easily guessed. On Zurich was turned all the fury of the famished Forest men, and they sent a challenge in October, 1531. A second time the hostile armies met at Kappel, but the positions were reversed. Zurich was unprepared to meet a foe four times as numerous as her own, and Bern hesitated to come to her aid. However Göldlin, the captain of the little force, recklessly engaged with the opposing army, whether from treachery or incapacity is not known, but he was certainly opposed to the reformed faith. Zwingli had taken leave of his friend Bullinger, as though foreseeing his own death in the coming struggle, and had joined the Zurich force. He was with the chief banner, and, with some five hundred of his overmatched comrades, fell in the thickest of the battle. Amongst the slain were most of the

[1] Traffic absolutely necessary to the Forest Cantons for supplying provisions.

foremost men of the city, councillors, clergy, Zwingli's friends and relations. Amongst these last was his beloved stepson who had been fighting by his side. A canon of Zug, seeing Zwingli's body, burst into tears, crying, "Whatever thy faith, I know thou hast been a brave Eidgenosse." According to the barbarous custom of the time the body was quartered, then burnt, and scattered to the winds. And the terrible disaster which befell Zurich was followed soon after by another.

But the reformation was far too deeply rooted to be thus destroyed. Bullinger, the friend of Zwingli, and, later on, of Calvin, worthily succeeded to the headship of the Zurich reformers. Keeping clear of politics, for which he had no propensity, he concentrated his attention on the perfecting of the Zwinglian ecclesiastical system; working for strict morality without narrowness of mind, for national independence, for inquiring after light and truth, and for true piety combined with benevolence and charity. Zwingli had made mistakes of policy, but his devotion to his cause, his self-abnegation, and his tragic death, made full reparation for them.

At Solothurn Catholicism again got the upper hand, and the reformers had to leave. Intestine feuds were breaking out, and indeed the first shot had actually been fired, when the noble-minded Schultheiss, Nicolas von Wengi, a Catholic, threw himself before the mouth of a cannon, and exclaimed, "If the blood of the burghers is to be spent, let mine be the first!" Wengi's party at once desisted from the attack, and matters were settled amicably.

XXIII.

THE REFORMATION IN WEST SWITZERLAND.

(1530-1536.)

THE history of French Switzerland has not yet been touched upon, and that for good reasons. It is difficult to realize that down even to the sixteenth century the French Swiss were still languishing under the ancient forms of feudalism, and this at a time when their German brethren had long been enjoying the blessings of national independence, and had filled the world with their military renown. But, in truth, the French were slow to awaken to republican freedom, and looked to East Switzerland rather than to themselves for deliverance from political bondage. It is a remarkable fact that the Reformation was made but with the assistance of those skilled statesmen, the Bernese, the connecting link between the eastern portions of Switzerland and the isolated west. That Bern rightly calculated on benefiting by this junction is well known.

Before passing to the Reformation itself, however, we must give a slight sketch of the political condition

MINSTER, BERN.
(*From a Photograph.*)

at that time of Vaud and Geneva, with which alone we have here any concern. Neuchâtel still remained in reality a separate principality, though temporarily (1512-1529) under Swiss rule. Vaud had in its time seen many masters which may perhaps account for its backwardness in adopting home rule. Its natural beauty and enjoyable climate have made it coveted at all times, in ancient, in mediæval, and, as we shall see, even in modern times. At first a scene of turmoil and tumult caused by the quarrels of its powerful nobles, it sank beneath the sceptre of Savoy, Peter, the eminent prince of Savoy—surnamed the "Petit Charlemagne"—having succeeded in establishing his authority over the native nobility. Once joined to Savoy, the fortunes of Vaud naturally depended on those of the Savoy dynasty. Peter attempted to annex the bishopric of Lausanne, but failing, Vaud was torn asunder, and there existed side by side a spiritual and a temporal lordship. Of the two portions that under ecclesiastical sway enjoyed the less liberty. Lausanne was a place much frequented by pilgrims, and was a mart for indulgences, but it possessed not a vestige of autonomy. It lay "dormant at the base of its many churches." When in the fifteenth century the power of the House of Savoy declined, the Vaud country speedily fell into a condition of anarchy, the nobility at daggers drawn against the burghers, and the mountain-dwellers at deadly variance with the vine-tillers of the plain. But early in the sixteenth century Lausanne was stirred from its lethargy by the attempts of Charles III. of Savoy to obtain the overlordship of the city. Thus threatened, and torn by intestine quarrels, Vaud in its helplessness seemed to invite the interference of Bern in this affair, and that city on its part was only too glad of an occasion of interfering.

Geneva was Vaud's companion in trouble, threatened by similar dangers, and torn by similar struggles. Here also the bishop was lord-paramount, but in this case the stout-hearted burghers had wrested from him a considerable amount of self-rule. Its inveterate enemy, too, was the Duke of Savoy. But the men of Geneva loved independence far too much to submit quietly to hostile aggressiveness and encroachment; for centuries even they had kept at bay the designing nobility. Yet at one time the Duke of Savoy had arrogated to himself the rights of vicedom, that is, temporal justice of the bishop as his vassal. Possessing thus temporal jurisdiction, *nomine episcopi*, over the city, he was anxious to annex it altogether. Geneva was almost entirely surrounded by Savoy territory. In the end Savoy arrogated to itself the right of appointing to the see, and its nominees were, it is needless to say, always members of its own house. Boys of twelve or fourteen, bastard sons even, were not unfrequently raised to the episcopal dignity. This did not add to the peacefulness of the district, and the adherents of the respective Savoy and Geneva factions went about armed to the teeth.

The accession of Charles III. in 1504 opened for Geneva a period of struggle. Anxious to maintain its freedom against a crafty and malignant prince, and his creature, the base-born bishop, the city split into two parties, the patriotic *Eidguenots*, so called from their relying for assistance on the Swiss Confederation, and the Savoyards, who were nicknamed the Mamelukes (knaves). Something like half the population were Savoyards by birth. Among the patriot party we find the "Children of Geneva," a gay and somewhat noisy band of patriotic enthusiasts, who loved fighting and did not fear death. At the head stood Thilibert the witty hotspur, François Bonivard, Prior of St. Victor, and a noteworthy Geneva chronicler, and Hugues Besançon, a clever statesman, and the father and deliverer of his country. When Charles required the Genevans to do homage they refused, answering sturdily that "Geneva would rather go begging and be free." In 1519, during his sojourn in the city, Charles punished with terrible rigour this bold stand for freedom; all were cowed into submission except Berthelier, who scorned to "bend to a man who was not his master." His head was one of the first to fall. But executions of one kind or another were soon of almost daily occurrence during Charles's stay. Four years later Charles and his beautiful bride, Beatrix entered Geneva with great pomp, and the princess even remained for the birth of her first-born. Charles desired the city to become accustomed to royal splendour, and to feel real sympathy for a native sovereign. But all his plans failed. By his eloquence and patriotism Hugues melted the hearts of the men of Freiburg, and succeeded in persuading them as well as the people of Bern to make an alliance with his own city. This alliance checkmated the plans of Savoy. But the success of the Genevans excited the jealousy of the "Ladle Squires." This curious nickname was given to an extraordinary band of the gentry and nobility living around Geneva. They met at a most frugal supper, and vowed the destruction of the city. A dish of rice was being served by the duke with a large spoon or ladle when one of the guests suddenly brandishing the implement fiercely exclaimed, "With this I shall swallow Geneva!" By an oath the men assembled bound themselves to seek the destruction of the obnoxious city, and hung their ladles round their necks in token of adherence. These "Seigneurs de la Cuiller," though unable to carry out their design, were yet able to work much mischief to Geneva, by cutting it off from the necessaries of life, and by keeping up a desultory but none the less harassing warfare against it. More than this, Bonivard was by order of the duke ousted from his living, and thrown into the castle of Chillon, in 1530.[1] In this same year, however, a new attack on the part of Savoy was checked by Bern and Freiburg, and Charles was forced to sign the treaty of St. Julien, guaranteeing the independence and freedom from molestation of Geneva. It was stipulated that should the treaty be violated by Savoy it should forfeit Vaud to Bern.

[1] For a fuller account of Bonivard the reader is referred to Marc-Monnier's "Genève et ses poètes." It is of course well known that though Bonivard's adventures suggested the idea of Byron's beautiful "Prisoner of Chillon," the story in the poem is almost entirely fictitious. In truth, Bonivard was liberated by Bern in 1536, and set himself to write the annals of his city of Geneva. He was married no fewer than four times. He seems to have been frequently cited before the Consistory for gambling and other like offences.

About this time Bern ventured on the introduction of the reformed faith into French Switzerland, hoping thereby to deepen her interest in that quarter. She found a suitable instrument in the person of Guillaume Farel, a fiery Frenchman from Dauphiné. The most intrepid and daring of champions of the gospel, he had fled from his native soil to Switzerland to avoid religious persecution, and had been expelled from Basel for his fanaticism. Supported by "Leurs excellences les Messieurs de Berne," as the government of that city was styled, he wandered about as an itinerant reformer, visiting Vaud and Neuchâtel. Through his efforts the latter canton adopted Zwingli's doctrines, in 1530, Vaud obstinately refusing the reformation, except in that portion of the district subject to Bern. Farel's preaching always excited the mob, and his harangues generally ended in a scuffle. He would often stop a priest on the road and fling into the river the host or the relics he carried. He had even been known to burst into a church during mass, and inveigh against Antichrist from the pulpit. Buffetings and prison alike failed to stop his efforts, for rough though his manner of controversy was, he was yet deeply in earnest. Going to Geneva, in 1532, his very name so stirred the Catholics there that he was obliged to flee for his life. The Protestant party in the city were strong and well organised, and they counted on the assistance of Bern, and that important state, anxious to convert the whole west, if possible, threatened Geneva with her displeasure should Farel not be favourably received. Thus Geneva was suddenly called upon to decide between the friendship of Bern, and that of Freiburg, where the Catholic party was dominant. Fear of Savoy decided Geneva in favour of Bern, which certainly was a more powerful ally than Freiburg. Furbity, an eloquent priest, who had been chosen to controvert the reformers' teachings, was to be discharged, and Farel, Fromment (another Frenchman), and Viret, a very able Vaudois, one of Farel's disciples, were established at Geneva, in 1534, by the desire of Bern. The new faith rapidly spread, and fresh attacks on the part of Savoy against Geneva only served to promote its extension. A religious discussion arranged by Bern, and conducted (on the reformed side) by Farel, took place at Geneva, in 1535, and resulted in the full establishment of the Zwinglian doctrine in that city. During the disputations an embassy from the Bernese attended the city council to make known the will of the ruling state, much after the manner of the proud and austere Roman senators of old.

But neither the ousted Catholics nor Savoy was inclined to submit tamely to this state of things. Geneva was a perfect hotbed of dissension. Duke Charles laid siege to the city, both by land and by water. A sudden change in French politics prompted Bern to show more active energy than it had lately shown. Two claimants for the Duchy of Milan appeared, Francis I. and the Emperor Charles V. To facilitate its conquest the former also planned the annexation of Savoy, intending to include Geneva as the key to Rhone valley. Bern thus seeing threatened the safety of a city which it was itself coveting, declared war on Savoy, and marched six thousand men into the Vaud country. The pretext set up by Bern was that Savoy had violated the treaty of St. Julien. Vaud was seized without striking a blow, and portions of Savoy, Gex, and Chablais, were annexed. In great triumph the Bernese army entered Geneva, but fear of France, and the proud and noble bearing of the Genevese, prevented the Bernese from attempting to put into execution any plans they might have had for annexing the republic. It was in this campaign that Bonivard was rescued.

Great was the disappointment of Vaud to find that it had only changed masters; had been rescued from the grasp of Savoy to fall beneath the sway of Bern, though the latter master was certainly in every way superior to the former. It will be well understood that this treatment on the part of Bern would later on give rise to serious troubles. Indeed to this day Vaud bears a grudge against her former master. However the powerful canton set up order and discipline in the disorganized district of Vaud, and gave it the *cachet* of its exemplary administration. It was divided into governmental districts and managed by eight Bernese landvögte. It agrees with the laws of Bern though its local administration was left it. Every effort was made to establish the reformed faith, and a disputation was held at Lausanne. In this Calvin took a part, but not a prominent one. The result was, however, the downfall of Catholicism in the district, deeply-rooted though it had been. Schools were established, and the Academy was founded by Bern. In this way the French position of the country was cemented to the eastern half. It was not till the Great Revolution that the prerogatives of the governing cantons were shaken, the immense wealth of the cathedral of Lausanne went to fill the state coffers of Bern, and the funds of the various churches were left to provide schools.

XXIV.

GENEVA AND CALVIN.

(1536-1564.)

POLITICAL and religious changes had brought about in Geneva a confusion which Farel felt himself incapable of lessening. By vehement intreaties, therefore, and even by threats, he induced Calvin to join him in his missionary work, Calvin being already known to the world as the author of "Institutio Christianæ Religionis," a work that fell on men like a revelation. John Calvin, or Cauvin, was born at Noyon, in Picardy, in 1509, and was a northern Frenchman of superior intelligence and learning, but of a gloomy, austere disposition, with a large admixture of fatalism in his views. Destined for the Church, he studied in Paris at the early age of thirteen, but by his father's wish he changed his intention, and applied himself to the study of law, at Orleans and Bourges. To these latter studies he owed that wonderful facility in systematic reasoning which is so noticeable in his writings. But the death of his parent in 1531 brought Calvin once more to Paris, where he speedily found himself drawn into the new religious movement which was winning its way in France. Profound theological researches and severe inward struggles caused his conversion to the reformed faith, in the following year. In 1535 we find him at Basel, whither he had retired to escape further persecution on account of his extreme views. Here he published his "Christianæ Religionis Institutio," which is his most celebrated work, and which has shed undying lustre on his name. Fascinating by its profound learning, its unflinching logic, and its wonderful fervour, the book became at once a general favourite, and was translated into all the civilized tongues. It is not necessary to do more than place before the reader one or two essential features of this great work. It is of mathematical exactness, and is the very base and foundation of his remarkable religious system, while it likewise maps out his scheme of reformation. This scheme was based on the doctrine of predestination, a doctrine Calvin had embraced with eagerness. Predestination was indeed with him a religious axiom, a self-evident truth which neither needed proof nor admitted of dispute, and he made it the corner-stone of his new religious system. His theory was that, of men all equally guilty *a priori*, some had from the beginning of the world been destined by God for eternal happiness, others for eternal perdition. Who were the elect and who the rejected was left an open question. However incompatible with humane feeling, however irreconcilable with the doctrine of the redemption, this belief might be thought by many, it yet sufficed for the eager minds of the sixteenth century, earnestly seeking as they were some practicable and, as it were, palpable, faith. Whatever the objections to the doctrine, it was on this that the Calvinistic Church was built, and by its spirit that that Church was swayed.

It was in 1536 that Calvin settled in Geneva. With Farel he undertook the reorganization of the Church on the lines marked out in his "Institutes," entirely sweeping away previous reforms. A "confession of faith" was drawn up and subscribed to by the people, and a new Church constitution was adopted which involved the establishment of a Church censorship, or rather a Church police. The rigorous discipline enforced, however, clashed with the Genevans' notions of present freedom, and the civil magistrates stoutly contested the right of the pulpit to find fault with the secular government, or interfere in the public administration. For the Genevese were a gay and pleasure-loving people, and they were moreover boisterous, undisciplined, and fond of disputation. A bold stand was made against the "Popery on Leman Lake," by the national party. The spirit of opposition was quickened by the disappointment of Bern at the overthrow of her reformation movement and ritual,[1] and the immigration of French refugees who strengthened Calvin's party. Bickerings, disorderly scenes, riots, both inside and outside the churches, followed, and

[1] The Bern, that is, the Zwinglian, ritual preserved several things which the French reformers rejected, amongst others, the four high fête days, the baptismal font, and the use of unleavened bread in the Communion.

the direct disobedience of Calvin and Farel to a civil decree of suspension prompted the government to pass sentence of banishment against them in 1538. Amidst the revilings and hootings of the mob they quitted Geneva, Farel going to Neuchâtel, where he remained till his death in 1565, and Calvin to Strasburg.

In this more tolerant German city he came into daily contact with the workings of the Lutheran and Zwinglian professions. He attempted to mediate between them with the view of reconciling their opposing views on the Eucharist, but failed. He admired Melancthon, but considered that his temporizing measures resulted in laxity of discipline. He was grieved, too, by the little regard shown to the clergy, and by their dependence on the courts, and the contemplation of all this served to confirm him in his own views. He never lost sight of the aim of his life—to make the Genevan Church, which he loved as his own soul, the rallying point for his persecuted countrymen. His plans were greatly favoured by several circumstances : the quarrels convulsing Geneva during his exile, and the incapacity of the new ministry there ; above all, the well-founded dread of Bern's supremacy. This fear brought into existence the party nicknamed the Guillermins, from Guillaume Farel, which literally drove the Genevans into the fold of Calvinism. Yet Calvin at first hesitated to return. "Why should I replunge into that yawning gulf," he writes to Farel, "seeing that I dislike the temper of the Genevese, and that they cannot get used to me?" But believing himself called by God, he yielded, and, amidst acclamations and rejoicings, he was welcomed back to the city in 1541.

Speaking roughly Calvin began his reforms where Luther and Zwingli had stopped; they had broken the ice for him, and shown him the way. He demanded implicit and unquestioning obedience to the Divine Word, for human reason, he said, was "as smoke in the sight of God." His aim was to found a kingdom of God in the spirit of the ancient prophets, and ruled by equally rigorous laws. Excluding the people from direct control in church matters, he lodged the chief authority in the clergy, a class which was also to have the preponderance in the state. By skilful organization he established a theocracy with strong aristocratic leanings, the democratic element being almost entirely excluded. Geneva became indeed "the city of the spirit of stoicism, built on the rock of predestination." But the most curious institution of the Calvinistic Church was the *Consistoire*, a body of twelve chosen from the oldest councillors and the city clergy, Calvin himself being usually at the head. This tribunal was of authority in spiritual and moral, and in public and private, matters alike. Calvin's intention was to change the sinful city into a sanctified city—a "city of God." The members of the Consistoire had power to enter private houses, and to regulate even the smallest concerns of life, and they admonished or punished offenders as they thought fit. Even the most trivial matters came within its ken; it prescribed the fashions, even down to the colour of a dress, and fixed the *menus* of the table, not less than it enforced attendance at religious worship. The table was by no means profusely supplied either, only one dish of meat and one of vegetables being allowed, and no pastry, and only native wine. We find girls cited before the Consistoire for skating, a man for sniffing in church, two others for talking business when leaving church. Every now and then Bonivard was brought up for card playing, and other disorderly deeds. A hairdresser adorning a lady's hair, together with the friends present, was sent to gaol. To the Genevans theatre-going was the chief occupation in life, but nevertheless theatrical performances were suspended, and remained so till shortly before the advent of Voltaire, who, indeed, gloried in leading back the strait-laced Genevans to worldliness and pleasure. But not only was the theatre forbidden, but likewise dancing, games, and music, except psalm-singing. No wonder the Muses left Geneva! Objects of art, and even those of home comfort, were objected to by iconoclasts like Calvin. The once gay Geneva sank into a dull, narrow-minded city of the true Puritan type. Indeed, as is well known, she furnished the pattern for later Puritanism. The Consistoire reserved to itself the right of excommunication, that is, of exclusion from the Communion, though secular or physical punishments were left to the Council.

The criminal history of the Genevan Republic reflects the temper of the time, and the spirit of the ecclesiastical leaders. Vice was mercilessly punished, and drunkenness, blasphemy, and unbelief were put in the same category with murder. One reads with dismay of the state of terrorism prevailing during the plague raging about the middle of the century. Superstition was rife and increasing, and every kind of torture was used to extort confessions from accused persons. Whilst the plague was at its worst the sword, the gallows, the stake were equally busy. The jailor asserted that his prisons were filled to excess, and the executioner complained that his arms were tired. Within a period of three years there were passed fifty-eight sentences of death, seventy-six of banishment, and eight to nine thousand of imprisonment, on those whose crime was infringement of the Church statutes. Offences against himself personally Calvin treated as blasphemy, as he identified himself with the prophets of old. Strange as this assertion is, it can be supported. A single instance will suffice. One Pierre Amicaux, a councillor, had once in company spoken of Calvin as a bad man. This the reformer declared to be blasphemy, and refused to preach again till satisfaction was done to him.[1]

In such manner was Geneva forced into obedience. However, there was one powerful check on Calvin's progress, viz., the efforts of the national party, the "Children of Geneva," as they called themselves, or the "Libertines," as their opponents nicknamed them.[2] An excellent way of neutralizing the influence of

---

[1] Amicaux was led in his shirt through the city, with a lighted torch in his hand, and was required to confess his fault in three different public squares.

[2] These "Lovers of Freedom" were stigmatized by the opposite party as "men of loose morals," but of such there were not a few amongst the Calvinists themselves.

these, Calvin tells his friend Bullinger, at Zurich, was to expel the natives and admit French *emigrés* to the Genevan citizenship. "The dogs are barking at me on all sides," he complains to the same friend, and now and then he made a clean sweep of his adversaries. The Genevans naturally looked with disfavour on Calvin's policy, objecting to the French refugees not so much from ill will as from a natural dislike to leaving a city to which they were so devotedly attached, and seeing the positions of honour and influence taken up by the strangers. At last, exasperated beyond measure by the admission of a fresh batch of refugees, the Libertines attempted a *coup de main* on the Calvin government, May, 1555. The attempt miscarried, and the ringleaders were put to death or imprisoned, and most of the rank and file expelled from the city. To fill the great gaps thus caused, three hundred and fifty-nine French families were admitted gradually to the citizenship, and in this way within a few years the population increased from thirteen thousand to twenty thousand. Such high-handed proceedings — wholesale proscriptions one might call them—caused the wheels to run smoothly enough, and Calvin was now completely master of the situation. The imprisonment and burning of Servetus for denying the doctrine of the Trinity once more ruffled the smooth surface of affairs, yet helped if possible to increase Calvin's prestige and influence. Every one knows of the endless discussions that have since taken place as to Calvin's part in putting to death the learned and unfortunate Spaniard. But Calvin's own defence would seem to show that it was he who was chiefly the leader in the matter.[1]

His pre-eminence now fully established and acknowledged, Calvin founded the Academy, in 1559, in order to provide ministers for the reformed churches generally. Learned French *emigrés* were appointed to the professorships, and Theodore de Bèze (Beza) was made rector, and the institution became the glory of the city. From all parts sympathizers flocked to Geneva—Italians, English,[2] Spanish, Germans, mostly French and Italians, however—and churches to suit the different nationalities sprang up. On Leman Lake they found another Rome, and another inspired and infallible Pope, albeit a Protestant Pope. At the first view of the sacred city they sank on their knees and sang songs of joy and praise, as if they had sighted a new Jerusalem. Wittenberg had witnessed similar scenes. No fewer than thirteen hundred French and three hundred Italian families had made Geneva their second home, and men of the greatest mark had settled there temporarily or for good. Missionaries went to France to rally and strengthen the Huguenots, and some two thousand communes were converted to the new faith. Religious champions, like the intrepid John Knox, Peter Martyr, Marnix (de St. Aldegonde), went to Scot-

[1] The Swiss churches under the ægis of Bullinger acquiesced, not so much from a spirit of intolerance, as from a fear that the influence of Servetus might undermine French Protestantism. Rome envied Calvin the honour of having condemned Servetus to the flames.

[2] Amongst the English we find the names of Spencer, Coxe, Chambers, Bishop Hooper, and the Bishops of Exeter, Norwich, Durham, and Salisbury.

land, England, or the Netherlands, to advance the cause of Calvinism. To Geneva as their mother church may look Puritans and Presbyterians.

Calvinism but little affected Switzerland at large during the lifetime of its founder. Its absolutism and narrowness clashed with the milder and more advanced, and, if one may say so, more ideal views of the Zwinglian system. It was due to the conciliatory spirit of Bullinger and to his noble efforts that the Churches of Zurich and Geneva — while other countries were distracted with religious differences — drew together as friends, and that their doctrines were blended in official "confessions" of faith. Viret's attempts to plant Calvinism in Vaud failed, as did those of Farel in Neuchâtel.

And if Geneva did not regard her great master with affection, she bowed before him in profound veneration. Without him the ancient, frivolous, and quarrelsome city could hardly have kept at bay her many foes. But trained in the school of Calvinism she gathered moral strength, and became the "abode of an intellectual light that has shone for three centuries, and that, though growing pale, is not yet extinguished."

Calvin was a prodigious worker, a profound theologian, an accomplished linguist, a statesman and organizer of consummate skill, and a most excellent correspondent. Twenty-four printing-presses were kept at work day and night multiplying his writings in different languages. No fewer than 2,025 sermons of his have been collected, and 4,721 letters. For the French language Calvin did much what Luther did for the German. His frame, at all times weak, became still more enfeebled by continued illness, and it seemed impossible that he should be physically fit to labour as he did, but his religious enthusiasm was able to triumph over bodily ailments. Bright, sparkling eyes lit up his pale and emaciated features. Averse to earthly pleasures, careless of popular applause, of strong and unbending will—though not devoid of deep feeling—he commanded men's awe

THALER OF 1564.
(*Laus et gloria soli Deo optimo maximo.*)

THALER OF 1564.
(*Moneta nova Civitatis San Gallensis, 1564.*)

rather than their affection. His near personal friends were devotedly attached to him, and on the death of his wife, who sank when bereaved of her children, his tenderness breaks forth in letters to his friends. "If I did not make a strong effort to moderate my grief," he writes to Viret, "I should succumb." He died in May, 1564, and even in his last moments had words of censure for those who had come to take leave of him. His death is registered in these curious terms: " Aujourd'hui spectable Jean Calvin s'en est allé à Dieu, sain et entier, grâce à Dieu, de sens et entendement." Beza was elected his successor; and, less severe and more conciliating than his friend and predecessor, he exerted great influence, both at Geneva and in the reformed countries generally. Beza's death occurred in 1603.

XXV.

THE CATHOLIC REACTION.

THE benefits conferred by the Reformation on Switzerland were counterbalanced by a religious schism which divided the land into two antagonistic moieties, and paralyzed political progress. The religious enthusiasm in Europe had spent itself in the first half of the sixteenth century, and the energy it had displayed had roused amongst the Catholics a corresponding activity. They were led by the famous Philip II. of Spain, but fortunately Queen Elizabeth of England was able to withstand the attack directed against her country. But the new order of Jesuits, lately launched on the world to undo the work of the religious reformers, took the field with united ranks; whilst, on the other hand, the Protestants, split as they were into sections, and stumbling over questions of dogma, lacked the unity of aim and purpose necessary to stand successfully an attack so formidable. The wars of Schmalkalden (1547–49) were as injurious to Protestant Germany as the catastrophe of Kappel had been to Reformed Switzerland. The tide of Reformation rolled back in Germany, and the men of Zurich beheld with grief and indignation the fall of their strong ally in the work of religious reform, Constance, after its desperate stand against the Emperor, Charles V. Zurich was prevented by internal dissension and Catholic intolerance from assisting Constance, and, moreover, was compelled to release Mulhausen and Strasburg from their evangelical union with her. Thus Geneva, which the Papists threatened to level with the ground, was forced into an isolated position, and was near becoming the prey of invading Savoy. Considering the internal condition of the Confederation, we may well ask what it was that saved the little republic from complete destruction in the terrible storm of the reaction which swept over Europe, if it was not the very strength of the Federal union, and the common possession of the different Swiss bailiwicks, which bound the parts so strongly together, and which triumphed over both party feelings and private interests. Thanks to the moderation of the Protestants, war was avoided, and the country settled into a state of comparative repose. Through Zwingli's efforts Switzerland extended the *droit d'asile* to all, and she henceforward followed out her mission as a neutral power. It is the protection so freely given to refugees by Geneva, Zurich, and other Swiss cities that brightens the history of this gloomy reaction period.

Henry II., anxious to win over Switzerland to the Catholic cause, requested the Swiss to stand as sponsors to his daughter, Claudia, and received their embassy with marked distinction. Bern and Zurich, however, were not coaxed into an alliance with France by these blandishments. France wished for the preservation of peace from self-interest. But she extolled greatly the prowess of the Swiss, and called them the very "marrow" of her army. The Swiss excelled in single feats of arms, and amongst the Catholic captains stands out conspicuously the valiant Ludwig von Pfyffer, of Lucerne, who played a part, as regards political influence, not unlike that of Waldmann, and was nicknamed the "Swiss King." The wealth he had hoarded up during his French service he freely spent in the Catholic cause.

Pre-eminent amongst those who worked for the Catholic revival was the famous Carlo Borromeo, Archbishop of Milan, and nephew of Pius IV. He lived the life of a saint, and in due time was canonized. To his see belonged the Swiss bailliages in the Ticino and Valtellina. Indefatigable in his labours, constantly visiting every part of his diocese, toiling up to the Alpine huts, he gathered the scattered flocks into the Papal fold, whether by mildness or by force. Shocked at the state of religious matters in the Forest Cantons, he founded a seminary for priests, to which Pfyffer at once gave a very large sum of money. For the spread of Catholic doctrines he hit upon three different means. He called into being the Collegium Helveticum in 1579 at Milan,[1] where the Swiss priests were educated free. He sent the Jesuits into the country, and

---

[1] This still exists in connection with the episcopal seminary.

placed a nuncio at Lucerne, in 1580. In 1586 was signed, between the seven Catholic cantons, the Borromean or Golden League, directed against the reformers, and in the following year a coalition was, by the same cantons, excepting Solothurn, entered into with Philip of Spain and with Savoy. The Jesuits settled themselves in Lucerne and Freiburg, and soon gained influence amongst the rich and the educated, whilst the Capuchins, who fixed themselves at Altorf, Stanz, Appenzell, and elsewhere, won the hearts of the masses by their lowliness and devotion. In this way did Rome seek to regain her influence over the Swiss peoples, and the effect of her policy was soon felt in the semi-Protestant and subject lands. To the impression made by the efforts of the Capuchins the great dissension in Appenzell bears witness, the canton actually breaking up into two hostile divisions. The Catholics removed to Inner, and the Reformers to Outer Rhoden, and each managed its own affairs independently of the other; the latter, however, soon began to prosper more than the former. In the Valais, the Protestant party, though strong, was quite swept out by the Jesuits, before 1630, and fled to Vaud and Bern. The history of lacerated Graubünden will occupy the next chapter.

It is painful to read of an act of violence committed by the Papists in the expulsion of the Evangelians from Locarno, in the winter of 1555, where a little band of two hundred adherents of the Zwinglian Church had formed round Beccaria. Zurich supported them, notwithstanding the opposition of France, and even of some of the Protestant cantons, and Bullinger was their comfort and strength in all transactions. However, Beccaria was compelled to flee to Misox valley, whence he ministered by stealth to his flock. In January, 1555, stronger measures were taken, and men and women were driven over the snowy heights to Misox, a sorry substitute for the luxurious homes some of them had left in Locarno. But they were soon moved on by the Papal legate, and in May some 120 of the band arrived at Zurich, where Bullinger had arranged for them a hospitable welcome. These new-comers revived the old trade with Lombardy, and reintroduced the silk manufacture, which, being a monopoly, became a source of great wealth to Zurich. Thus the town was rewarded for its hospitality. Some of the aristocratic Zurich families of to-day trace their origin to these Locarno refugees.

The city of Zurich was indeed at this time a general asylum for religious refugees from all quarters. Germans, Italians, and English fled there, and especially the Marian exiles from England. We find Peter Martyr from Oxford established as a professor at the Carolinum; and Occhino as minister to the Italian congregation in Zurich; Socinus and other famous Italians.[1] Martyr and Socinus both died at Zurich, and lie buried in its minster. For several years Peter Martyr and Bullinger had lived on terms of the closest friendship with each other, and their

---

[1] Faustus Socinus, the nephew of this Laelius Socinus, formed into a regular system the ideas of his uncle, and really prepared the way for modern Unitarianism.

letters show how close was the tie between them. Their respective religious views naturally tended to greater mutual resemblance. Bullinger, like Calvin, kept up an immense correspondence with the reformed churches, and was in frequent communication with monarchs, princes, powerful nobles, and learned doctors. The readers of the present story will naturally feel most interest in the relation between the Swiss and the English Churches, and it will perhaps be better to leave on one side the tangled skein of religious dissensions which agitated Europe, and show from authentic sources [1]—letters chiefly—how the Swiss Churches and Swiss divines influenced the Reformed Church of England.

Though the English Reformation under Henry VIII. was greatly influenced by Luther, under Edward VI. the Church veered round more to the Swiss views, Cranmer especially leaning strongly towards Zwinglianism. Since 1536 the prelate had been on most friendly terms with Bullinger, and in this same year some young Englishmen, Butler, Udrof, and Partridge, by Cranmer's desire, settled in Zurich, to study its religious aspect and enjoy intercourse with the distinguished Bullinger. In the following year Eliot and others arrived with similar intent, and a great attachment sprang up between

[1] The Zurich archives are remarkably rich in materials relating to the Reformation period. The Simmler collection contains copies of eighteen thousand authentic letters. The "Epistolæ Tigurinæ," published by the Parker Society, London, in 1842, contain copies of original letters from the Marian exiles to Zurich divines. At Zurich are preserved original letters from Erasmus, Henry the Fourth of France, Lady Jane Grey, &c.

the young men and their spiritual guide. At the request of the students, Bullinger addressed to Henry two treatises on the "Authority of the Scriptures," and on the "Dignity and Office of Bishops," respectively, and was afterwards told that the treatises greatly interested both the king and the archbishop. "It is incredible what fame you acquire in England by your writings," says Eliot in his letter to Bullinger in 1539; "the booksellers are growing rich through you." Under Edward VI., Bullinger's relations with Cranmer and Hooper, with Warwick and Dorset, and with Coxe and Cheke, grew closer and closer, and the Church of Zurich regained its ascendency. At Bullinger's house Hooper passed his second exile, and he says he was received with delight, "being a true Christian," and he states that his faith was greatly quickened by the writings of the famous Zurich divine. The friendship between the two men was most intimate. At Hooper's desire, Bullinger dedicated a series of his sermons on the "Christian Faith" to Edward, who was greatly delighted with them, and had them translated into English. During his imprisonment Hooper composed a remarkable treatise addressed to Parliament in defence of the Zwinglian teaching with regard to the Lord's Supper, and Traheron states (1548) that England at large was inclined towards the Zwinglian view. In 1550 King Edward sent an envoy to ask the state of Zurich to unite with England with regard to a Church Council, and, curiously enough, with regard to reconciling that country with France.[1]

[1] Pestalozzi's "Life of Bullinger," Zurich.

A charming episode in the life of Bullinger was the springing up of the friendship with Lady Jane Grey, then a young and studious girl of fourteen. Three letters written by her hand, and still treasured up at Zurich, bear witness to this friendship. Of the treatise on "Christian Marriage" dedicated to her, she translated a portion into Greek, and presented it as a Christmas present to her father. Bullinger's sermons and letters were a delight to her, and were to her "as most precious flowers from a garden." She asked his advice as to the best method of learning Hebrew, and regarded him as particularly favoured by the grace of God. He it was whose teaching quickened her love for Christ, and gave her and her family such support in their great trials later on. Even at her last hour her thoughts were of him, for at the block she took off her gloves and desired that they should be sent on to her Swiss friends.[1]

It was on the Continent, among the Reformed Churches, that Hooper and others gained their taste for a simple form of religious worship. When Hooper was made Bishop of Gloucester, in 1550, he refused both the oath and the episcopal vestments, and was sent to prison for his refusal. His opposition, indeed, sowed the germs of that religious development which so strongly agitated the Church under Elizabeth, and which, breaking into open schism, resulted in the rise of Puritanism, and, later on, of the dissenting movements generally. And, as is well known, the Puritans fled to New England

[1] Pestalozzi's "Life of Bullinger."

rather than give up their religious liberty. Hooper was exempted from taking the oath, but had to give way in the matter of the vestments. During his episcopacy Bullinger was ever his faithful and wise counsellor, and when the martyr's death overtook him, he recommended his persecuted country to his Swiss friends. "Of all men attached to thee," he assures Bullinger in 1554, "none has been more devoted than myself, nor have I ever had a more sincere friend than thee."

Many other Marian exiles settled in Zurich, to whom, however, only a passing word can be devoted. Bullinger alone accommodated often as many as twenty guests at a time, and both ministers and magistrates—Gualter, Lavater, and others—received the English exiles "with a tenderness and affection that engaged them to the end of their lives to make the greatest possible acknowledgment for it," to quote the words of one Englishman. The correspondence between the Swiss hosts and their English guests proves how close were the friendships formed between them. Amongst these correspondents we find the English archbishops, Grindal and Sandys, Bishop Pilkington, the Earl of Bedford, and other notable men. Other proofs without number might be given of the close connection between Switzerland and England in religious matters in the sixteenth century, but what has been said must suffice.

Enough has been said to show how the influence of the Reformed Swiss Churches was brought to bear on English Protestantism; on the Anglican Church in respect of doctrine; and on the dissenting Church, that is, Puritanism, in respect of both doctrine and form of worship. The Reformed Church is the result of an amalgamation between the two mother Churches of Geneva and Zurich, the union being brought about by the desire of the leaders Calvin, Farel, Beza, Bullinger, who, anxious for peace and concord, made mutual concessions.[1] Thus in Switzerland the narrowness of Calvinism has been tempered by an admixture of the broader and more enlightened teachings of Zwinglius, or rather the basis of the teaching is Zwingli's, and Calvin has confirmed, intensified, and completed it. Over France, England, Scotland, Holland, and North America the reformed faith spread its roots "to grow up to trees of the same family, but of different shape and size according to the soil from which they started up." That Switzerland, with the exception of Geneva, inclined strongly to Zwinglianism we have already shown. To deal adequately with the question of the religious influence of Switzerland on other European countries would be impossible within the limits of this work. But that its influence was very great needs no saying. And not in Europe alone, for the Puritan spirit was carried beyond the ocean, and the reformers of Switzerland had their disciples in far-away New England. Even modern Unitarianism is, in a sense, the direct descendant of the reformation of Zurich, and its apostles—Williams, Channing, Parker—are so far the successors of Zwingli and Bullinger.

The revival of learning witnessed by the sixteenth

---

[1] In England the general name Calvinistic is applied to certain doctrines of the Reformed Churches, but not altogether appropriately, seeing that Calvin was only one of the teachers of these doctrines.

REVIVAL OF LEARNING. 301

century had its full effect in Switzerland. The thirst for knowledge was so great that men would undergo almost any privations in their pursuit of it. Thomas Platter—to cite but one instance out of many—rose from the humble position of goatherd to be a prominent master of Hebrew and the classics at Basel. In early life he laboured at rope-making, or turned serving-man, or even begged in the streets. His son Felix was a notable physician. The great reformers have already been spoken of. Besides the above,[1] we may just mention among the Catholics, Glarean, the foremost classical scholar of his country, crowned poet-laureate by the Emperor Max. I.; and Tschudi, of Glarus, the brilliant narrator, author of the national epic, Tell, and for centuries the first authority on Swiss history; Paracelsus of Einsiedeln: of Protestants, Manuel (Bern), the satirical poet, and painter of the *Todtem Tänze à la* Holbein; and, above all, Gessner, of Zurich, scholar, philosopher, naturalist, the "Pliny of Germany."

Kleinkunst, lesser or practical art, also made brilliant progress in Switzerland. Painting on glass, wood-carving, manufacture of painted-tile stoves developed into industries almost peculiar to the country in their excellence. This is shown by an inspection of the magnificent specimens of these arts with which the country abounds—splendid painted windows, beautiful wainscots, exquisite relievi, beautiful tiled stoves, and so forth.

A few words respecting affairs in Geneva must close our account of the sixteenth century. The

---

[1] Glarean and Tschudi were Catholics, Manuel a Protestant.

Dukes of Savoy, unwilling to renounce their claims, continued to harass the city. Henry IV., of France, came forward as a protector, and Elizabeth, of England, addressed to the Swiss cantons and reformed cities letters remarkable for the noble sentiments and clear judgment displayed in them.[1] She urged them not to throw away the key of Switzerland. However, on the night of the 21st of December, 1602, Duke Charles Emmanuel ventured on a treacherous *coup de main* on the city known as the famous "Escalade." Eight thousand men had been drawn up before her gates, and some three hundred had already scaled her walls, when the sudden firing by a watchful guard roused the citizens to a sense of their danger. A fierce conflict took place in the streets, and the intruders were fortunately overpowered. This event caused the greatest indignation throughout Europe, but it sealed the independence of the Republic. The anniversary of the victory is still regarded by the Genevans.

[1] Copies are preserved among the Zurich letters.

XXVI.

THE ARISTOCRATIC PERIOD.

(1600-1712.)

In the life of nations no less than of individuals there are vicissitudes, alternations of prosperity and adversity. If the fourteenth and fifteenth centuries witnessed the glorious rise of the Swiss people, the seventeenth and eighteenth saw the political decline of the Republic. Even the Reformation itself led the way to this decline by lodging all power—political, fiscal, moral, and educational—in the Protestant cantons in the hands of the governments. Patriotism was on the wane, and the old mania for foreign service as a means of securing foreign gold was again breaking out. Even Zurich, which for well-nigh a century had steadfastly borne in mind the patriotic maxims of Zwingli, now yielded to the persuasions of France. Indeed the Swiss Commonwealth was rapidly becoming a mere vassalate of that country, under the despotic Louis XIV. Swiss rule was taking that tinge of absolutism which was colouring the governments of almost all European states.

Louis, the personification of absolute rule, had stamped the century with his *cachet*, and aristocracies and oligarchies were taking the place of the old democratic governments. This seems incompatible with the old Swiss republican tenets. Yet, drawn within the influence of the monarchical states, how could Switzerland escape the effects of that influence any more than Venice or Genoa?

The political and religious passions and animosities of the previous century now found vent in the terrible Thirty Years' War, which from 1618 to 1648 convulsed Europe. Thanks to its good fortune and far-sightedness, Switzerland was not drawn into the conflict, save as to its south-eastern corner, close as it was to the theatre of the great struggle. Most anxiously was the neutrality of the country maintained, yet its territory was not unfrequently violated. To give one instance, General Horn led his Swedes into Swiss territory to besiege Constance. Germany and Sweden—Gustavus Adolphus especially[1]—did all they could to draw Switzerland to their side, but the Swiss had the good sense to resist all blandishments, and bear patiently with vexatious intrusions. The terrible scenes that were taking place across the Rhine were enough to quell all intestine disputes in Switzerland itself, and the comparative peace and prosperity found within its borders was the envy of the neighbouring lands. A German traveller chronicles his surprise at finding in Switzerland neither rapine nor murder, but security and content. How-

---

[1] Appealing to the absurd pretended national relationship between Swedes and Switzers, an etymology of the Middle Ages.

ever rough and rugged its surface, the little republic seemed to him an earthly Paradise.

Different, however, was the experience of Graubünden, then a separate free state, and a connection only of the Confederation. In truth, the history of that old Rhætian land at that time forms a striking pendant as it were to the great drama of the European struggle. The Latin-German inhabitants, combining northern prudence with southern passion, had since the middle of the sixteenth century been steeped in internal dissension, owing to the religious divisions caused by the Reformation. The Protestant party under Von Salis, and the Catholics headed by Von Planta, were at deadly enmity with each other, and sided with France and Venice, and with Austria and Spain respectively. John von Planta, head of his clan, and solicitor-general of the Papal see, was suspected of intending to reintroduce Popery into the Grisons. The mountaineers accordingly descended from their Alps in crowds, and flocked to Chur. There they brought to trial Planta and sentenced him to death, and his fall struck the keynote to the tragedy that followed. With the opening of the seventeenth century the conflict grew fiercer, national interests and foreign policy being now inextricably mixed. Mistress of the beautiful Italian Signory Valtellina, Bormio, Chiavenna, and the Alpine passes commanding the entrance into the Tyrol and Italy, Graubünden became the apple of contention between the southern states of Europe. Austria and Spain possessing Milan were not without hopes of joining hands across Graubünden, and France was sanguine of her success

HIGH ALTAR, CHUR CATHEDRAL.
(*From a Photograph.*)

in preventing it. This latter state with Venice had effected an alliance with Protestant Bünden, and that party strongly opposed the Spanish union for which the energetic but headstrong Rudolf von Planta was working. Fuentes, a Spaniard, Governor of Milan, furious at the resistance offered, erected a chain of strong forts on Lake Como, with the view of cutting off the Valtellines. Before long, George Jenatsch from the Engadine, Tschusch, and other high-minded and patriotic Protestants, began to decry the Spanish scheme, and tumults arose. An attack on Planta's manor, Zernez (1618), having failed through the escape of Rudolf, Zambra, Landammann in Bregaglia, and Rusca, a priest in the Valtellina, both greyheaded old men, were seized. They were sentenced to death by a new court which had been set up at Thusis, a court which raged against popery and spread terrorism for some months. In the Engadine a strange thing happened. The respective chiefs of the hostile clans were the two brothers Von Travers, and a hand-to-hand fight between the opposing parties having begun, suddenly the wives, daughters, and sisters of the combatants rushed amongst them like the Sabine women of old, and checked them. Foremost amongst these noble women was the spirited Anna Juvalta. The Plantas were now in exile, and were conspiring with Austria. Their cousin Robustello (Valtellina) at a given signal broke into the houses of the Protestants, and, with the help of hired assassins, put the inmates to the sword. This was on the 19th of July, 1620, and throughout the whole valley no quarter was given. Zurich and Bern on hearing of this shocking massacre—the "St. Bartholomew of the Valtellina"—sent troops, but they were defeated at Tirano by the Spanish forces and adherents. The Plantas returned from exile and asked the Forest Cantons to give their countenance to their party, and these were not unwilling; but the plot itself was opposed by the Protestant Grisons with scorn and fury. Jenatsch penetrated to the castle of the Plantas at Rietberg, and Pompejus fell by his hands (1621). The Catholics were defeated at Valendas, and the country was cleared of the troops of the Forest Cantons and of Spaniards. However, Jenatsch failed to take Valtellina.

The Austrians still claimed supremacy over part of the *Zehngerichte*,[1] and we find them, from 1620 to 1629, twice invading and occupying Graubünden. The most dreadful cruelties marked the passage of their general, Baldiron, and Catholicism was reintroduced by force. In 1629, the Emperor Ferdinand had reached the height of his success and greatness, and Bünden with all its dependencies lay prostrate at his feet. France came to the rescue. Richelieu pursued the policy of Henry IV. to re-establish the balance of power by breaking down the prestige of the Habsburgs. With the view of gaining supremacy for France, he had drawn Sweden into the Thirty Years' War; and on the death of Gustavus Adolphus, when the zeal was somewhat flagging, he revived it by sending French troops into Alsace, South Germany, and the Grisons. The command of the Franco-Grison army was entrusted to Duke Henry

---

[1] See the chapter on the Swabian wars.

de Rohan, godson of Henry IV. of France (and godfather to Charles I. of England), one of the noblest characters of his age. De Rohan was also appointed ambassador to the Eidgenossen states in 1631. He had been leader of the Huguenots, and had supported the Edict of Nantes in opposition to Louis XIII. Becoming obnoxious to the king in consequence, he withdrew to Venice. There he wrote a treatise on the strategical importance of the Grisons, as if he foresaw his future mission.[1] During his residence in Switzerland he watched zealously over its interests, smoothing over difficulties in the Diet to avoid war. Richelieu sent him neither money nor help, but left him to extricate himself as best he could from his position in that isolated mountain fastness; yet Rohan was the idol of his soldiers and of the people of the Grisons, and was always spoken of by them as the "good duke." In 1635, when France was doing its utmost to oust Austria, open war broke out, and Rohan gained four brilliant victories in succession—Jenatsch serving as local guide and combatant in advance, his superior tactics proving too much for the Austro-Spanish forces. Yet the "good duke" was soon to fall a victim to the perfidious policy of Richelieu, and the treachery of Jenatsch. This latter was a strange mixture of the noble and the vile—fierce, and ambitious, a seeker of gain, yet a man of honour,

---

[1] Rohan was a great friend to Zurich, and presented to its city library which was then forming his "Parfait Capitaine," a Hebrew Bible, and his portrait. He was by his own request buried at Geneva, and his death was greatly regretted by the reformed cities. The letters written by his family in reply to the "Condolence of Zurich" are still preserved in the library. See pamphlet on Rohan by Professor von Wyss.

full of a wild patriotism and thirst for freedom. Eager to free his country from the grasp of the stranger, he and the hot-tempered Bündner, at whose head he was, suddenly found that they were but exchanging masters. Sticking at nothing to gain his ends Jenatsch entered into a secret understanding with Austria and Spain, and even turned Catholic to win more favour with them. Then, forgetting the many kindnesses he had received from his friend Rohan, he betrayed him to his enemies. It should be observed, parenthetically, that the question in dispute was that of the Valtellina, and Rohan had had no instructions from Richelieu to return that territory. Suddenly the French general found himself surrounded by hostile troops from the Grisons, and was compelled to capitulate (1637). Unable to bear the sight of France again, he fought for her under the banner of Bernhard von Weimar, and fell at Rheinfelden, in Aargovy, seeking rather than fearing death. Jenatsch, however, did not long enjoy the fruits of his guilty action. Two years later he was stabbed at an officers' banquet, during the carnival, by some masked figure. Rudolf Planta, son of Pompejus, was said by some to have done the deed, whilst another story has it that the avenger was Rudolf's sister, Lucretia, who was burning for vengeance on the slayer of her father.[1] One of the first German novelists of our time, Ferdinand Meyer, of Zurich, has worked these thrilling episodes into his fine story, " Jenatsch." The hero was buried

[1] In Meyer's novel, Lucretia is betrothed to Jenatsch and takes the veil after the murder of Jenatsch, but this story has no foundation in fact.

with pomp at Chur, but his murderer remained unpunished. Thus Graubünden, after a struggle of nearly a hundred years, recovered both its independence and its lost territory.

That memorable event of the seventeenth century, the signing of the Peace of Westphalia, which concluded the Thirty Years' War, whilst, on the one hand, it sanctioned the dismemberment of the German Empire, yet ratified the independence and autonomy of the Swiss republics. This result was chiefly due to the noble efforts of two men—Wettstein, Burgomaster of Basel, who most effectively championed Swiss interests at the Congress; and Henry d'Orleans Longueville, count and reigning prince of Neuchâtel, the French representative at the same conference, who supported the Swiss claims.

The religious strife of Villmergen in 1656, which ended in the defeat of the Protestants, cannot be gone into here. Suffice it to note that this defeat was fully repaired by the second war of that name in 1712. A more important matter was the Peasants' Revolt, in 1653. It promised to grow to alarming dimensions, but was put down by the Government. This rising, however, is noteworthy, as marking the vast chasm which had formed between the labouring and the governing classes. The peasantry were now in a state of complete subjection, and patiently awaited the dawn of a brighter day, which nevertheless came only with the French Revolution. What they claimed was the restoration of their old liberties, relief from the excessive taxation, and the general improvement of their material interests. But many of the governing classes, councillors, *landvögte*, and others, had served abroad at foreign courts, and had drunk in the spirit of absolutism, and were as much imbued as any James I. or Louis XIV. with notions as to the "divine right" of the privileged classes to govern. They claimed seats on the administration as a right. From their superior positions they looked down on the labouring classes, and had little or no sympathy with them. Except in name the Swiss cantons were as absolutely governed by aristocracies as France was by Louis XIV. Nothing is more ludicrous, or more clearly shows the affectations and narrow pedantries of the age, than the childish delight in long or high-flown titles, by which the Swiss "regents," as they were called, were wont to address each other, and be addressed even by foreigners. "Leurs excellences," "noble-born," and so forth, were as common amongst Swiss republicans as in any monarchy.[1] Nor were they behindhand in the adoption of court fashions, wigs, frills, and the like; whilst they hunted eagerly for patents of nobility, and placed the "von" so unblushingly before their names that the higher classes, and really well-born for the most part dropped it for a time.

The Eidgenossen, however, were eminently useful soldiers, and Louis XIV. in 1663 wheedled or tricked them into the renewal of the alliance with France, an alliance into which Le Barde had tried in vain for thirteen years to coax them. The wily Louis invited a Swiss embassy to his Court, and for a whole week

---

[1] A few of these magnificent titles, or epithets, may be noted: "Hoch," "Wohlgeachtete," "Edle," "Fromme," "Fürsichtige," "Fürnehme," "Weise Herren," and many more such like.

amused and flattered his guests with a succession of banquets, ceremonies, and entertainments. Molière played before them by royal command. The ambassadors were thus beguiled into admitting some of the most important points in the treaty, the neutrality of Burgundy, the liquidation of the old debt, &c. On the 18th of November, in the presence of the whole French Court, at Notre Dame, the Swiss representatives agreed to a disgraceful and humiliating bargain with Louis. The king was not, however, inclined to lavish money on them like his predecessors had done. One day Louvois complained to him that his Swiss troops stood him dear, that for the money they had cost him and his predecessors the road could be paved with crown-pieces from Paris to Basel. Stuppa from the Grisons, overhearing this, quickly retorted, "Sir, you forget that with the Swiss blood spilt in the French service you might fill a canal from Basel to Paris."

Despite the engagements to France which Switzerland had entered into, it never ceased to give shelter to the French refugees who fled to escape the persecutions of Louis—to the Waldenses and the Huguenots. After the revocation of the Edict of Nantes, sixty-six thousand emigrants are said to have found shelter in Switzerland. Amongst the Swiss cities Geneva stands out conspicuously and honourably by her great benevolence. Not to speak of the vast amount of private assistance given, the municipality spent on the relief of the religious refugees no less a sum than five million florins between 1685 and 1726. Gradually the Eidgenossen became alive to the real character of Louis and his negotiations with them, and ashamed of their own lack of patriotism. As early as 1689, indeed, we find Swiss envoys from Bern and Zurich at Paris, rejecting his bribes, his golden chains, and what not. And on their return home they received the eulogies of their people for their integrity and independence. Gradually the league with France was set aside, or ignored. Nevertheless, the system of mercenary service remained an evil—one may say a cancerous evil—in the Swiss policy of the later centuries.

XXVII.

POLITICAL MATTERS IN THE EIGHTEENTH CENTURY.

POLITICALLY Switzerland presents much the same aspect in the eighteenth as in the previous century, and it needs here only a few words to indicate more clearly the temper of the times. In Swiss lands, as elsewhere, we have the inevitable division into the two classes of governor and governed. The rank and file of the "reigning families," *regiments-fähig*, patricians or plutocrats, rigorously kept all power to themselves, and held sway over the ordinary burghers and common folk. Unchecked rule and superiority and a life of ease and luxury on the one side; blind submission and toil on the other, especially in the rural districts. Even in the professedly democratic cantons the same despotism is met with; chieftains and family "dynasts" seizing the reins of government, and overruling the *landsgemeinde*, whilst they contend with each other for supremacy. Just as in the case of the oligarchies, the *laender* make the most of their "divine right" to govern. No wonder risings took place, as that of the Leventines against the harsh *landvögte* of Uri, and that of the Werdenberger (St. Gall) against Glarus, though these revolts were in vain. In Zurich, Schaffhausen, and Basel, there was less oppression, the guilds keeping the nobility at bay, though this guild system itself was not without blemish. The chief cities or cantonal *chefs-lieux* one and all held sovereign sway over the country districts attaching to them, but, like the old nobility of France, shifted off their own shoulders nearly all taxation, whilst they monopolized trade and industry. Thus the peasantry were crushed with the weight of taxes, imposts, tithes, and what not.

Religious differences had deepened since the second war of Villmergen (1712), which had brought the Protestants to the fore, and had established the principle of religious equality. The Catholics, having lost their supremacy in certain bailiwicks or subject districts, began to dream of regaining their lost position. To this end they entered into a secret agreement (*ligue à la cassette*) with Louis XIV. of France shortly before that monarch's death. It was not till 1777, however, that France really gained her point. In that year the common fear of Austria induced both Protestants and Catholics to enter into a league with Louis XVI. Thus, for the first time since the Reformation, the Confederates were a united body, or at any rate were agreed as to their joint plan of action.

Interesting though the task might be, it is here impossible to investigate the various conditions of the government in the subject lands — Aargau,

Thurgau, Ticino, Vaud, part of St. Gall, portions gained by conquest, or fragments acquired by purchase. We should meet with curious remnants of feudalism, and strange mixtures of the mediæval and the modern. But our space will permit of only a glance. The subject lands were deprived of all self-government, and the *landvögte* ruled them as an Eastern satrap might rule his satrapy. A somewhat strange arrangement for a republic to make and allow; but yet, on the whole, the government was excellent, and this state of things continued for a long period. Abuses, bribery, extortions, and the like of course crept in, but it is to be remembered that the *landvögte* were strictly controlled by the central government.[1] Many of them, especially at Bern, kept up much state; possessed horses, carriages, and livery-servants, and kept open house. In their lordships they ruled as veritable sovereigns, but they cared for their people, as good sovereigns should. They were, indeed, more like the patriarchs of old, rewarding or admonishing their peoples as circumstances required. One specimen of the class was greatly admired by Goethe, viz., Landvogt Landolt von Greifensee (Zurich). A few traits will serve to mark the man and the system. This governor was of the old school, and hated enlightened peasants and modern revolutionary ideas. He advocated compulsory attendance at church, and firmly believed in flogging as the most rational form of punishment. On the other hand, he was both

---

[1] The unrighteous and cruel Landvogt Tscharner was punished with death by the Bernese Government in 1612.

benevolent and humane, and watched over his
people with a fatherly care. He was equally
anxious to improve their farms and their morals.
He was wont to go about *incognito*—generally
dressed as a Tyrolese—and visited the printshops
to find out the gamblers and the drunkards. The
latter he had put into a revolving cage till they got
sober. Quarrelling couples he shut up together, and
forced them to eat *with the same spoon!*[1] But among
many subject lands the system had greatly changed.

The greatest holder of subject territory was Bern,
with its forty-four lordships or bailiwicks, Zurich
coming next with twenty-nine. The largest subject
district was Vaud, and, thanks to its thriving agriculture, and the wise, though harsh, administration
of Bern, it flourished greatly. The Vaudois had
on the whole submitted quietly to Bernese rule,
though the upper classes amongst them did not
relish their exclusion from the conduct of State
affairs. However, bowing to the inevitable, they
gave themselves up to the enjoyment of a life of
pleasure and to intellectual pursuits. About this
time Lausanne, their capital, had become the resort
of men like Gibbon, Fox, Raynal, Voltaire, and
many men of lesser mark. They were attracted
by the beauty of the scenery and by the high repute
of the Vaud gentry for good breeding and affability.
These noble families opened their salons to the distinguished foreigners who resided among them, and

---

[1] For further particulars about this original man the reader is referred
to the charming novel bearing his name, by Keller (Keller's "Zurcher
Novellen").

Gibbon seems to have particularly appreciated their good qualities.[1] The historian spent much of his life at Lausanne. An unlucky attempt had been made by Major Davel, in 1723, to rescue Vaud from the grasp of Bern. This enthusiastic patriot had himself concocted the plot, and attempted to carry out his plans without informing a single person of his intentions. Mustering his men, Davel, on some pretence, led them to Lausanne, where the council were then sitting, the *landvögte* being up at Bern, and informed the board what he proposed to do. But the members of the council were not yet prepared to seek emancipation, and, simulating an understanding, betrayed the luckless patriot to the Bernese authorities. " Leurs Excellences " — such was the official title of the Bernese rulers—made use of the rack, with the object of extorting from him the names of his accomplices, but in vain, and he was beheaded.

Amongst the leading cities of the Confederation, Zurich was conspicuous as the centre of Liberal tendencies and intellectual progress, whilst Bern was the political centre, and the leading financial focus.[2] Like a modern Rothschild, Bern then lent to various European states. Part of her treasure went towards paying the cost of Napoleon's expedition to Egypt. Among her sister cities, Freiburg, Solothurn, and Lucerne, Bern presented the most perfect example

[1] Madame de la Charrière, the novelist, writes : " Nous vivons avec eux, nous leur plaisons, quelquefois nous les formons, et ils nous gâtent."

[2] The Bernese peasantry had attained unusual wealth by its excellent management and the strict administration of its government.

of an oligarchy, admired by Montesquieu, Napoleon,
and even Rousseau. Her decided bent was for diplomacy, and she was completely absorbed in rule and
administration, and she had few other tastes. Trade
and industry she considered beneath her dignity;
even literary pursuits to a great extent. The Bernese
aristocrats were politicians from birth, so to speak,
and the young men had a curious society amongst
themselves, "Äusserer Stand," a society formed for
the purpose of cultivating the diplomatic art and
practising parliamentary oratory and tactics, especially their more formal outward side. Thus trained
in bearing and ceremonial they acquired their much-
admired political *aplomb*. Bern was French in fashion,
in manners, and in language, and the German tongue
was as little appreciated amongst the Bernese patricians as at the Court of Frederick the Great. The
constitution presents some features quite unique in
their way. There was an exclusiveness which has
lasted in all its force even down to our own days;
and three classes of society sprang up, as widely
separated from each other as the different castes in
India. All power was vested in the 360 "reigning
families"; the number of these was at length, by
death and clever manipulating, reduced to eighty,
and even fewer. From these families alone were
the councils selected, and to the members of these
only were governorships assigned. If male heirs
were wanting, then the seats on the council were
given to the daughters as dowries. So exclusive
was this governing body, that even Haller, the great
poet, was not allowed to enter it. The class next

lower in rank was that of the burghers, *ewige habitanten*, with no political rights, and with not a vestige of power in the commonwealth. They were not allowed to hold officerships abroad, but trade, industry, and the schools and churches were theirs. Lastly came the Ansässige (settlers), the proletariat, including the country labourers, foreigners, refugees, and commoner folk generally. Many were their disabilities; they were not permitted to buy houses, to have their children baptised in the city, to have tombstones set up over the graves of members of their family.[1] They might not even appear in the market till their betters had done their business, viz., 11 a.m., and they were strictly forbidden to carry baskets in the archways (*les arcades de la ville*), in order that these should not damage the hooped petticoats of the patrician ladies.[2] Bern has often been compared with ancient Rome, and certainly its stern council somewhat resembles in its austerity, solemnity, and pomp the august Roman Senate. It is not surprising that many attempts should have been made to induce the Government to relax its severity. In 1744 certain citizens petitioned the council to that effect, but were banished for their pains. Five years later a famous man named Henzi, with several associates, formed a plot against the council, but they were detected and executed.

But in truth there were risings in almost every one of the cantons. Of these only the most remarkable

[1] Prof. Vögelin, "Schweizergeschichte," p. 344.
[2] See "Die Patrizierin," a recent fascinating novel by Widmann, a Bernese writer.

can be touched on here, those of Geneva. These are real constitutional struggles, and, indeed, form the preliminaries in their way to the French Revolution, on which indeed their history sheds no little light. These troubles in Geneva are not unlike those of the Gracchi period in Roman history. By the Constitution of 1536 Geneva had been granted the right of a "Conseil Général," but this council had never been allowed to act or meet. The patricians who occupied the *haut de la cité* had arrogated to themselves well-nigh all power. But as early as 1707, the burghers, ever on the alert to regain their liberties, rose with the view of re-establishing the General Council of 1536. The movement was headed by the generous and noble-minded Pierre Fatio, himself a patrician. In fiery speeches, made in the open places of the town, he championed the popular rights, asserting with vehemence that the rulers were not the masters and tutors of the people, but the executors of its sovereign will. The attempt to gain popular liberty miscarried, Fatio was shot in prison, and his followers were exiled. Yet Fatio's idea lived on amongst the working classes, and later were again advocated in the pamphlets of Micheli du Crêst. In the years 1734 and 1737 the insurrections burst out afresh, and resulted in the establishment of the Constitution of 1738, which secured for a quarter of a century a happiness it had never before known.

However, the second half of the century witnessed new troubles between the burghers and the patricians. These latter were called, by way of nickname, "Négatifs," because they denied the people reform, whilst the burghers were styled "Représentants," because they presented petitions for political liberty. The artizan class were nicknamed "Natifs." It is impossible here to follow closely these "tea-cup squabbles," as Voltaire called them, but the philosopher's sympathies were with the *haut de la ville*, while Rousseau, on the contrary, sided with the *bas de la ville*.

Of all the Swiss lands the most equitable and righteous government was that enjoyed by Neuchâtel, under Frederick the Great (1740–1786). This state had of its own free will in 1707 accepted the ducal sway of the kings of Prussia, in order to escape the grasp of Louis XIV. At one time, however, Frederick II. so far forgot himself as to infringe the "states'" right of taxation, and the semi-republican duchy at once rose in rebellion. Gaudot, the vice-governor, Frederick's devoted minister, was shot in the fray (1768). Yet, thanks to the monarch's wise moderation, and the intervention of the Swiss Confederation, the storm was calmed, and Neuchâtel continued in her peaceful and happy condition. It is clear that there was in Switzerland plenty of combustible matter, needing only the French Revolution to raise a conflagration.

XXVIII.

SWITZERLAND AND THE RENAISSANCE. INFLUENCE OF VOLTAIRE AND ROUSSEAU.

BARREN and uninviting is the waste of politics in Switzerland at this period of our story, and it seemed as if the republic was quietly crumbling out of active existence. But the literary and scientific renaissance runs through it all like a fertilizing stream, and saves it from utter sterility. Feeble though it was politically, Switzerland yet produced on all sides men of mark in science, in literature, in philosophy. Time would fail to tell of them all, and we must be content to follow briefly the three great currents of the movement, which centred respectively around Geneva, Zurich, and the Helvetic Society. The two former of these may indeed be said to form a part (and an important part) of the great general awakening of the eighteenth century, an awakening beginning with the French "period of enlightenment," and crowned by the era of German classicism. Yet the French movement itself was based on English influence. Just as, at the Restoration, England had copied the France of Louis Quatorze, so France in return drew intellectual strength from the England of the second half of the eighteenth century—England was then vastly ahead of the Continent—and brought forth the "*siècle de la philosophie.*" Of the great Frenchmen who learned in the school of English thought, Montesquieu, Rousseau, and Voltaire stand foremost, and of these again Voltaire occupies indisputably the highest place. Voltaire was not only the founder, but the very heart of the philosophic school which reared its front against the statutes and traditions and pretensions of the Church. He had drunk deeply of the spirit of Newton and of Locke during his exile in England, and spread abroad their views and discoveries, assisted by his genius, his sparkling wit, his lashing satire, and his graceful style. None equally with him naturalized on the Continent English free thought and English rationalism. Voltaire and Rousseau were as two great beacons planted in the century guiding as they would the course of philosophy. Both were champions of personal freedom and religious tolerance in a benighted and down-trodden age. But the influence of the two men worked in very different ways, for in the one it was based on the head, in the other on the heart. Voltaire, the realist, by his venomous and even reckless satires on the Church and on Christianity, dealt a severe blow to religion at large. Rousseau, the idealist, plunged into the mystery of good and evil, and was wrecked by the very impracticability of his system.

Voltaire, as is well known, spent the last twenty years of his life—his "*verte vieillesse*"—almost at the gates of Geneva, and Rousseau, actually one of its citizens, passed the greater part of his life wandering abroad, though he loved Geneva so dearly that he once fainted with emotion on leaving it. Yet while both did battle so to speak from Geneva, neither of them was reckoned as a prophet in that city. After Voltaire had spent a couple of years at "Les Délices" —this was subsequent to his break with the great Frederick—he bought Tournay and Ferney, close to Geneva, to "keep aloof from monarchs and bishops, of whom he was afraid." Ferney, with its *parc à la Versailles*, and its fine castle, he made his residence; and there his niece did the honours of the house to the countless visitors who came from all parts to do homage to the illustrious "Aubergiste del' Europe," as he pleasantly styled himself. It was not the salons of Ferney that induced him to reside there, but care for his health and a wish to be free from all fear of bastilles.

Geneva was not inclined to bow in admiration before her famous neighbour, as has been already stated. She had by this time become a great intellectual centre. Men of science, naturalists, and philosophers there congregated, and a reaction against the everlasting study of theology, of which the fashion had been introduced by the Huguenot refugees, having come about, the study of nature had taken its place. Whilst France was being governed by the Pompadours, Geneva was ruled by a society of savants, inclined, it is true, to absolutism and narrow Calvinism, but still savants. It is a common error to suppose that Voltaire's influence took deep root in Geneva. Voltaire set the current running for the world at large indeed, but Geneva was not specially affected. In truth, most of her learned men were disinclined to do more than follow Voltaire half way, as it were, into his philosophy, whilst some of them, as, for instance, Charles Bonnet, were particularly narrow in their views, and were even heretic hunters.[1] Voltaire's contest with the city authorities respecting the establishing of a theatre is a good illustration of his want of real authority and influence there. It greatly tickled his fancy to seduce the "pedantic city still holding to her old reformers, and submitting to the tyrannical laws of Calvin" from the ancient path, and to make war on her orthodoxy. And as part of his plan he determined to introduce theatrical performances into the city. The ball was set rolling by an article in the "Encyclopédie" by D'Alembert, but the arguments there adduced in favour of the theatre proved of no avail. Rousseau made a furious reply, and averred that a theatre was injurious to the morals of a small town. In a large city, where the morals were already corrupt, it did not signify. The Consistoire was in a flutter, for it had pretended that the Genevans had a prodigious love for light amusements. However, one day Voltaire invited the city authorities to "Les Délices," and there treated them to a representation of his "Zaïre," and it was no little triumph to the wily old schemer that his

[1] Hettner's "French Literature in the Eighteenth Century."

audience were overcome with emotion. "We have moved to tears almost the whole council—Consistory and magistrates; I have never seen more tears," he delightedly reports; "never have the Calvinists been more tender! God be blessed! I have corrupted Geneva and the Republic." Nevertheless he was not to triumph. The theatre at "Les Délices" had to be closed. He opened his theatre several times elsewhere in Genevan territory, and began to draw crowds, but in every instance was compelled to close again. In truth, it was not till 1766 that Geneva had a theatre of its own, and even then it lasted but two years. The building was set on fire by some Puritans, and, being only of wood, was rapidly consumed. Crowds ran to the conflagration, but finding that it was only the theatre that was on fire, they emptied their buckets, shouting, "Let those who wanted a theatre put out the fire!" "*Perruques* or *tignasses*," exclaimed Voltaire, with irritation, " it is all the same with Geneva. If you think you have caught her, she escapes."

Rousseau (1712-1778) was the son of a Genevan watchmaker, and received but a very desultory education in his early days. Whilst yet but a boy he had drunk in the republican and Calvinistic spirit of his native town, hence his democratic leanings. He was a lover of nature, and fond of solitude, and was possessed of a deep religious feeling, even though his religion was based on sentiment. He witnessed the revolt of 1735-37, and, *enfant du peuple* as he was, rebelled against the tyranny of the patricians, and gave vent to his indignation in his writings. He thus became the mouthpiece of a down-trodden people craving for liberty, of a society satiated with culture. His prize essay on " Arts and Sciences " is an answer in the negative to the question propounded by the Dijon Academy, Whether the New Learning had resulted in an improvement to morals. His next essay on " L'origine et les fondements de l'inégalité "

ROUSSEAU.

is a sally against the state of society. In it he advocates a return to the condition of nature, on which Voltaire sarcastically retorted, "I felt a great desire to go on all fours.". " Emile " (1762), which Goethe calls the "gospel of education," declares against the hollowness of our distorted and over-refined civilization, and advocates a more rational training based on

PORTRAIT OF PESTALOZZI.
(*From a photograph of the statue, at Yverdon, by Lanz.*)

nature. And Pestalozzi, pedagogue and philanthropist, though he styled "Emile" a "book of dreams," was yet nourished on Rousseau's ideas. "Emile" is opposed to deism and materialism on the one hand, whilst on the other it objects to revelation and miracles, and declares that existing religion is one-sided and unable to save mankind from intellectual slavery. The excitement the book created was immense on both sides, and it was publicly burnt both at Paris and Geneva. Its author was compelled to flee.

A similar untoward fate befel the same author's famous "Contrat Social," perhaps the most important political work of the eighteenth century. In this Rousseau advances much further than Montesquieu. Indeed the former was a strong Radical, whilst the latter might be more fittingly described as a Whig. Rousseau advocates republicanism, or rather a democracy, as the best form of government; whilst Montesquieu points to the constitutional government of England as his model, insisting on the right to equality of all before the law. The "Contrat Social," as is well known, did much to advance the revolutionary cause, and became indeed the text-book of the democracy, and formed the principal basis of the Constitution of 1793. But Rousseau himself was no agitator. On the contrary, when the burghers of Geneva rose on his behalf, to save "Emile" and the "Contrat" from the flames, he hesitated hardly a moment, but begged them to submit to order, as he disliked disorder and bloodshed.

His novel, "La Nouvelle Héloïse" (1761), introduced the romantic element, and opened a new era in literature. It was, in fact, a manifesto against a bewigged and bepowdered civilization. Poetry was invited to withdraw from the salons and come once more to live with nature. But this sudden onslaught on the stiff conventionalism and narrowness of the time was too much, and there ensued an outburst of excitement and feeling such as we in our day can scarcely realize. A great stream of sentiment poured into literature, and gave rise to that tumultuous "storm and stress" (*Sturm und Drang*) period in Germany, out of which sprang Schiller's "Räuber" (Robbers). Goethe caught up the prevailing tone of sentimentality and supersensitiveness in his "Werther" (1774). This tearful, boisterous period is but the outrush of a nation's pent-up feelings on its sudden emancipation from the thraldom of conventionalism. And it led the way to the golden era in German literature, the era of Schiller and Goethe.

The brilliant literary court of Madame de Staël at Coppet succeeded that of Voltaire at Ferney. Though born in Geneva she was in heart a Frenchwoman, and her native country but little affected her character. "I would rather go miles to hear a clever man talk than open the windows of my rooms at Naples to see the beauties of the Gulf," is a characteristic speech of hers. Yet amongst women-writers Madame de Staël is perhaps the most generous, the most lofty, and the grandest figure. Her spirited opposition to Napoleon, her exile, her brilliant *coterie* at Coppet, and her famous literary productions, are topics of the greatest interest, but as they do not specially concern Switzerland, they cannot be more than hinted at here.

From the very depression, political and social,

HALLER.

prevailing in Swiss lands arose the yearning for and proficiency in letters and scientific culture which in the period now before us produced so prolific a literature in the country. And it was not in West

Switzerland alone that this revival of letters showed itself. Basel prided herself on her naturalists and mathematicians, Merian, Bernoulli, and Euler; while Zurich could boast of her botanists, Scheuchzer and John Gessner. Bern produced that most distinguished naturalist, Haller, who was also a poet; Schaffhausen claims Johannes von Müller, the brilliant historian; and Brugg (Aargau) Zimmermann, philosopher and royal physician at Hanover. Bodmer and Breitinger formed an æsthetic critical forum at Zurich. And no country of similar area had so many of its sons occupying positions of honour in foreign universities. A whole colony of Swiss savants had settled at Berlin, drawn thither by the great Frederick, others were to be found at Halle. Haller, who had lived at Göttingen ever since 1736, likewise received an invitation from Frederick, but found himself unable to accept it, being greatly averse to Voltaire and his influence. A perfect stream of Swiss intellect poured into Germany, and by its southern originality, greater power of expression, and its true German instinct, quickened German nationality, and witnesses to the fact that there is ever passing between the two countries an intellectual current.[1] It is impossible within the limits of the present volume to do more than touch upon the most characteristic literary movements of the period.

Amongst the upper classes in Switzerland, French culture reigned supreme, just as did French fashions,

[1] Switzerland was the cradle of the German drama in the sixteenth century; even the Oberammergau Passion play can be traced to a Swiss origin (Bächtold).

French manners, and it may almost be said, the French language. Nevertheless, the Swiss were the first to throw off the French supremacy in literature, turning rather to England as a more congenial guide and pattern. Bodmer speaks of Shakespeare and Milton "as the highest manifestations of Germanic genius." As for German literature itself, it was still in a state of helplessness—what with the Thirty Years' War, and the German nobility given over to French tastes and French influence—and fashioned itself in foreign modes till the close of the Seven Years' War, in 1763, when it took the leading position it has ever since maintained.

Bern and Zurich, which had both risen to wealth and independence, were stout opponents of the French policy. Both cities were homes of the *belles lettres*, and Zurich was a veritable "poets' corner." The chief figure there was Bodmer, who wielded the literary sceptre in Switzerland and Germany for well-nigh half a century. A fellow-worker with him, and his well-nigh inseparable companion, was Breitinger, and these two more than any others helped to break the French spell. Bodmer (1698-1783), was the son of a pastor of Greifensee, and had himself been at first destined for the church, though he was at length put to the silk trade. But neither calling could keep him from his beloved letters, and in 1725 he became professor of history and political science at the Zurich Carolinum. His aim was to raise literature from its lifeless condition. As far back as 1721, he had joined with Breitinger and others, in establishing a weekly journal on the model of Addison's *Spectator*

—" Discurse der Maler." Breitinger was professor of Hebrew, and later on, canon of the minster of Zurich, and was a man of profound learning and refined taste. The new paper treated not only of social matters, but discussed poetry and *belles lettres* generally. Gottsched (1700 – 1766), who occupied the chair of rhetoric at Leipzig, was supreme as a literary critic. His tastes were French, and he held up the French classics as models. In his "Critical Art of Poetry" (1730), he tries to teach what may be called the *mechanics* of poetry based on reason, and pretends that it is in the power of any really clever man to produce masterpieces in poetry. In 1732, appeared Bodmer's translation of "Paradise Lost," to the chagrin of Gottsched, who, feeling that he was losing ground, furiously attacked the Miltonian following. His mockery of the blind poet roused Bodmer's anger, and he replied with his work the "Wonderful in Poetry." A fierce controversy raged for ten years. In the name of Milton the young men of talent took the side of Zurich, that is, of the German, as opposed to the French influence in literature. The result was that by the efforts of such men as Haller, Klopstock, Wieland, and Kleist, the French influence was ousted and the national German influence came to the front.

Albrecht von Haller (1708–1777), whom Goethe calls "the father of national poetry," was the first representative of the new school of poets which began to turn to nature for inspiration and illustration rather than to mere dead forms. His poems on the Alps (1732) paint the majestic beauty of the Bernese highlands, and contrast the humble and peaceful but natural life of the shepherd with the luxurious and artificial life of the patrician, and the dweller in cities. Haller's writings made a great impression on the polite world.[1] Klopstock it was, however, whom Bodmer welcomed as the harbinger of a new era, as the German Milton. Klopstock had been trained in the Swiss school of thought, and regarded Breitinger's "Critical Art" as his æsthetic bible, whilst Bodmer's translation of "Paradise Lost" inspired his epic, "Messiah." The first three cantos appeared in the "Bremer Beiträge" in 1748, and created such a *furore* that he was declared to be an immortal poet. Wieland's first poems were, in 1751, published in the "Swiss Critic," and met with a reception hardly less favourable if somewhat less enthusiastic. A strong friendship springing up between Bodmer and the young Klopstock, the former offered the poet a temporary home at his Tusculum (still standing) on the slopes of Zurichberg, that he might go on with his great epic. The fine view of the lake and mountains, the "highly cultivated city beneath," was greatly prized by Goethe who sounds its praises in "Wahrheit und Dichtung." However, Bodmer was disappointed with his young guest, for Klopstock loved the society of the young men and young women of his own age, and the progress made with the "Messiah" was well-nigh *nil*. However, it is to Klopstock's sojourn there, that we owe some of his

---

[1] Haller, anxious to return to his native land, accepted an inferior post as director of salt-mines at Bex (Vaud), Bern, his native town, disregarding his great merits, declining to offer him either a professorship or a seat on the governing board.

fine odes, especially that on Zurich lake. But meanwhile Bodmer's friendship had cooled, and Klopstock went to the house (in Zurich itself) of Hartmann Rahn, who later on married the poet's sister. With this same Rahn was some years afterwards associated the philosopher Fichte, when he lived at Zurich (1788). Fichte in fact married Rahn's daughter, Johanna. In 1752, Wieland [1] repaid Bodmer for his previous disappointments, by staying with him for some two years.

Bodmer's zeal for the advance of literature was unremitting. Though he could not himself boast of much poetic genius, he was a prolific writer in both prose and verse. His great merit is his bringing to light again the fine old mediæval poetry long since forgotten. The manuscript of the " Minnesänger " and the famous " Nibelungen " he had dug up from the lumber-room of Hohenems Castle. He moved heaven and earth to obtain royal protection and patronage for German literature. But little did he gain at the court of the great Frederick. To Müller, who presented the " Nibelungen," his majesty replied in characteristic fashion that the piece was not worth a single " charge of powder." Not less characteristic was Voltaire's reply when a request was made for the royal favour to Klopstock. "A new 'Messiah' is too much of a good thing, the old one has not been read yet."

Bodmer's influence on the young man of parts is noticeable. He gathered round him a large following of young Zürcher who had a taste for letters.

---

[1] A daughter of Wieland was also married to the son of his great friend Gessner, the poet.

Crowds of them would accompany him in his evening walks in the avenue Platzspitz, drinking in his words of wit and wisdom. Of the disciples thus gathered round " Father " Bodmer—for so he was affectionately styled—some attained no little eminence in later life. Amongst them we may mention Sulzer, who became art professor at Berlin, and stood in high favour with the king; and Solomon Gessner, the painter poet, whose word pictures are hardly less beautiful than the productions of his brush. His " Idylls," published in 1756, gave him a European reputation. The work was translated into all the literary languages, and in France and Italy was read with great eagerness, a first edition in French being sold out within a fortnight. Another important work is Hirzel's " Kleinjogg," or the " Socrates of the Fields." In this Hirzel, who was a physician and a philanthropist, brings to the fore the despised peasantry. " Kleinjogg " is not a work of fiction solely, but an account of Jakob Gujer who lived in a small Zurich village. Jakob was a man of great intelligence, indomitable resolution, and practical wisdom, who by his admirable management raised a wretched country home into a model farm. Goethe, who on a visit ate at his table, was delighted with the philosophic peasant, and called him " one of the most delicious creatures earth ever produced."

Heinrich Pestalozzi, the philanthropist, but better known for his efforts in the cause of education, was also a Zurich man. His principles of education are embodied in his novel of rural life, " Lienhard and Gertrude " (1781). His ideas are partly borrowed from Rousseau, but he failed to realize them in practice. The work at once won for Pestalozzi European fame. Ludwig Meyer von Knonau, a country magnate, was a poet and a painter, and wrote "Fables." Johannes Casper Lavater Bodmer's

LAVATER.

favourite pupil, stirred to their depth the patriotic feelings of his countrymen by his famous "Schweizerlieder," which he composed for the Helvetic Society, in 1767. Indeed literary tastes seem to have been very prevalent amongst the Swiss at that time.

More of Winkelmann's great work on Æsthetics were sold in Zurich and Basel then would in our own day probably be sold in such cities as Berlin and Vienna. And Solothurn, we find, produced thrice as many subscribers to Goethe's works as the great cities just mentioned.

After Bodmer Lavater became the chief attraction at Zurich, and strangers flocked thither in great numbers to see him. He was the founder of the study of physiognomy, and his works on it were very largely read at the time. Goethe himself joined with Lavater in his "Essays on Physiognomy." The philosopher's personality being singularly charming and fascinating, he was one of the most influential men of his time. He was the pastor of St. Peter's church, and was full of high religious enthusiasm. He desired to take Christianity from its lifeless condition and make it a living thing, and was strongly opposed to rationalism—Anglo-French deism—then slowly creeping in, notwithstanding severe repressive measures against it. Goethe was for many years the close friend of Lavater, and carried on with him a brilliant correspondence. The great poet, it may be stated, paid no fewer than three visits to Zurich, viz., in 1775, 1779, and 1797. He considered his intercourse with Lavater the "seal and crown" of the whole trip to Switzerland in 1779, and calls the divine the "crown of mankind," "the best among the best," and compares his friendship with "pastureland on heaven's border." Lavater's later years were marked by many eccentricities, and he fell into religious mysticism. But his sterling merits will not readily be forgotten by the Swiss.

A word respecting the Helvetic Society must close the present chapter. This society was founded in 1762, with the view of gathering together those who were stirred by political aspiration. It gradually united all those who desired the political regeneration of their fatherland, and the most prominent men of both East and West Switzerland, and of both confessions, joined the new society. The young patriots regularly met to discuss methods of improving the country and its institutions, and this in spite of the prohibitions of a narrow-minded executive, and the close control of the press. Stockar's scheme for amalgamating the free states into one republic mightily swelled the hearts of both Catholic and Protestant, and their efforts gave rise to many practical reforms. The most prominent result of these efforts was the rise of national education. Zurich with its higher schools occupied a leading position in the work of reform, and Pestalozzi established on his own estate a school for the poor. Unfortunately this admirable institution failed for want of a proper manager. Later on, after the Revolution, when the soil was better prepared for it, Pestalozzi's system took vigorous root.

XXIX.

THE FRENCH REVOLUTION AND SWITZERLAND.

(1790-1798.)

NONE of our readers will need to be told the story of the French Revolution, nor shown that it was the natural outcome of previous misgovernment and oppression. Every one has read of the miseries of the lower classes—intolerable beyond description; of the marvellous inability of the nobles and clergy to see that amidst all their selfishness and pleasures they were living on the very edge of a frightful volcano; of the *tiers-état* and its emancipatory movement, which, outgrowing its primary intention, brought about a series of stupendous changes; of Napoleon, how he stopped this disorder and how he made all Europe into one vast theatre of war. All this, in so far as it is the history of France, can only be alluded to here, but, inasmuch as Switzerland was dragged into the whirlpool of changes, we must dwell upon some of the effects of the great Revolution. Not less clearly than in France itself did the cry of "*Liberté*,

THE LION OF LUCERNE.
(*From a photograph of the original.*)

and égalité!" resound through the Swiss lands, filling the hearts of the unfree and the oppressed with high hopes. Yet it was only after terrible sufferings and endless vicissitudes that the liberal principles of the Revolution came to the front, and admitted of that practical realization which was to lead up to a nobler and happier life for men.

Of the many popular risings in Switzerland due to the influence of France, we may briefly touch on those which precede the Bern catastrophe in 1798. In September, 1791, Lower Valais rose against the *landvögte* of Upper Valais, but the intervention of Bern checked the revolt. In the April of the following year, Pruntrut (in the Bernese Jura) renounced its allegiance to the prince-bishops of Basel, and set up as an independent territory, under the style of the "Rauracian Republic," and three months later the widely-extended bishopric itself was amalgamated with France as the "Department Mont Terrible." It was on August 10th of this same year (1792) that the Swiss Guards defending the Tuileries against the Paris mob were massacred. Every one knows the story. "We are Swiss, and the Swiss never surrender their arms but with their lives," were the proud words of Sergeant Blaser to the crowds furious against the protectors of royalty, and claiming that their arms should be put down. When Louis was in safety, the Swiss Guards were withdrawn. But on leaving the palace they were suddenly attacked by thousands of the mob. Resistance was plainly useless, yet the Swiss would not fly, and were ruthlessly slaughtered. Of the 760 men and twenty-two officers, but few escaped that terrible onslaught. The beautiful and far-famed Thorwaldsen monument—the "Lion of Lucerne"—with its inscription, "Helvetiorum fidei ac virtuti," still keeps up the memory of the heroic courage of the Swiss Guards.[1] The outrage aroused intense indignation at home, but could not be avenged. The subjects of the prince-abbot Beda, of St. Gall, secured under his mild rule the abolition of serfdom. His successor, Forster, however, refusing the measure his sanction, was driven from his see—till he returned under Austrian auspices—and a large rural district of St. Gall gained autonomy and freedom from the rule of the abbey in 1797. Geneva saw almost every possible change. At one time she was rescued by Bern at Zurich, but was, in 1798, absorbed by France. The singularly harsh bearing of Zurich towards the country districts brought about the widespread insurrection of Stäfa, in 1795; an insurrection vigorously suppressed however. The Italian lordships, severely treated by Graubünden, desired to be included in the Cis-alpine republic Bonaparte was forming, and the general advised that free state that it should be admitted into their pale as a fourth member of equal rank. Finding that his advice was not taken, he suddenly proclaimed the memorable maxim, "that no people can be subject to another people without a violation of the laws of nature," and joined Valtellina, Bormio, and Chiavenna to Lombardy. This arrange-

---

[1] This grand work of art is carved out of and on the face of an immense rock, after a model by Thorwaldsen—a wounded lion with a broken spear, representing hapless but noble courage. The work was executed in 1821.

ment he had ratified by the treaty of Campo Formio, in 1797, which destroyed the Venetian republic, handing it over, indeed, to Austria, France taking the Netherlands and Milan as her share of the plunder.

Few things served to draw the attention of France to Swiss lands more than the Helvetic Club at Paris. This famous club was founded in 1790, by malcontents, chiefly from Vaud, Geneva, and Freiburg. They were bent on the liberation of Switzerland from aristocratic domination, and desirous of assimilating the form of government with that of France. This suited the French Directory exactly, their aim being to girdle France with a strong belt of vassal states. Among these Switzerland was to serve as a bulwark, or at any rate as a battle-ground, against Austria; and France was not without hope of filling her *coffres-forts* with Swiss treasure, now grown, after long years of peace, to great dimensions. Amongst the band of patriots two men stand out as leaders. One was César de La Harpe, a noble-minded and enthusiastic Vaudois, who, however, was more concerned for his own canton than for Switzerland at large. The other was Peter Ochs, of Basel, a shrewd and able man, but ambitious, and a creature of France. La Harpe had once been taunted by a Bernese noble, who reminded him that Vaud was subject to Bern, and this he never forgot. Even at the Court of Catherine II. of Russia, to which he had been called as tutor to the imperial grandchildren, he never forgot his republican principles. In 1797, returning from Russia, and being forbidden to enter Vaud, he joined the Helvetic Club at Paris, and thence launched forth his pamphlets against Bern. And in the Directory things were making against that hapless canton, Reubel, a declared enemy, gaining a seat. Napoleon too was no lover of Bern. On his way to the Congress of Rastatt, in 1797, he passed through Switzerland, and,

LA HARPE.

while accepting the enthusiastic welcome offered by Basel and Vaud, he declined altogether to respond to that of Bern and Solothurn. Peter Ochs enjoyed Napoleon's full confidence, and was by him summoned to Paris, and charged with the drafting of a new constitution for Switzerland, on the lines of the Directory. La Harpe and Ochs thus worked towards the same end, though the motives of the two men differed greatly.

Vaud hailed with delight the French Revolution, and celebrated the fall of Bastille in the most ostentatious manner; Bern, on the other hand, looked with dismay on the march of events, and, in Jan. 1798, sent Colonel Weiss with troops into the province. France replied by immediately sending men to occupy the southern shore of Lake Geneva. This was done at the request of the Helvetic Club, which gave as a pretext an old treaty of 1564, by which France guaranteed her support to Vaud. In vain did Weiss issue manifestoes; Bern was irresolute, and Vaud, feeling herself safe under the ægis of France, proclaimed the establishment of the "Lemanic Republic," with the seat of government at Lausanne (Jan. 24, 1798). A simple accident which resulted in the death of a couple of French soldiers was by their general magnified into an *attentât* of the "Bernese tyrants" against a "great nation." The French troops marched on Weiss, ousted him without the necessity of striking a blow, and then charged Vaud with a sum of £28,000 for services rendered. Such proceedings struck terror into the hearts of the Swiss, and many of the cantons—Basel, Schaffhausen, Lucerne, &c.—set about reforming their governments. With matters at this pass the Diet ordered that the national federal oath should be sworn to, a proceeding which had been neglected for three hundred years. But this pretence of unity was a mere sham, as indeed were all these hasty attempts at reform. They failed to avert the coming storm, as the rulers failed to read aright the signs of the times. The Tagsatzung distracted and helpless dissolved on Feb. 1st.

In the operations which followed, the chief command of the French forces in Switzerland was transferred from Mengaud to Brune, a Jacobite of the school of Danton. Brune directed his main attack on Bern, which, torn by dissensions, was wavering between peace and war. With Machiavellian astuteness Brune enticed the city into a truce. This truce, which was to last till the 1st of March, was most injurious to the interests of Bern, as it allowed time both for Brune to increase his own forces, and for Schauenburg to join him with a body of troops from Alsace. The Bernese were well-nigh paralyzed, and not unnaturally suspected treason amongst their own adherents. Unluckily, too, for her, Bern was far from popular amongst her sister cantons, and was well-nigh left to her own resources. Her chief allies were Solothurn and Freiburg, but these surrendered to Schauenburg and Brune at the first shock, on March 2nd. The French troops next marched to Bern, destroying on the way the national monument at Morat. But Von Grafenried secured a decided victory against Brune at Neueneck. On the other hand, Ludwig von Erlach, who attempted a stand against Schauenburg at Fraubrunnen, quite failed to hold his own, and was driven back on Grauholz, a few miles from Bern. A life-and-death struggle followed, even women and children seizing whatever weapons they could and fighting desperately, many of them even unto death. For three hours the combat lasted, and the Bernese fighting with their old bravery, maintained their honour as soldiers. Old Schultheiss von Steiger, "trembling in body, but stout in heart," cheered on his men regardless of the hail of bullets falling, but harmlessly, around him. Four times did the Swiss stand against the terrible onslaught of the French, but were at length compelled to yield to a force so superior in numbers and tactics to their own. And even whilst the clash of arms was still sounding the news came that Bern had surrendered. Erlach and Steiger fled to the Oberland, intending there to resume the combat; but the troops, mad with suspicion that the capitulation was the result of treason, murdered the former, Steiger narrowly escaping a similar fate. On the 5th of March, 1798, the French entered Bern in triumph, Brune, however, cautiously keeping up strict discipline. On the 22nd of the previous month at Lausaune, Brune had caused it to be proclaimed that the French came as friends and bearers of freedom, and would respect the property of the Swiss citizens. Notwithstanding this he emptied the treasuries and magazines of Bern, and on the 10th and 11th of March, sent off eleven four-horse waggons full of booty, nineteen banners, and the three bears—which they nicknamed respectively Erlach, Steiger, and Weiss—the French carried off in triumph.

Thus fell Bern, the stronghold of the aristocracy, and with its fall the doom of Switzerland was sealed, though more work remained to be done before it would be complete. The Directory now abolished the old Confederation, and proclaimed in its stead the "one and undivided Helvetic Republic," forcing on it a new constitution elaborated from the draft by Peter Ochs. Brune himself had had a scheme for a triple division of the territory, but a preference was given to a united republic, as more easily manageable from Paris. The thirteen old cantons, together with the various subject lands and connections were formed into twenty-two divisions. After the failure of the *laender* the number was reduced to nineteen, the three Forest Cantons with Zug being thrown into one, as a punishment. Some of the rearrangements and partitions were very curious. A few may be cited. Oberland Canton was lopped off from Bern, and Baden from Aargau proper. Säntis included Appenzell and the northern portion of St. Gall, and Linth comprised the rest of St. Gall and Glarus: Tessin was split into Bellinzona and Lugano; Vaud, Valais, and Bünden were added intact. Geneva and Neuchâtel were left outside. In this manner the united Helvetic commonwealth was formed, the central government being fixed at Aarau, Lucerne, and Bern in succession. The passing of laws was vested in a senate and great council. There was a Directory of five members to whom were added four ministers of state—for war, justice, finance, and art and science. A supreme court of justice was made up of nineteen representatives, one from each canton. These were sweeping changes, and the unadvised manner in which they were forced on the people prevented their meeting with general approval. And then France gained the hearty dislike of the Swiss generally by her treatment of the country. Switzerland was regarded as a conquered and subject land, and was ruthlessly despoiled by the French. A contribution of sixteen million francs was imposed on the Swiss aristocracy—besides the eight million francs carried off from Bern at her fall.[1]

Ten cantons, notably Bern, Zurich, Lucerne, and Vaud, *i.e.*, the city cantons, feeling that resistance was impossible, and reform was necessary, acquiesced in the new arrangement; but the *laender*, except Obwalden, stirred up by the priests and local patriots, and fearing that religion and liberty would die together, offered a most uncompromising resistance. They preferred, they said, "to be burnt beneath their blazing roofs, rather than submit to the dictates of the foreigner." Very noble was the defence made by the Forest folk, but we can only touch briefly upon it. After a brave resistance Glarus was defeated at Rapperswyl, on the 30th of April, 1798, and then Schauenburg proceeded with his whole strength against Schwyz. In its defence a band of some four thousand stout-hearted men was collected under the command of Reding, a young and handsome officer, who had just returned from Spanish service. Reding was an enthusiastic patriot of the old stamp, deeply imbued with conservative principles. Men rallied to his standard eagerly, and swore a solemn oath, "not

---

[1] The exact sum paid by Bern is not known, but probably it reached seven or eight million francs. The Bernese losses, up to 1813, were estimated at seventeen million francs. One hundred and sixty cannon, and sixty thousand muskets were also captured. Bern had kept three bears (in the Bärangraben of the town) ever since the battle of Novara, in 1513. Strangely enough the bears carried off in that battle were French trophies.

to flee, but conquer." Reding and his little army gained three brilliant victories, at Schindellegi, Arth, and Morgarten, respectively, showing themselves worthy descendants of the old heroes of 1315. However, the French effected an entrance by way of Mount

REDING.

Etzel, through the failure of the priest Herzog to hold his own against them, and poured through the gap in overwhelming numbers. For the moment they were thrust back at Rothenthurm, but Schwyz was too exhausted to continue the unequal struggle, and

Reding was forced to enter into negotiations, though negotiations of an honourable character, with Schauenburg.

Then followed the gloomy 9th of September, written down as "doomsday" in the annals of Midwalden,[1] a day that well-nigh blotted that semi-canton out of existence. Having set up a wild opposition to the "Helvetic," this district drew down upon itself the wrath of France. Animated by the spirit of Winkelried, one and all—its worthy sons, its women and children even—the little band—they were but two thousand as against sixteen thousand—for some days kept up the unequal struggle. The little bay of Alpnach (Alpnacher See) and the Wood of Kerns (Kernserwald) were red with the blood of the enemy. But this state of things could not last long. Suddenly the French broke through, and poured in from all sides. Terrible conflicts took place at Rotzloch and Drachenried, and a rush was made on Stanz, the chief place of the district. By noon this town was really taken, but notwithstanding this the combat continued in furious fashion till evening. This was the 9th of September, 1798, a day which Schauenburg called the hottest of his life. "Like furies," the report says, "the black legion of the French galley-slaves slew and raged the district through." When night set in Stanz looked a devastated, smoking city of blood and death. Europe

---

[1] The mountain range, running from Titlis north-west and then north-east to Stanzer Horn, with the Kernwald at its centre, separates Unterwalden into Obwalden (above the wood) and Midwalden (below the wood).

looked with amazement, yet with admiration and sympathy, on this heroic spot of earth. Both England and Germany sent provisions and money, and even Schauenburg was moved with compassion towards the poor Midwaldeners, and had food distributed to them. It may perhaps here be noted that Stanz shortly figures again in Swiss history, but this time in a far more peaceful and humane manner. It was here that Pestalozzi resumed his noble work of education. To heal the wounds of his noble country as far as was in his power the minister Stapfer founded an educational establishment for the orphan children of the district. And here it was that Pestalozzi ruled, not so much as a mere pedagogue, but as a veritable father, the little unfortunates committed to his care.

XXX.

THE "ONE AND UNDIVIDED HELVETIC REPUBLIC."

(1798-1803.)

THE day of the "one and undivided Helvetic Republic" was a period of "storm and stress," short-lived, full of creative ideas and vast schemes, with much struggling for what was most noble in the principles of the Revolution. Yet Helvetia was torn by inner dissensions, and its energies paralysed by civil and foreign war, by its position of dependence, and by financial difficulties. The Helvetic scheme of pounding the various members of the Confederation into one state wiping out the cantons—a scheme often planned since then, but to this day unrealized, and as yet unrealizable—by its inevitable levelling tendencies, roused intense disgust and hatred amongst the more conservative of the Swiss. In truth, it went too fast, and too far in the direction of centralization. The *laender* were robbed of their *landsgemeinde*, the city cantons of their councils, and the independent states of their sovereignty. Everything seemed to be turned topsy-turvy. Cantons became mere administrative districts.[1] The barriers between them, and likewise between the various classes of society, were broken down. Subject lands were recognized as equal in status to the rest, and the inhabitants given full rights of citizenship. Amongst the many beneficent measures brought forward the principal may be mentioned. All restrictions on trade and industry were removed, tithes, bondservice, and land taxes could be redeemed at a small cost; freedom in religious matters, freedom of the press, and the right to petition were guaranteed, and torture was suppressed. That child of the Revolution, "the Helvetic," indeed, advocated many reforms and gave birth to many new ideas which required time and thought and peace to bring to maturity and usefulness. But the time was not yet ripe, and peace was lacking, and many things were suggested rather than put into practice. Yet we look back with interest on many of the ideas of the time, for they paved the way for and led up to much of our modern progress.

Excellent men, men of parts, wise and moderate, watched over the early days of the young republic; amongst them Usteri, Escher (of Zurich), Secretan and Carrard (Vaud), and Mayer (Bern). But gradually French partisans, nominated from Paris, were returned to the Swiss Directory, and Ochs and

[1] The utter failure clearly shows how little such a centralization of government, leaving the cantons no scope for action, could suit the separate states of the Confederation at any time. The name "canton" was first used in French treaties with Switzerland, and became thenceforward the general term. It had not come into use even so late as the Helvetic.

La Harpe were promoted to the leadership of Helvetic affairs. Soon a "reign of terror"—of a milder form, perhaps, but none the less a rule of terrorism—was set up, with the view of dragooning the country into submission to the "*grande nation.*" A levy was enforced in order to make up a total of eighteen thousand men, a number the Swiss were loth to produce for the foreigner. They objected to this forced service, and took up arms abroad, whilst men like Lavater and Reding, who defied both French tyranny and "Helvetic" despotism, were transported, or thrust into the filthy dungeons of the fortress of Aarburg. On the 19th of August, 1798, was concluded the fatal Franco-Helvetic Alliance—offensive and defensive—despite the supplications and warnings of the more far-seeing patriots, such as Escher (von der Linth) for instance. Swiss neutrality being thus abandoned, the door was opened to the Austro-Russian invasion, planned by the second European coalition with the view of ousting France from Swiss territory. Hating the new *régime* exasperated at French supremacy and French extortion, and desirous that the *status quo ante* of 1798 should be re-established, the reactionists hailed with delight the coming of the Austrians, quite as much as the "Patriots" had before welcomed the interference of France. A legion of Swiss *emigrés* abroad collected by Roverea, at Vaudois, who had sided with Bern in the previous struggle, joined the Austrian army. The foreign occupation which took place and turned Switzerland into one military camp cannot be followed in all its details here. Yet one or two points must be noted, above all, those remarkable Alpine marches carried out, though against his own will, by Suwarow. These marches are quite unique in military history.

After the defeat of the French in Southern Germany, the Tyrol, and Italy, by the Archduke Charles, Hotze, and Suwarow, they were to be driven out of Switzerland. Marshal Massena, who had succeeded Schauenburg in the command of the French troops, had at the commencement of the war seized Graubünden, and forced it, free state though it was, to join the Helvetic Republic to which it so strongly objected. But in May, 1799, it was recaptured by Hotze, a gallant swordsman of Swiss birth;[1] who had risen to the rank of field-marshal in the Austrian army. Hotze drove the French from the central highlands, Roverea likewise taking a prominent part in the expedition. About this time the Archduke Charles entered Switzerland at Schaffhausen, and, carrying all before him, advanced to Zurich. This city, after various skirmishes in its neighbourhood, he seized on the 4th of June, forcing Massena to retire to the heights beyond the Limmat river. But now a cessation of hostilities intervened for some months, owing to differences between Austria and Russia, and with this came a change of tactics. Archduke Charles withdrew, and his place was taken by Korsakow with a Russian army forty thousand strong. A plan was now agreed upon under which Suwarow should join Korsakow from Italy, and they should then combine their forces in a grand attack on the French, on September 26th. This Massena was

---

[1] He was a native of a large village in the Zurich district.

determined to prevent. By admirable manœuvring he disposed his eight divisions about Eastern and Central Switzerland, his force amounting to no fewer than seventy-five thousand men. The highlands of Schwyz, Uri, and Glarus, were held by Lecourbe, a skilled strategist, thoroughly at home in the Alps, and the entrance to the St. Gothard pass was blocked. Marshal Soult gave battle to Hotze in the marshy district between Lake Zurich and Walensee, on the 25th of September, with the result that Hotze was slain, and the Austrian force retired from Swiss soil. Wherever the Austrians had gained a footing, the reactionists had taken advantage of it to re-establish the *status quo*. On the 25th and 26th of September, Massena attacked the Russian forces under Korsakow, at Zurich. This second battle of Zurich—the fighting was continued (from outside) into the very streets—resulted in the complete defeat of Korsakow. Fortunately the city itself, having remained neutral, escaped violent treatment, but Lavater was unfortunate enough to be struck by a shot during the engagement, whilst carrying help to some wounded soldiers.[1]

Quite unaware of what was being done in Switzerland, Suwarow reached the heights of St. Gothard on the 24th of September, and, finding the pass occupied by the enemy, cut his way through in brilliant style. Whilst some of the Russians—at Teufelsbrüche, for instance—held in check the French, the larger portion of their army scrambled down the

---

[1] He lingered on suffering from his wound for a whole year, and then died, distinguished to the very last by his love for all mankind, and for his country especially.

DILIGENCE CROSSING THE SIMPLON PASS.

steep rocks lining the Reuss, amidst the French fire. Wading across the rapid torrent they hurried down the valley to Flüelen, intending to push on to Lucerne and Zurich. But to their great dismay they found no road skirting Uri lake, and all the boats removed. They were thus locked up in a labyrinth of mountain fastnesses, the outlets from which were blocked by their foes. In this desperate strait there was nothing for it but to proceed over the mountains as best they might, by any rough path which might present itself. In reality, however, these passes were no highroads for armies, but only narrow paths used by occasional shepherds or huntsmen. Devoted to their leader, the Russian troops toiled up from the sombre Schächenthal, and along the rugged Kinzig pass, pursued by their enemies. On reaching Muotta they learned the disheartening news that Korsakow had been defeated. No wonder that down the weather-beaten face of the brave old general, the tears rolled as he gave the order to retreat. But Suwarow was not inclined to sit still and repine, and undaunted by his recent terrible struggle against nature, at once resumed his march across the toilsome Pragel pass into the canton of Glarus, where he had good hopes of finding Austrian friends. But on his arrival he learnt that the Austrians had left the neighbourhood. Thus baffled once more, and unable to get to the plains at Naefels on account of the enemy, he was compelled to retreat again, and again attempt the terrible passage across the mountains. Striking across the Panixer pass, which rises to the height of eight thousand feet, he found himself confronted by greater difficulties than before. Snow had lately fallen, and all traces of the path had disappeared. For five terrible days the force decimated, dying with cold, hunger, and fatigue, unshod—their boots were entirely worn out—struggled along those wintry regions, creeping like caterpillars up walls of snow and over icy peaks. Hundreds of men and horses fell into the hidden crevices, down which also many a piece of artillery fell with sudden crash. Fully one-third of the gallant band perished during that fearful passage. The worn and famished survivors reached Graubünden on the 10th of October, and thence made their way into Austrian territory. Suwarow had failed, but immortal glory attaches to the memory of the dauntless and resolute old general. The non-success of the foreign invasions meant also the failure of the reactionists in their attempt to overthrow the "Helvetic Republic."

Indescribable misery was the consequence of the foreign wars, and it was intensified by the French occupation, and especially by the disgraceful system of spoliation practised by the French generals and agents, Mengaud, Lecarlier, Rapinat, &c. A few examples of the treatment Switzerland received at the hands of the French "liberators" may be given. Urserenthal, one of the Uri valleys, was called upon during the year Oct. 1798 to Oct. 1799, to provide food for a total of 861,700 men, and a pretty hamlet in Freiburg for twenty-five thousand, within half a year. During four months, Thurgau spent one and a half million francs, and the Baden district well-nigh five millions, in provisioning French troops within a year. All protestations of inability on the part of the inhabitants were useless; Rapinat[1] and others, like vampires, sucked the very life-blood out of the unfortunate Swiss. The "Helvetic Republic" had its noble side, it is true, but the French occupation, by which it was maintained, and which indeed was the outcome of it, caused the Helvetic scheme to be regarded by the people at large with disgust and hatred.

The brightest side of the "Helvetic Republic" was seen in the remarkable efforts of noble patriots—foremost amongst them Rengger and Stapfer—to mitigate the effects of all these calamities by promoting, in spite of all difficulties, or against all odds of the time, the material and ideal interests of the people. Both Rengger and Stapfer were highly cultivated men, and both were ministers of state, the former holding the portfolio of finance, the latter that of arts and sciences. Rengger directed his efforts to the improvement of trade and agriculture; one of his practical efforts being the introduction of English cotton-spinning machines. Stapfer, on the other hand, worked for the spread of popular education. "Spiritual and intellectual freedom alone makes free," he maintained. He himself had been born in one of the new enfranchised subject lands, it may be noted parenthetically. He drew up a remarkable scheme of national education, a scheme embracing the child in the

---

[1] The following lines, common in men's mouths afterwards, tell their own tale:—

"La Suisse qu'on pille et qu'on ruine
Voudrait bien que l'on decidât
Si Rapinat vient de rapine,
Ou rapine de Rapinat."

primary school, and the young man in the National University. This dream of a national university, by the way, is still unrealized,[1] but Stapfer intended that it should crown his whole system of national education, and should combine German depth with French versatility and Italian taste. Most of Stapfer's grand scheme remained untried through want of means and time, but it was a very remarkable scheme for that day. Yet much was done. Numerous schools sprang up, and every canton had its educational council and its inspector of schools. Lucerne, which had hitherto been quite behindhand in these matters, now founded schools in all its communes (by 1801), and Aarau established a gymnasium. Some four thousand children from the wasted and ruined country districts were brought into the towns and educated; whilst numerous journals were started, and many literary and art societies founded. Perhaps Stapfer's chief title to honourable remembrance is his appreciation of, and his assistance to, Pestalozzi. Leaving Stanz on account of confessional differences, the great philanthropist established his famous school at Burgdorf, winning for himself by it European renown.

These noble efforts towards national advancement intellectually are the more admirable as the country was convulsed with constitutional struggles. From the first days of the Revolution, there had sprung up two political schools, the Centralists, who[2] wished to see one single state with one central government; and

[1] And not very likely to be realized, as the respective cantons cling to their four universities and two academies, which are their pride.

[2] In German, *Centralisten* or *Unitarier*.

the Federalists, who clung to the historical traditions of their fatherland, and to the *status quo ante* of 1798. These latter desired to see cantonal self-government preponderating over the central authority. It was a struggle to the death between advanced Liberals and stout Conservatives. Within the short space of five years, the country saw no fewer than four *coups d'état*, complete overthrowings of government and constitution. We can notice only the chief points in the history of these changes. The first shock came with the change in France from the Directory to the Consulate, and the return of Napoleon from Egypt, on the 9th of November, 1798. Ochs, detested as the tool of France by nearly all the Swiss, was hurled from his eminence; and La Harpe following suit, the Swiss Directory was replaced by an executive committee. The Peace of Lunéville, February, 1801, left the Swiss free to chose their own form of government, but Napoleon himself gradually went over to the Federalist view. Drafts of new constitutions followed each other in quick succession, each in its turn being upset by that which followed. The sketch of La Malmaison, drawn up by the Federalists, restored the Tagsatzung, and the independence of the cantons, May, 1801. Another overthrow, and then Alois Reding rose to the position of first Landammann, and head of the Conservative government (Oct. 28, 1801). Chivalrous and of unflinching resolve, Reding lacked the pliancy necessary for a statesman, and desired to see Vaud again placed under the rule of Bern. "Sooner shall the sun turn from west to east," fiercely exclaimed Napoleon, "than Vaud shall go back to Bern." Reding was deprived of his office, and shut up at Aarburg, a fate that befell him on several other occasions under Bonaparte. In July, 1802, Napoleon withdrew the French troops from Swiss territory, with the view ostensibly of complying with the treaty of Amiens, but in reality to show the Swiss how powerless they were without his help. This was the signal for a general outbreak of civil war, humorously called *Stecklikrieg*, or *Guerre aux bâtons*, in allusion to the indifferent equipment of the soldiery. The Helvetic Government which was then in power fled from Bern, and took up its quarters at Lausanne. Its small force was defeated at Avenches by the Federalists, who pushed on to the Leman city, when an order to lay down their arms reached them from Paris. Through the medium of General Rapp, Napoleon offered his services as "mediator" in the civil troubles of Switzerland, and at his heels followed Marshal Ney, with an army of forty thousand men to enforce order.

XXXI.

THE MEDIATION ACT AND NAPOLEON.

(1803-15.)

FROM a constitutional point of view this period—the mediation period (1803-13)—is the most satisfactory portion of the epoch between the French revolutions of 1789 and 1830. It suited Napoleon's fancy to assume the position of a directing providence to the Alpine lands. And, finding that the federalists and the centralists of Switzerland—the *laudatores temporis acti* and the progressivists—were quite unable to agree upon a compromise, it pleased him to give the country a new constitution. He stopped their squabbles by summoning the "Helvetic Consulta" to Paris. Sixty-three deputies, of whom but fifteen were federalists, obeyed the call, many of the foremost statesmen among them. Those who disobeyed the summons, like Reding and his party, were arrested (Nov., 1803). In the official gazette Napoleon was pleased to speak of the Swiss nation as one that had "always stood out in history as a model of strength, courage, and good manners," and he expressed a wish that the Swiss should "aim at good government, and should sacrifice their party feelings to their real interests, to glory, and independence." Thus complimentary was his language, and the painstaking care and thoughtful consideration he brought to bear on the re-organization of Swiss affairs presents the great despot under a singularly amiable aspect; and the Mediation Act which he drew up would, but for the selfish *arrière pensée* running through it, be one of his noblest and most beneficent political acts.

From the drafts and data presented by the Conference Napoleon, in two months (Nov. 25th-Jan. 24th), drew up his famous scheme. Laying it first before the whole assembly, he then had selected an inner committee of ten for a further and final consultation. This took place on Jan. 29th at the Tuileries, the sitting lasting from one o'clock to eight in the evening. The French commissioners[1] afterwards stated that they had never witnessed such a scene, and that "never had the First Consul devoted such close attention, even to the most important matters of European politics." The Swiss party, representing both the political sections, and the four French Commissioners, sat round the table, Napoleon himself in the middle of them, beaming with graceful amiability. The proposals respecting the three classes of cantons were read out, and two of the delegates, Stapfer of whom we have heard before, and Hans von

---

[1] Barthélemy, Röderer, Fouché, and Desmeunier.

Reinhard,[1] were called upon to express their respective views. A general discussion followed, the Consul giving the closest attention to every detail. His own speeches showed an intimate acquaintance with Swiss matters, and whilst full of practical wisdom, also evidenced his real interest and sympathy with the little republic. He pointed out that Switzerland was quite unlike any other country in its history, its geographical position, in its inclusion of three nationalities and three tongues. The characteristics and the advancement of three nations had, in fact, to be considered and maintained. Nature itself had clearly intended that it should be a federal state. To the Forest Cantons, to which he avowed the whole republic owes its characteristic hue, he restored the time-honoured *landsgemeinde*, "so rich in memories of the past"; to the city cantons he gave back their ancient councils, re-fashioned in accordance with modern ideas; and to the subject lands he gave autonomy. The position of these last in the past was, he averred, incompatible with the modern character of a republic, and his elevation of them into new cantons is the special merit of his scheme. Meeting the views of the federalists by giving independence or home-rule to each canton, he also met those of the centralists by planning a well-organized central government in the form of a *Tagsatzung* with enlarged powers. At the head of this he placed a Swiss Landammann with almost *plein pouvoir*.

[1] This Hans von Reinhard was burgomaster of Zurich and Landammann; he belonged to one of the old aristocratic families of his native city.

Napoleon selected as first Landammann a man he highly esteemed—Louis d'Affry, of Freiburg, son of Count d'Affry. Both father and son had served in France as officers and statesmen, and Louis was one of the few who had escaped the massacre at Paris in 1792. He was a perfect courtier, mild and conservative in his views. It is worth mentioning that during the *intermezzo*, which occurred at five o'clock, when refreshments were handed round, the Consul, standing by the mantelpiece, with a circle of delegates round him, talked incessantly on Swiss politics and spared no pains to impress on his hearers how much Swiss interests were bound up with those of France. There was no mistaking his meaning, which, to do him justice, he did not attempt to conceal. The members of the Conference, whom Napoleon treated all through with marked distinction, were quite alive to the danger threatening their country, but trusted that some turn of the wheel might avert it. After this parley the Consul redrafted the Mediation Act, and presented it in person on the 19th of February for signature, afterwards taking leave of the whole deputation.

La Harpe gained for the Swiss the countenance of the Emperor Alexander, and Prussia and Austria were engaged in a territorial squabble, and no interference took place. An epoch of peace and prosperity followed the general amnesty (April 15, 1803) granted by the Mediation Act. The period of quiet was broken only by the Bockenkrieg in 1804, a rising in which an attempt was made by the country folk of the Zurich Canton to stand against the unredeemed land rents and tithes still due to the city.¹ The insurrection was put down by force.² Six new cantons were formed by the new Act—Bünden, St. Gall, Thurgau, Aargau, Vaud, and Ticino; and these were added as equals to the thirteen *Alte Orte*, the management of its own affairs being granted to each. The liberal principles inaugurated by the "Helvetic" were to a great extent borne in mind, though the lower orders were still excluded from direct political representation. Mercenary wars, military movements, and leagues between separate cantons, were strictly forbidden; but so, also, was forbidden the maintenance of a federal army, save a small force to maintain order, and thus the country was robbed of adequate means of defence. Freiburg, Bern, Soleure, Basel, Zurich, and Lucerne, became in their turns managing or dictatorial cantons for one year at a time. That is, they were the seats of the Diet, and their chief magistrate—schultheiss or burgomaster, as the case might be—became Landammann. To the larger cantons, *i.e.*, those having not less than one hundred thousand inhabitants, two votes at the Diet were

---

[1] The liquidation of this territorial debt was a most complicated matter, and plays an important part in the risings of the rural districts, yet the rightly cautious city had to consider various other interests besides those of the country folks. Many benevolent city institutions for the sick and poor were maintained by the income drawn from country dues.

[2] "It is meet that the country districts should cease their antipathy to the city, or they deserve to fall again under its authority," Napoleon had remarked, during the Paris Conference, to the Zurich representatives, Reinhard and Paul Usteri. He added that the personal character of the representatives was a guarantee that they would reconcile the two parties they represented.

assigned, to the smaller, one vote. It is not necessary to go into more minute details here, as there are numerous constitutional changes to be noted between that period and the year 1874.

Thus, whatever may be thought of Napoleon's ultimate aims, it was owing to him that Switzerland enjoyed quiet, prosperity, and perfect self-government at a time when Europe generally was torn by quarrels and steeped in war. The Swiss people gave their whole attention to home affairs, and to the striving after intellectual and material progress, as they had done in the Helvetic days, but now with more success. Benevolent societies were founded, high schools established, and institutions for the advancement of letters, science, and art, sprang up. Many men of note mightily stirred the ideal side of life; amongst them we may mention the novelist, Zschokke,[1] of Aargau; Martin Usteri, the poet-artist; and George Nägeli, the Sängervater, or "Father of Song." Both these latter were of Zurich, and Nägeli gave a great impulse to the founding of musical societies, and did much to spread the art of singing so common in the German districts, and especially cultivated at Basel and Zurich. Pestalozzi established a new school at Yverdon in Vaud; and his friend and former pupil, Von Fellenberg, of Bern, the superior of his master in practical management, founded his famous institution at Hofwil. This comprised a whole series of schools, high schools, schools for the middle class, agricultural schools, and elementary schools for the poor. Pater Girard, a friend of Pestalozzi, at Frei-

[1] A German by birth.

burg, did for the Catholics much what these men did for the Protestants. Another noble and devoted man was Escher, who, though of aristocratic birth himself, was yet an ardent worker for the benefit of the poorer classes. His chief work was the canalization of the Linth between Walensee and the Lake of Zurich, by means of which some twenty-eight thousand acres of unhealthy swamp became valuable agricultural land. For this labour of love, to which he sacrificed his health, the Diet decreed to him and his family the honourable addition of "Von der Linth."[1] The introduction of machinery gave a great impetus to trade and industry. In 1800 the cloisters of St. Gall were turned into the first Swiss spinning mill, and during the following decade four more mills were started in the canton. In 1808 Heinrich Kunz, the "King of spinners on the Continent," laid the foundations (Zurich) of the first of his numerous mills. In 1812 the great firm of Rieter and Co., whose machines soon gained a world-wide reputation, started business at Winterthur.

Yet all was not smooth in the little Swiss state. Switzerland was compelled not only to enter into a close defensive alliance with France, but to keep the French army constantly supplied with sixteen thousand Swiss soldiers. So great was the drain of

[1] Escher died soon after the completion of the Linth Canal (1822), and the Diet erected to his memory a monument in Glarus Canton. A characteristic story respecting him is worth repeating. Some poor man seeing him standing hard at work up to his waist in water exclaimed, "Why, sir, if I were as rich as you, I shouldn't work at all." "That's just why God has given you no wealth," was Escher's quiet reply.

this "blood-tax," that in some cantons even the prisons had to be opened to enable the levy to be made up. Switzerland was made an *entrepôt* for English contraband goods; and the decree of Trianon, in 1810, ordered the confiscation of these, and placed a tax on English goods of half their value. All this weighed heavily on Switzerland, and the Landammann's touching representation to Napoleon, that twenty thousand families were rapidly becoming breadless, passed unheeded. In 1806 the despot gave Neuchâtel to his favourite general, Berthier, and in 1810 he handed over Ticino to Italy, on the pretext that that district was harbouring English contraband goods. The same year he joined to France the Valais district, where he had a few years earlier (1802) constructed the famous Simplon road into Italy. The Swiss naturally protested against these mutilations, but he threatened to annex the whole country, and D'Affry and Reinhard, who stood in favour with him, had much ado to calm his temper. When, however, the impetuous Sidler, of Zug, and the heroic Reding, defied him, and advised an armed resistance at the Diet, Napoleon sent word to Reinhard that he would march fifty thousand men into the country, and compel the Swiss to unite with France.

But the tide was beginning to turn; Napoleon had passed his zenith. The fatal Russian expedition, into which his pride and reckless ambition tempted him in 1812, was followed by the terrible disaster of Leipsic, "the battle of the nations." The allied armies marched to Paris, and compelled the abdication of the emperor. This turn of events naturally affected the position of the Swiss very greatly, but, quite content with their new constitution, they declined to join the allied states. At the command of the Landammann, Von Reinhard, General von Wattenwil placed his scanty forces, numbering some fifteen thousand men, along the frontier to enforce neutrality if possible. But on the approach of the allied forces Wattenwil saw that resistance would be madness, and gave orders to his men to withdraw, and be careful not to provoke hostilities. About Christmas time in 1813, the combined Austrian and German troops—Alexander was for sparing the Swiss —to the number of one hundred and seventy thousand, marched right across the country on their way to the French capital. On the whole little material injury was done to the country, but the Mediation Act, by the very reason of its origin, was bound to fall. On the 29th of December the Diet was compelled to decree its own extinction. The Peace of Paris, on the 31st of May in the following year, guaranteed Switzerland its independence. A new constitution was to come later on.

The overthrow of the Mediation Act plunged Switzerland into fresh troubles. All the reactionary elements came to the surface. Bern revived her old pretensions to the overlordship of Vaud and Aargau ; and Freiburg, Solothurn, Lucerne, and the Forest Cantons, acting on the same lines, supported Bern in her claims. Zurich, on the other hand, stood out for the nineteen cantons, and headed the opposition to Bern. Again there was seen the deplorable spectacle of a divided state, with two confederations and two diets. One of these, with its headquarters at Lucerne, was, however, forced to dissolve, by foreign pressure, chiefly through to the influence of D'Istria, the Russian ambassador at Zurich. All the cantons now sent representatives to the Diet held in this last-named city, with the view of drawing up a new federal pact. But party strife was very bitter, and the session lasted from April 6, 1814, to the the 31st of August, 1815, an extraordinary length of time hence it was called the " Long Diet." The protracted proceedings were caused chiefly by Bern, which obstinately refused to abate her pretensions to the two districts (Vaud and Aargau). There were, however, many minor points of difference, all tending to embitter and prolong the session. It was clear that a settlement could only be brought about by a compromise, and great concessions on the part of some of the members. As a matter of fact several things were left unsettled. This Zurich constitution was to be laid before the Vienna Congress, which opened on the 3rd of November, 1814, and which was to disentangle many knots in European politics.

Monarchs, princes, ambassadors, ministers, and generals, from all the states, met at the gay city on the Danube, to rearrange the map of Europe. The story of this strange international gathering is well known, with its Vanity Fair of fine ladies and gentlemen, its magnificent fêtes, balls, masquerades, steeplechases, and gaities innumerable. It is said that Francis I. spent no less than thirty millions of florins on entertaining his guests, and the gay scene and high spirits formed a strange contrast with the previous despondency prevailing on the Continent generally. The "*Congrès danse, mais ne marche pas*," was the saying that went abroad. Yet it was not strange that men felt glad. The weight of Napoleon's hand was now removed, and the world breathed more freely. All the sufferings of the last quarter of a century were forgotten, and, it is to be feared, the lesson to be learnt from them was not learnt. The changes were too many, too sudden, and too sweeping to permit anything to take root. But the seeds left behind by the revolutions and wars will blossom and bear fruit later on. Every sound movement must develop gradually. In this way only can we account for the reactions, the return to the old lines of constitution and social life, after the fall of Bonaparte.

Switzerland had many points to settle at the Congress, and, indeed, to the despair of the members, seemed inclined to bring forward all her domestic squabbles. On the whole, the commissioners showed much goodwill towards Switzerland, and took great pains to make that country a strong outpost against French extensions. Von Reinhard, the first Swiss representative at the Congress, gained much praise by his dignity and astuteness, and the Emperor Alexander entered fully into his liberal views and aspirations, coinciding with those of La Harpe. Bern and her pretensions, which were as strong as ever, gave most trouble, Vaud and Aargau naturally insisting on retaining their independence. At length a compromise was arranged, and the larger portion of the see of Basel (Bernese Jura, &c.), and Bienne being given to Bern. The bailiwicks of the *laender* redeemed their freedom by purchase; the rest of the cantons, more generous, required no compensation. Subject lands were set free for good, and the country received its present boundaries. Ticino had been restored by Napoleon, and Valais, Geneva, and Neuchâtel, were admitted as cantons on an equality with the rest, and thus we get the now familiar number of twenty-two cantons. The list was closed, though by a strange anomaly Neuchâtel still continued to be not only a Swiss canton, but a Prussian duchy. Geneva was, as it were, rounded off by the addition of Versoix (Gex), and some Savoy communes.[1] Geneva had long wished to be received into the Federation, and great was her rejoicing now that her dream was realized. Thus Switzerland received the great boon of independence, and was placed under the protection of the Great Powers. Bünden lost her appendages, Valtellina, Chiavenna, and Bormio, which went to Austria, but gained in return the district of Räzuns. The new constitution assigned to Switzerland is decidedly inferior to the "Mediation Act." There was a revival of the old system of narrow prerogatives; the several cantons gaining *plein pouvoir* as against the federal authori-

---

[1] She objected to receiving the larger strip of Savoy and French land (on the lake and the Rhone), which the Congress wished to assign her, for fear of being absorbed by Catholicism, and, moreover, she was anxious not to alarm her old friends. The facts were and are often misrepresented. Chablais and Faucigny, once temporarily held by Bern, were declared neutral, and placed under the guarantee of the Powers. That is, in case of war, Swiss troops quarter the district, as in 1870-71.

ties; the cities retaining their preponderance over the rural districts, and the wealthy and the aristocracy their power over their poorer brethren. Military matters alone were better provided for. Thus we shall presently find that Revolution had to begin her work over again. Bern, Zurich, and Lucerne became in turn the seat of the Diet, and one vote only was allotted to each canton. Midwalden offered a fanatical opposition to the new constitution, but was compelled to give way, and had to forfeit Engelberg, with its famous cloister and the whole valley, which was given to Obwalden.

XXXII.

SWITZERLAND UNDER THE CONSTITUTION OF 1815–48.

THE history of the thirty-three years following 1815 may, so far as Switzerland is concerned, be summed up in this description—it was a protest, latent at first and afterwards open and declared, of the Swiss people against the decrees of the Vienna Congress, which tended to stop the wheel of progress. The Swiss struggled onwards through the conflicts of political development, and battled against all that was a hindrance to them in the constitution of 1815, the Powers looking on with misgiving if not with dismay the while not understanding the signs of the times. Yet, by 1848, when the thrones of Europe were again shaken by revolutions, Switzerland had gained that for which it had been struggling, and had settled down into a peaceful and regenerated *Bundestaat*. We have shown how the settlement of 1815 was in many ways a return to old lines in both Church and State. Speaking generally, the Church gained greatly by the new constitution, the return of the Jesuits was favoured, the religious establishments were still maintained at a rate which really exceeded the financial possibilities of the state, and the clergy were given a free hand. Then the old power of the aristocracy was largely re-established, and the cities were given their former great preponderance over the country districts. Bern, for instance, receiving two hundred seats in the Council, as against ninety-nine. The reactionary *régime* from 1815 to 1830, was, in fact, politically a blank, though towards its close some of the cantons began to carry measures of reform. Amongst these was Ticino, into which some fatal abuses had crept. To make up for their political deficiencies, and to rekindle their smouldering patriotism, the Swiss, as they had done before, turned to the past history of their country. They founded patriotic and literary clubs, and established liberal and benevolent institutions. Monuments were erected at classical spots—Morat, St. Jacques, the lion monument, and so forth. Eminent painters like Vogel and Didary chose national historical events for their canvas; and Rudolf Wyp composed the fine national anthem, " *Rufst Du mein Vaterland.*" [1] A naturalists' club at Geneva, a students' association at Zofingen, and a society of marksmen—still in existence—were started, whilst the old Helvetic Society of the eighteenth century left behind its mere theorizings and discussions, and became an active political club.

[1] Wyp had studied at Göttingen, which was still under English rule, and had there been impressed by the English national anthem, of which his own is an imitation, the air being borrowed from "God save the Queen."

All these things tended greatly to spread and promote Swiss liberalism, of which many noble champions had sprung up, now and in the previous period, like the veteran trio—Victor von Bonstetten, the friend of Madame de Staël, La Harpe, and Usteri; like Troxler, Zschokke, Monnard, Von Orelli and others, far too numerous even to name here. Under such men Switzerland moved on. "No human efforts can succeed in permanently leading back mankind to the old lines of a past and less enlightened age. To struggle onwards, and to reach the end aimed at is the quickening stimulus in every thinking being." Such were the encouraging words of Usteri, a champion whom the party of progress regarded as an oracle. Military matters received a great impetus by the formation of a central school for officers at Thun, and the increase of the army from fifteen thousand to thirty thousand men. It hardly needs to be said that when the struggle of the Greeks for independence began they had the hearty sympathy and support of the Swiss.[1]

In 1830 the revolution of July hurled from his throne Charles X., and raised to his place Louis Philippe. Strangely enough the effects of this movement were felt almost more abroad than in France itself. Certainly its influence on Switzerland was very considerable, and it hurried on various changes of a sweeping character in that country, changes, however, which had been long preparing.

[1] One of the leading collectors of subscriptions in aid of the Greeks was Eynard, a wealthy Genevese, whose own contributions were most munificent.

Constitutional struggles, both federal and cantonal, crowded the next few years, and confessional difficulties tended not a little to quicken them. With nearly all the states, excepting some of the *laender*, the chief object now became the revision of their charters, so as to make them more consistent with the principles of popular rights and equality. Glarus, Uri, and Unterwalden were as yet averse to making changes, however justifiable and desirable they might seem to the rest of the country. The reforms were for the most part quietly carried out, but there were popular oppositions and stormy disputes in places. Bern was at first inclined to be conservative, but once embarked on the sea of reformation, sided strongly with the more progressive Zurich. Freiburg returned a crowd of fifty-seven priests and seventeen professors, all of the Jesuit order, and these ousted Girard, the Catholic Pestalozzi, from his noble work at St. Michael's College. Zurich proceeded in a peaceful and interesting fashion. Here as in other cases the city had a great preponderance of political power over the country districts of the canton. The fourteen thousand citizens elected one hundred and thirty representatives, as against the eighty-six assigned to the two hundred thousand rural inhabitants. The cause of the country folk was ably and without bitterness championed by two eloquent speakers, Guyer and Hegetschweiler; and a motion was carried which allotted to the rural districts two-thirds of the seats on the council board. This "day of Uster," as it was called, proved a great landmark in political development. The sovereignty of the people was

INTERLAKEN, FROM THE FELSENEGG.

now the basis on which reforms were made. The foundation was laid for better administration, and social improvement and provision was made for necessary revisions of the constitution. To safeguard their constitutions against the influence of reactionists, seven cantons entered into a league—*Siebner-Concordat*—March, 1832. They were Bern, Zurich, Lucerne, Solothurn, St. Gall, Aargau, and Thurgau.

Less satisfactory was the course of events in Schwyz, Basel, and Neuchâtel. In Schwyz a temporary separation into the two semi-cantons of Inner and Outer Schwyz was caused by the refusal of the former to grant equal rights to the latter, which had been formerly subject or purchased land mainly. Basel, the city of millionaires and manufactures, was able by her overwhelming importance to hold her supremacy over the rural districts, and thus arose the division into Baselstadt, and Baselland, which latter had Liestal as its *chef lieu*. But all this after a civil strife of three years. Basel city joined the Catholic League formed at Sarnen, in November, 1832, as a counterblast to the *Siebner-Concordat*. Uri, Inner-Schwyz, Unterwalden, Valais, and Freiburg also joined this league. The inhabitants of Neuchâtel had a double object, the reformation of their constitution, and their separation, if possible, from Prussia, the double *régime* being greatly disliked. An attempt was made on the castle, but it failed, and the Federation re-established order, and the old *status quo*. The royalist party in Neuchâtel now aimed at a severance from Switzerland.

But the natural consequence of constitutional revision in the separate cantons was the revision of the federal pact, with the view of strengthening the bonds which joined the states. The draft of a new constitution for Switzerland was presented at Lucerne in July, 1832, by the moderate party, but it failed, as so many other attempts have done which clashed with the selfishness of those cantons, that thought more of the question of cantonal home-rule than of the weal of the country as a whole. A far-seeing policy required that the central government should be strengthened, that the Diet should be made thoroughly capable of protecting Swiss interests, both in the country itself and abroad. That the Diet was quite incapable of enforcing its decrees for the general good was plainly shown by the condition of things in Basel, alluded to above.

With all these drawbacks, however, the period from 1830-1848 witnessed a true regeneration—social, political, intellectual. Never had education made such marvellous progress. It is to this period that the country owes that revival of educational zeal and that improvement in schools and methods of teaching, which are the great glory of modern Switzerland. Canton vied with canton, and authority with authority, in their noble enthusiasm for education. Zurich, Bern, Thurgau, Solothurn, Vaud—all these founded excellent teachers' seminaries. Primary schools were improved, and secondary schools established in every canton, and in all the more important cities gymnasiums were founded. At Zurich these time-honoured institutions, the Chorherrenstift and the

Carolinum, were in 1832 converted into the present gynmasium and university, and Bern made similar establishments in the following year. Thus were being gradually realized the noble aspirations of the " Helvetic " period, those of Stapfer particularly.

Unfortunate conflicts with foreign powers, however, not seldom arose. Fugitives from other countries then as now made Switzerland their abode, and many of them abused her hospitality, and entangled her in dissensions with foreign governments, exactly as we find happening at the present moment. Many of the political *emigrés* were men of great note, but space will permit of our noticing only two, Louis Philippe, and Louis Napoleon, afterwards Napoleon III. The Prince de Chartres lived for some years in Graubünden, occupying under the name of Chabaud, the position of mathematical master in an educational establishment of repute at Reichenau. Singularly enough he afterwards refused to the man who was to succeed him on the throne of France, the privilege of shelter in Swiss lands, that is to say, he objected very strongly. For in 1838 he suddenly requested that the Swiss Diet should give up Louis Napoleon, on the plea that he was an intriguer. This request was in reality a demand, and was more than the Swiss could stand. Napoleon was in fact a Swiss burgess, having become naturalized, and having passed through the military school at Thun, and become a captain in the Swiss army. His mother had for some time lived with her son in the castle of Arenenberg (in the Canton of Thurgau), which she had purchased soon after 1814. Thanks to the efforts of Dr. Kern, representative of that state in the Diet, the Swiss Government were able to disprove the charge made against Louis Napoleon, and the Diet firmly refused to expel the prince. France enraged threatened war to her "turbulent neighbour," and actually set on foot an army of twenty-five thousand men. Thoroughly roused, the Diet sent troops to the frontier, amidst general acclamations, Geneva and Vaud being conspicuous in their endeavours to protect their boundaries. These two cantons were specially thanked by the central government. The prince, however, cleared away difficulties by quitting the Swiss soil.[1]

The Zurich conflicts of 1839, called "Zurichputsch," from a local word meaning push or scramble, claim a moment's attention. That canton had perhaps more thoroughly than any other carried through a reorganization of its legislature and administration. It had establishment a most complete system of schools, graded from the primary school up to the University, whose chairs were occupied by men who made the city a real intellectual centre—by Oken, Hitzig, Schweizer, Von Orelli, Bluntschli, and others. Things marched too rapidly however. Dr. Scherr, a rationalist German *emigré*, was at the head of an

[1] "La Suisse a montré qu'elle était prête à faire les plus grands sacrifices pour maintenir sa dignité et son honneur. Elle a su faire son devoir comme nation independente ; je saurai faire le mien, et rester fidèle à l'honneur. . . . le seul pays où j'avais trouvé en Europe appui et protection. . . . Je n'oublierai jamais la noble conduite des cantons qui se sont prononcés si courageusement en ma faveur . . . surtout Thurgovie" (Extracts from Napoleon's letter of thanks to the Landammann of Thurgau, published in Dr. Kern's "Souvenirs politiques").

excellent training-college for teachers, but refused to allow biblical teaching to be given. Then the Government, anxious to make the city of Zwingli a centre of freethought, appointed the famous Strauss, author of the "Leben Jesu," to a vacancy on the university staff, despite the warnings of the native professors. The country people rose in wild frenzy, being urged on by the reactionary party, which desired to regain the reins of government. So great was the feeling against the appointment, that Strauss was pensioned off even before he saw the city. Even yet the excitement was very great, and, led by Pastor Hirzel, the rural inhabitants flocked into Zurich in great numbers. The Council was obliged to resign, and for a considerable period the reactionists had the power in their own hands. A few persons, but not many, were killed during the disturbances. The effects of this *contre-coup* in the most advanced city of the republic were soon felt in other places, in Ticino, Lucerne, and Freiburg, where conservative governments were returned, and codes altered accordingly. Zurich and Lucerne left the *Siebner-Concordat*.

But the event which stands out more prominently than any other during this period is the Sonderbund war of 1847. This conflict, which threatened the very existence of the state, forms the prelude to the European disturbances of the following year. This dispute of 1847 is the old struggle between the centralists and the federalists, or rather the progressivists and the reactionists, the dispute being intensified by religious differences. The chief points in the conflict must be briefly noted. In some of the cantons the Catholics, though in a minority, had advantages over the Protestant population, and when, in 1841, Aargau was revising its constitution, the latter demanded to be put on an equal footing with their Catholic brethren. This was flatly refused, and an embroilment took place in the canton, some of the monasteries taking a leading part in fomenting the quarrel. The rising, however, came to nought, and the Diet, on the motion of Keller, suspended the monastic houses, on the plea that they were hotbeds of intrigue. This step was clearly in opposition to the principles of the Constitution of 1815, and for years caused great trouble. It is impossible to give here minutely the story of the disputes: suffice it to say, the Diet compromised matters by extending forgiveness to four of the cloisters that had kept aloof from the rising (1843). But in 1844 Uri, Schwyz, Unterwalden, Zug, Freiburg, and Valais, formed a secret league—that of Sarnen had long since fallen through—to protect Catholic interests, and appointed Jesuits to the highest offices in the state. The entrance of the order at the Vorort created great excitement, but the Diet abstained from intervening, fearing to make matters worse. Two hapless expeditions of "Free Lances" now took place, the liberals from Lucerne and other cantons attempting to carry that city. The attempts utterly failed, and naturally so, seeing in how disorganized a condition the partizans were. But in January, 1847, the Protestants managed to get a majority at the Diet, and demanded the dissolution of the Sonderbund, as it had got to be called by that time. The foreign courts—Paris, Vienna, Berlin, and others—sided with the Swiss Sonderbund, being anxious to retain the *status quo* of 1815; France and Austria particularly sending money and promises of further support. England alone favoured the Protestants of Switzerland, and rendered them a great service. Palmerston was all against foreign intervention, and when the Powers issued a manifesto against the Swiss, he kept it back till Nov. 30th, when all was quietly settled. Meanwhile the Sonderbund organized a Council of War, and prepared for action. The Diet did all in its power to reconcile the contending religionists, and the English ambassador at Bern strongly recommended moderation and mutual concessions.[1]

Seeing that in spite of all their efforts war was inevitable, the Diet levied an army of ninety-eight thousand men, at the head of which was placed General Dufour of Geneva. The Sonderbund raised seventy-five thousand men, under General Salis-Soglio, a Protestant from Bünden. Dufour was a soldier of the old Napoleonic school, and a consummate tactician, and was revered by his fellow countrymen for his patriotism, lofty character, and high culture. It was under his management that the Swiss topographical maps bearing his name—the first of their kind—were executed. His selection as general gave great satisfaction. Thanks to Dufour's ability the campaign was short, lasting only from the 4th to the 29th of November, 1847, and the losses

[1] See "Souvenirs Politiques de 1838-83," by Dr. Kern, Swiss Ambassador at Paris, Bern, and Paris, 1887, pp. 51, 52.

were comparatively small. Honours were lavished on Dufour on all sides, even they of the Sonderbund heartily acknowledging his great services.

Heartburning and jealousy enough and to spare there had been between the opposing religious parties. On the 29th of October, 1847, the last occasion on which the Diet had attempted to reconcile Catholic and Protestant, there had been the utmost dissension and rancour. But such is the nature of Swiss patriotism that when, three short months after, the countries around Switzerland were convulsed with revolutions, and the Swiss lands were threatened with invasion, the contending religionists forgot their domestic quarrels entirely. And the glorious sight was seen of Catholic and Protestant standing shoulder to shoulder, ready to vie with each other in meeting danger and death in defence of their common and beloved fatherland. Not a vestige of hostile party feeling was left. It has ever been thus in Switzerland.

XXXIII.

UNDER THE CONSTITUTION OF 1848.

THE year 1848, which crowned the noble aspirations of the Regeneration period in Switzerland, marks a fresh starting-point in the history of the country. Providence had dealt graciously with the little republic. France, Prussia, and Austria were battling with the "February Revolution," and were thus prevented from dealing out to her the fate of unhappy Poland. Meanwhile eminent Swiss statesmen were drafting the new Federal Constitution which was to bind the various nationalities into one people, and the twenty-two cantons into a well-riveted Bundestaat, a state which, thanks to its policy, its prosperity, and its independent spirit, was soon to command the esteem of even the most antagonistic Powers.

On the 12th of September, 1848, the new pact was proclaimed, amidst cannonading, illumination, and general rejoicing. The old and crippled Tagsatzung was abolished. The new constitution borrowed some features from that of the United States, and, though greatly on the lines of the Mediation Act, blended far more happily the central and federal systems. Only the essential points can here be noted.

The Central Government, whose *raison d'être* is the maintenance of peace and order at home, and the upholding of the national honour abroad, divides itself into three authorities or divisions, the Federal Assembly, the Legislative body; the Federal Council, which is the executive body; and the Federal Tribunal. The Federal Assembly consists of two chambers, the National Council, and the Council of the States; the former elected by the Swiss people at large, the latter representing the different cantons. The Nationalrath is elected by ballot for three years, one member to every twenty thousand souls. At present (1889) there are 145 members. The cantonal governments elect the members of the other chamber, two to each canton, one to a semi-canton. The Federal Council (Bundesrath) is the Executive, and consists of seven members. Its chairman or president holds the highest dignity in the country, though his powers do not exceed those of his fellow-ministers. The whole Cabinet is *collectively* responsible for the conduct of all public business, and holds the *summum imperium*. Thus the *whole Federal Council, and not its president only*, occupies the position similar to that of the President of the United States.[1] There are various departments of the Executive — Foreign Affairs,

---

[1] There is, in fact, no office in Switzerland similar to that of the United States President, though foreigners nearly always speak of the *President of the Swiss Republic*, when they mean simply the *Chairman of the Cabinet.*

Interior and Education, Justice and Police, Military, Finance and Customs, Industry and Agriculture, Post and Railway. The Federal Assembly sits twice a year, and elects both the Bundesrath, and Bundesgericht (Tribunal). The Cabinet is subject to re-election every three years, but the same ministers are commonly chosen again and again. The Tribunal, or judiciary body, consists of nine members, who are elected every six years, with headquarters at Lausanne (since 1884).

POLYTECHNIKUM AT ZURICH.

Bern, on account of its position between the German and French-speaking districts, was chosen as the seat of the central government. Zurich was to have been the home of the National University, but the plan failed, and it is now the seat of the National Polytechnikum, or technical university. Thus the two leading cities of the Confederation keep up their old characteristics, as governmental and intellectual respectively. Zurich's claims to intellectual distinction are unquestionable. Its magnificent system of schools, &c., is probably one of the most complete in Europe, if not in the world.

It would be tedious as it is unnecessary to enter in detail into the powers of the central government as compared with those of the separate cantons. Suffice it to say, that the Bund reigns supreme in all relations with foreign states—it is only through the medium of the central government that any canton can treat with a foreign Power—that it controls all military matters, regulates coinage (Mints), weights and measures, posts and telegraphs, and fixes customs duties. It also partly controls the national education —the Polytechnikum at Zurich is wholly a federal affair, for instance—but in general each canton is left to its own devices in the matter. Thus, though every Swiss takes a pride in his schools, there in not one uniform standard throughout the state.

Every burgess is bound to perform military service, and at any time a force of 200,000 men of the *élite*, and first reserve, can be placed in the field, not including the Landsturm. Since the Franco-German war military matters are engaging the serious attention of the country, seeing the central position of Switzerland, and the unsettled state of Europe.[1] It remains to be said that the new Constitution secured freedom in religious matters, though the Jesuits were denied free settlement, and the Jews were not recognized till 1866. The *Octroi*, or duties between the

---

[1] The reader is referred for fuller information to the most interesting account by Sir F O. Adams and Mr. Cunningham in "The Swiss Confederation" (Longmans).

cantons, was not removed till 1887, and then only after a hard fight on the part of some of the cantons, notably Bern, to whom these dues were a great source of profit.

It is a problem requiring all the powers of the skilled statesmen to make the two Swiss sovereignties—the federal and cantonal—run side by side without allowing either to trench on the other's ground. And it is a much disputed point how far it is to the national benefit to increase the powers of the Federal Government. The centralization of the Government undoubtedly secures a better administration in most points, but the canting jealously guard against any infringement of their rights by the Federation. They believe that a healthy rivalry and emulation between the states is a good thing, and one not lightly to be given up.

The new Bundesrath was soon called upon to prove the quality of its mettle, for troubles arose in Neuchâtel. This canton was, up to 1848, a veritable mediæval relic in its form of government—a mixture of monarchy and free state. Few spots in Europe have had a more typical and characteristic history than Neuchâtel, and did space permit it would be most interesting to trace that history downwards, from its junction with the empire in 1033; through its rule by native lords, the counts of Neuchâtel, till their extinction in 1395; its vassalage to the house of Châlons; the suzerainty of the Orleans-Longueville family; the regency of Marie de Nemours (1679-1707). But here suffice it to say, that through fear of the designs of Louis Quatorze, Neuchâtel gladly

accepted the ducal supremacy of the kings of Prussia.
In 1815 it was incorporated with the Confederation,
as a canton with equal rights and standing to the
rest. Notwithstanding this, Prussia still claimed to
be its overlord, and thus arose a double *régime*,
a condition of things plainly untenable. In 1848 the
Confederation endeavoured to obtain the release of
the canton from Prussian rule, and this by the peaceful methods of diplomacy, but in vain. In 1856 a
conspiracy was set on foot to undo the work of 1848
—the granting of a more democratic constitution to
Neuchâtel. At the head of these royalist plotters were
Count Poustates and De Meuron. However, their
plans failed, and five hundred prisoners were taken.
Out of these, twenty-five were by order of the Federal
Government kept back to be tried as insurgents.
Frederick William IV., of Prussia, demanded their
unconditional pardon and surrender, an order obedience to which would have been a renunciation of the
canton, and a defiance of the Federal rule. The
demand was refused, and the question of the release
became the centre about which all the negotiation now
turned. In this emergency Napoleon III., of France,
offered his services as mediator, mindful of the hospitality shown to him of old by Switzerland. He
further promised to espouse the Swiss cause if the
prisoners were released, and to Switzerland his offer
carried greater weight than all the promises of Prussia.
" I shall act in the matter as if I were the Swiss Government," he assured Dr. Kern, who had been sent as
special envoy to the French Court, and in a further
conversation tried in every possible way to prove his

sympathy with the little republic.[1] England made similar promises. However the Prussian king made no overtures, and neither France nor England gave sufficient guarantee that Neuchâtel should be ceded to Switzerland, and the Swiss Government therefore declined to proceed further on these vague terms. Frederick William threatened war, and began to mobilize his troops. The Federal Council likewise began its preparation, and without outward sign of fear or hesitation, but with a unanimous feeling of heroic enthusiasm though the length and breadth of the country, the Swiss went on with their military organization. Most touching instances of devoted patriotism were witnessed—from the greyhaired old man to the mere boy the people offered their services; fellow-countrymen abroad sent large sums of money; even school children offered their savings. Catholic and Protestant, French and German, Italian and Romansch, all were animated by one spirit, all were equally ready to defend the honour and independence of their beloved country. Dufour was again elected Commander-in-chief of the Federal forces. To the crowds who gave him a splendid ovation he replied in these memorable words: "I rejoice to end my life in the service of my country. I am old"—he was seventy —"and my task is heavy, for the enemy is powerful, but I trust I shall carry on my mission in the name of the God of our Rütli, who has never ceased to protect our Fatherland." Such has ever been and ever will be the love of the Swiss for their native soil, a love

---

[1] Kern, "Souvenirs Suisses," pp. 124-129, where other instances of Napoleon's goodwill in 1848-9 are mentioned.

not based merely on the beauty of their land, nor on the perfection of its institutions, but on the knowledge that it is a stronghold of noble freedom, and one of their own rearing. The proud bearing of the Swiss made a great impression on the Powers, and particularly excited the admiration of Napoleon, who, forgetting the former distrust shown towards him, again offered his services as mediator. By his advice the prisoners were conducted to France, and there set free, on January 16, 1857, and they remained in banishment till the settlement of the dispute. This was finally accomplished on May 26th, at the conference of Paris, when the Prussian king formally renounced for ever all claims on Neuchâtel, whether duchy or canton, retaining, however, the title of Furst von Neuenburg. Thus the district was entirely ceded to Switzerland.

The cession of Nice and Savoy to Napoleon III. by Victor Emmanuel in 1859-60, led to dissensions with the emperor, which might have turned out serious, the Swiss having some claims on Chablais and Faucigny. The point is not settled even yet. There have also been disputes with the Papal See, consequent on the development of the Old Catholic movement, and the Pope's encroachments. Though the old diocese of Geneva had been long abolished, Pius IX. appointed Mermillod as bishop. Lachat, Bishop of Solothurn, turned out of their cures several priests for declining to accept the dogma of infallibility. The exasperation in the country was great, the two bishops were banished from Switzerland, and the Papal Nuncio was discharged. It was not till 1883 that Mermillod was allowed to return.

It remains to speak briefly of some of the constitutional revisions which have taken place, up to 1883, or even to the present moment. In 1874 the Federal Pact was amended. Briefly the improvement on the pact of 1848 consisted mainly in arranging a better and more effective centralization in financial, military, and judicial matters. Experience had brought to light many defects in the representative system. Personal, local, or class interests often weighed more with delegates than national interests; or occasionally a minister would assume too great powers to himself. To give the people a more direct share in the legislation, two institutions were set on foot which are peculiar to Switzerland. These are the "Initiative" and the "Referendum." They are perhaps the furthest developments of democracy yet reached, and are exciting considerable interest in English-speaking countries at the present time.

The Initiative is a development of the right of petitioning. By it any voter or voters may propose new legislation, and if the requisite number of voters can be got to support the proposal by signing the formal petition in its favour, the matter must be put to the popular vote. The number of signatures necessary is five thousand in the case of cantonal legislation, and fifty thousand in Federal matters. The people have thus always the power to bring on the discussion of any matter, however much the Council, or the legislators may object.

The Referendum, which by the way is far more frequently applied, secures that any law passed by the cantonal assemblies, or by the Federal Assembly,

VIEW OF SION. (*From a Photograph.*)

shall be put before the forum of the whole people [1]—*referred* to the whole body of voters—if again the required number of supporters can be got together. In cantonal matters this number is the same as in the case of the Initiative; in matters relating to the Confederation, thirty thousand votes, or eight cantons are necessary. There are two kinds of Referendum, adopted by different parts of the country, the "facultative," or optional Referendum, by St. Gall, Zug, Lucerne, Baselstadt, Schaffhausen, Vaud, Neuchâtel (1882), Geneva, Ticino (1883); and the "obligatory" or compulsory Referendum, which obtains in Zurich (1869), Bern (1869), Thurgau, Aargau, Solothurn, Schwyz, Graubünden, and Baselland. Uri, Glarus, the two Unterwalden, and the two Appenzell cantons, still cling to their old *landsgemeinde*, whilst Valais has a *financial* Referendum, and Freiburg is content with its older representative form of government. Opinion is much divided in Switzerland as to the value of the Referendum. In this, probably, most Swiss agree, that an arrangement which places the sovereign will of the people above that of the authorities and legislative bodies is a good arrangement, providing the people at large are intelligent and educated. And here Switzerland shows to great advantage. Probably no people in the world have so fully and so clearly recognized that "education alone makes free." The Swiss educational system is such,

---

[1] Legislative Acts are, in fact, referred *to the whole people* for approval or disapproval, as in limited monarchies they are referred to the *sovereign*. But in Switzerland the veto possessed by the people is a *real* thing, and not a virtual impossibility, as in England for instance.

that it reaches down to the poorest child and penetrates into the remotest valley. All primary education is gratuitous and compulsory. If any people deserve by education and intelligence to be entrusted with powers like that conferred by the Referendum, it is the Swiss. Yet men of every political shade admit that the Referendum is a two-edged weapon which may cut both ways. It is at any rate no new thing in Switzerland. It may be styled a *landsgemeinde by ballot*. And, as far back as the sixteenth century, the question of the Reformation was put to the Referendum—in a somewhat different way, it is true—both in Zurich and Bern. In its present form, of course, the Referendum is modern. It is curious to find that though introduced by the advanced democratic party it turns out in actual working to be a decidedly conservative measure. It may stop a sound and beneficial measure occasionally, but it is more likely to check rash and insufficiently considered legislation, as the Swiss are naturally averse to needless changes. An example or two may serve to illustrate this. Baselland thrice brought forward a Bill for the revision of its cantonal code; thrice the Bill was rejected, under the compulsory Referendum. At Zurich quite recently (spring of 1889), the Grand Council wished to bring in a new law for bettering the education of the masses by improving the supplementary schools. The country labourers had a majority, and rejected the measure, objecting, it is said, to the additional expenditure. It is to be hoped, however, that this measure will be carried eventually. On the whole, perhaps, the "facultative" Referendum is to be preferred to the obligatory. We may mention, in conclusion, that out of 107 Bills passed by the Federal Council, between 1874 and 1886, nineteen were submitted to the Referendum, and of these nineteen, but six were ultimately adopted by the whole body of voters thus appealed to.[1]

[1] For further notes on the Referendum, see Adams and Cunningham's "Swiss Confederation," alluded to above. The Referendum seems likely to attract increasing attention, in England and America especially.

LAW COURTS AT LAUSANNE.

XXXIV.

INDUSTRY, COMMERCE, RAILWAYS, EDUCATION THE "RIGHT OF ASYLUM."

OUR story must be brought to a close with a short account of several important matters on which nothing has as yet been said, viz., the industrial condition of the country, and its material progress. Hardly any other country has had to contend with so many natural disadvantages as Switzerland, in prosecuting her industries and establishing her trade. The difficulty of the country, the absence of coal and iron, the want of navigable rivers, the scanty produce of the soil in the more elevated districts, the want of seaboard—all these and other things increased the severity of the struggle in the race for wealth. Then she is fenced in as it were by protection. As a set-off against these drawbacks, there is an abundance of water-power. But it is evident that agriculture alone could not suffice to provide for all the inhabitants, and thus it comes to pass that the Swiss have turned their energies in a remarkable manner to the establishment and development of manufactures. It may here be pointed out parenthically that the poverty of the country in the pre-manufacturing days accounts for, and to some extent excuses, the old and reprehensible practice amongst the Swiss of hiring themselves out as soldiers to the highest bidder. Raw material in vast quantities is imported, and finished goods sent out. Switzerland competes successfully with some of the greatest manufacturing countries—England, Belgium, France—nay, considering her population, she almost surpasses them. Putting imports and exports together, Switzerland does a trade of £60,000,000 annually, the imports consisting mainly of coal, iron, raw silk, cotton, gold, and other raw materials, the exports of manufactured goods. The value of the imports exceeds that of the exports by no less a sum than six and a half millions sterling (Federal Statistics, 1887), the counterbalance being supplied by the tourists, and by the interest on foreign investments. The Swiss are a stirring and business-like people, and had already in the first half of the present century carried their enterprises abroad, especially in the principal seaports. As early as 1812, Egg, a citizen of Zurich, took two hundred operatives, and started a cotton factory at Piedimonti, near Naples, notwithstanding the blockade, the machinery being taken by way of Trieste and the Adriatic. Now the Swiss are to be found all over the world, as every one knows.

A few figures in detail respecting the imports and exports may be interesting. They are from the official statistics for 1887.

IMPORTS.

Food stuffs	242,935,277 francs.
Raw materials	330,324,615 ,,
Finished or partly-finished goods ...	263,775,024 ,,
Total ...	837,034,916 ,,

EXPORTS.

Food stuffs	78,565,548 francs.
Raw materials	95,922,106 ,,
Finished products	496,604,979 ,,
Total ...	671,092,633 ,,

Switzerland imports chiefly from the neighbouring countries, but her export trade is largely with England and America, as well as with Germany and France. Of the industries of the country, the largest as well as the oldest is the production of silk goods, dating back to the thirteenth century, the chief seats being Zurich and Basel. Cotton manufacture is carried on at Zurich, Aargau, St. Gall, and other places; embroidery is made at St. Gall and Appenzell; and watches at Neuchâtel and Geneva. This last town has also a great trade in jewellery and musical boxes. Then there are considerable manufactures of machinery, cheese, condensed milk, and other things, and wood carving is carried on to a large extent. The last returns give the exports of silk as 198,768,230 francs, cotton as over 158,000,000, and watches over 84,000,000.

This is not the place for details respecting the railway system, but it may be noted that the total length of the Swiss lines is now over three thousand kilometres. A special feature of the Alpine lines is, as every one is aware, the skill with which the

"VICTIMS OF THE WORK," ST. GOTHARD TUNNEL, FROM A BAS-RELIEF BY VELA.
(*Photographed by Guler. By permission of the Sculptor.*)

engineering difficulties have been surmounted. The St. Gothard line, with its fifty tunnels, is the most conspicuous of these successes. This grand international enterprise owes its execution to Dr. Alfred Escher of Zurich, and the famous engineer, Louis Favre of Geneva. Vela, the Ticinese sculptor, has produced a fine group of relievi as a memento of the many poor victims of the great undertaking. The tunnel is between nine and ten miles long, and was completed in seven and a half years.

There is no doubt that the thriving condition of Switzerland is chiefly due to three causes—the thriftiness of the people, their natural ability, and perhaps, more than all, the excellence of the educational system. On this last point much has been written by the late Matthew Arnold and Sir F. O. Adams, and to their works the reader must be referred for details. We may here mention, however, that besides the primary, secondary, and high schools, which are to be found in every canton, Switzerland stands out conspicuously by the number and excellence of its technical and trade schools. The great Polytechnikum of Zurich is the pride of the country, and Basel, Zurich, Bern, and Geneva have universities, and Neuchâtel and Lausanne academies.[1] Primary education is entirely free, and to it the greater share of the education vote is assigned—in 1887, nearly seventeen and a half million francs out of a total of twenty-six and a half millions given to education. Attendance at school is compulsory, and there were

---

[1] That of Lausanne is to be made into a university.

PORTRAIT OF GOTFRIED KELLER, THE POET.
(*After a Photograph.*)

in 1887, 467,597 children attending the primary schools.

Of men of intellect, of talent, of artistic, scientific, or literary skill, Switzerland has produced many, and has sheltered many more. The numerous academical institutions, literary, scientific, and musical societies, draw together large numbers of superior intellects. Amongst the numberless men of science now or lately living may be mentioned Agassiz, Desor, De la Rive, Heer, Merian, Studer, and Dr. Ferdinand Keller, the discoverer of the lake dwellings. In literature we have Viet, Marc Monnier, Zschokke, as well as Leuthold, Gotfried Keller, and Ferdinand Meyer. Keller has a reputation more than European; he has been called the German Shakespeare. He belongs to Zurich. The occasion of his seventieth birthday (on July, 1889), brought a remarkable demonstration. The Assembly voted him an address, and enthusiastic congratulations poured in upon him from all quarters. From Germany Von Moltke himself headed the list of admiring friends who sent messages. Keller is acknowledged to be the greatest living German poet. Amongst painters are Calaine, Diday, Girardet, Gleyre, Vautier, and Böcklin, whom the Germans consider one of their greatest living painters; and of sculptors, there are Vela and Lanz. Gustave Weber and Joachim Raff are well-known musical composers, with whom we must name Baumgartner, who has raised Keller's "Oh, mein Heimatland," into the position of a second national anthem.

We see in Switzerland a nation which once played

a conspicuous part in European military affairs, but which has now become a land of peace, whose neutrality the Powers vouchsafed at the Vienna Congress. In the exceptional position she holds, she deems it part of her mission of peace to promote the general welfare of the world, so far as lies in her power. Most important international institutions owe their origin, or at least their successful establishment, to Switzerland. Thus she started the Geneva Convention, under the presidency of General Dufour, in 1864. This Convention had for its object the mitigation of the horrors of war, and every European nation was represented at it. The declaration of the neutrality of all nurses, medical men, hospitals, &c., on either side, and the adoption of the distinguishing badge, the Geneva cross, are too well known to need description here. Then at the suggestion of Germany the International Postal Union was founded at a meeting at Bern. And quite recently the International Congress of labour delegates is under consideration to be called with the view of settling some of the social questions affecting labour. A particularly interesting Swiss foundation was started in 1886, to provide for poor soldiers incapacitated by war, and to assist relatives dependent on those killed in battle. It was founded to celebrate the five-hundredth anniversary of Sempach, and is appropriately named the *Winkelriedstiftung*.

The right to offer an asylum in time of war she considers one of her most precious privileges. Seeing, however, how frequently her well-meant intentions are misinterpreted, and her hospitality abused, she may probably have to restrict her offers of asylum. In fact, the Bundesrath have even now under consideration the question of how best to maintain her rights in this respect, whilst seeing that no injury is done to foreign interests. One thing is certain, she will not give up the right of asylum. Meanwhile the refractory foreign elements residing in Switzerland are not only endangering her safety, but doing harm to the character of her people. The confusion of 1848–9 brought to Swiss territory fugitives from all parts of Europe. As many as ten thousand fled from the Grand Duchy of Baden, when the Prussian troops checked the rising there. Many distinguished men, who would otherwise have met with death, or lingered indefinitely in prison, found a safe retreat in Switzerland. We need only mention the great composer, Richard Wagner, and Rüstow, Mommsen, Semper, Joh. Scherr, Kinkel, Köchly, from amongst a host of scholars who took refuge there, and settled for years at the Swiss universities. Köchly's scholarship and activity brought in a conspicuously successful period of classical study at Zurich University (1850–64),[1] and his successor, Arnold Hug, was no less devoted and successful.

In 1853 Austria turned out six thousand Swiss (Ticinese) in the harshest manner from Lombardy, on the plea that Italians had been allowed to combine on Swiss ground against Austria. Six years later the Swiss had an opportunity of heaping coals of fire on the head of Austria, for when the Austrian garrison was driven from Fort Laveno, on Lake

[1] "Life of Köchly," by Prof. A. Hug, 1878.

SWISS HOSPITALITY. 417

Maggiore, the soldiers were not only freely admitted into Swiss territory, but were liberally treated. Mazzini, too, the Italian patriot, sought safety in Switzerland, causing her, by the way, considerable trouble. The Franco-German war, again, offered the Swiss many opportunities of showing their usual benevolence and charity towards distressed foreigners. To the Germans who had to leave France on the outbreak of war, making their way home through Switzerland, the Swiss people showed innumerable kindnesses, many of the people being poor, and destitute of even necessaries. And when they heard of the siege of Strasburg, their old friend and ally of centuries ago, the Swiss sent a deputation to invite the weak and tender to go home with them. This was done with the consent of both belligerents, and fourteen hundred persons, chiefly women and children, and old men, accepted the invitation. It was a touching scene when they left with their protectors, and few eyes were dry. Every one knows how Bourbaki, failing to relieve Belfort, was compelled to flee into Swiss territory, with his eighty-five thousand men and nine thousand horse (February 1, 1871). The troops were disarmed, and quartered all over the country, and remained till peace was concluded. High and low, rich and poor, the Swiss vied with each other in showing kindness to the refugees. Miserable in the extreme had been their condition on their arrival, but they left recruited in health, improved in appearance and full of gratitude. As they departed the air was filled with shouts of "Vive la Suisse." That same spring, too, when seed was wanting with which to sow the ground in many districts of France, the Swiss sent large quantities of potatoes, oats, barley, and beans, and other seed corn, besides money and clothing. And during the war Swiss aid was distributed amongst French and Germans impartially.

It is not from self-interest or vain-glory that the Swiss act thus, but from motives of humanity and benevolence. And, though the "right of asylum" is liable to be abused, its nobler side is not to be forgotten. It is to be hoped that Switzerland will ever keep her present independence and neutrality, the very existence of which bears witness to the more human tendencies of modern European politics.

It remains only to give a few figures respecting the present numbers of the population. They are taken from the official returns, and though the report is only provisional,[1] it may be taken that the figures are substantially correct. It appears, then, that the total population of the Republic, on December 1, 1888, was 2,934,057 actually, or 2,920,723 in regular residence. In 1850 the actual population was 2,392,740, thus the increase during the thirty-eight years has been over half a million. Of the 2,934,057 enumerated on December 1, 1888, 1,427,377 were males, and 1,506,680 females; 2,092,530 were German-speaking, 637,972 French-speaking, 156,606 Italian-speaking, 38,375 Romansch-speaking, 8,574 were of other nationalities; 1,724,957 were Protestants, 1,190,008 Catholics, and 19,092 of other religions, or

---

[1] "Vorläufige Resultate der eidg. Volkszählung vom 1 Dezember, 1888."

INTERIOR OF LAUSANNE CATHEDRAL.
(*From a Photograph.*)

of none. The canton with the largest population was Bern, with 539,271, Zurich coming next with 339,014, whilst that with the smallest number of souls was Lower Unterwalden, with 12,524. The most populous town is Zurich, with 90,111 inhabitants, those coming next in order being Basel, with over 69,000, Geneva 52,000, Bern, 45,000, Lausanne, 33,000.

Here must end our short sketch of this remarkable little state. From the very earliest times its peoples have been particularly interesting—from its prehistoric lakemen with their almost unique series of settlements, down through successive nationalities of Helvetians and Romans, Alamanni and Burgundians to the modern Germans, French, Italians, and Romansch. Switzerland has bred or has been closely connected with some of the proudest ruling families in European history—Habsburgs and Zaerings, Carlovingians and Burgundians, Hohenstaufens and Savoys. Some of the most glorious victories recorded in history have been gained by the little Swiss nation in defence of their beloved fatherland; the fame of Morgarten, Sempach, Grandson, and Morat is not likely to die out while European civilization lasts. Constitutionally the history of Switzerland is of surpassing interest. Step by step we have seen a handful of gallant people free themselves from oppression by emperor or duke, by prince or lord, by prelate or cloister. Inch by inch the people at large have gained their political rights from foreign overlords or from native aristocracies. We have seen how a tiny confederation of three petty states has grown into a league of eight, and then of thirteen independent districts, and how this has developed into the federal state of twenty-two cantons of our own day. Lastly, some of the institutions of the country, notably the Initiative and the Referendum, are well-nigh unique of their kind, and certainly are of the greatest interest to the student of political history and development; whilst Switzerland's noble efforts for the amelioration and benefit of mankind at large cannot but command our admiration.

> "Il est à nous, notre libre avenir;
> Morgarten, Grandson, jours de fête,
> Si vous ne deviez revenir,
> O Saint Jacques, O sainte defaite,
> Dans ton pourpre linceul, tu nous verrais dormir."[1]

[1] De la Rive, Genevan poet.

THE END.

INDEX.

A

Aargau, subject land, 186
Adams, Sir F. O., 412
Adolf of Nassau, 131
Æneas Sylvius, 203, 253
Ætius defeated Huns, 45; gave Savoy to Burgundy, 51
Agassiz, 14
Agen, battle of, 20
Agnes of Königsfelden, 141
Alamanni, 39, 46, 47, 49
Albrecht of Habsburg, 113, 120, 131, 132
Alcuin, 64
Allobroges, 21
Allmend, or common land, 48, 126
Alpinus, 37
Alpnach, bay of, 355
Ambühl of Glarus, 176
Amman chosen in Uri, 127
Am Stoss, battle of, 181
Appenzell, 181; admitted as an ally, 182; admitted as a canton, 237
Aquæ (Baden), 35
Aquæ Sextiæ, battle of, 21
Arbedo, engagement at, 188
Arelatisches Reich founded, 73
Arnold of Brescia, reformer, 100, 152
Arnold von Melchthal, 120
Arnulf of Kaernthen, 76
Arth, Battle of, 354
Asylum, Right of, 416, 418
Augusta Rauracorum, 35, 39

Augusta Vindelicorum, 32
"Ausserer Stand," Society, 320
Austria, 143, 146, 166; defeated at Sempach, 172; defeated at Naefels, 177; claims the Forest, 178
Autun, battle of, 55
Avars, the, 76
Avenches, 97, 213; battle at, 368
Aventicum, 14, 34, 39

B

Baden (Zurich), 186
Barbarossa, 96
Basel, 14; treaty of, 236; divided, 387
Bayard, 240
Beccaria, 294
Bellinzona, 188
Bern, founded, 97; defeated at Schosshalde, 158; forms Burgundian Confederation, 159; rules over Hasle, 163; League with Austria, 166; power over house of Kyburg, 166; seizes Habsburg, 186; fortifies Morat, 212; natural bent for rule, 245; governing families of, 320; plundered by French, 351, 353; population, &c., 420
Berchtold V. founds Bern, 97; defeated by Savoy, 98
Bertha, the "Spinning Queen," 74, 86
Bertold I., Duke of Zaeringen, 93

Bertold II., 94
Bertold IV., 96
Beza, 287, 290
Bibracte, battle of, 23
Bituitus, 19
Bockenkrieg, 372
Bodmer, 334, 338
Bonivard, 273
Borromean League, 294
Borromeo, Archbishop of Milan, 293
Bourbaki, General, 417
Breisach, rising at, 205
Breitinger, 334, 336
Brun, Burgomaster of Zurich, 140, 146, 155, 157
Bubenberg, Hans von, 164; Adrian von, 206, 212
Bullinger, Reformer, 268, 296
Bund ob dem See, 181
Burgdorf, 97, 166
Burgundia Transjurans, 73
Burgundy takes West Helvetia, 40; defeated by Huns, 50; defeated by Franks, 55; two kingdoms of, 73; its wars, 200
Burkhard of Alamannia, 74
Burkhard of Chur-Rhætia, 78, 80, 81

C

Caecina ravages Helvetia, 36
Campo Formio, treaty of, 347
Calvin, 279; his writings, 280; settles at Geneva, 281; banished, 282; founds the Consistory, 283; burns Servetus, 286; his policy, 287; death, 289
Carlomann, 58
Carmagnola, General, 188
Carolinum founded, 67
Catalaunian Plain, great battle on, 45
Catholic League, 387
Catholic Reaction, 291, 294
Central Government, 396
Centralists, the, 365
Chablais, 380, 402
Charlemagne, 59; Emperor of the West, 60; legends concerning, 62; zeal for education, 64

Charles the Bald, 72
Charles the Bold, 200, 205; defeated at Grandson, 211; at Morat, 213; death, 215
Charles IV. of Germany, 141, 143
Chiavenna, 241, 346, 380
Chillon, 109, 274
Christianity, introduction of, 40
Christian League, 264
Codex Manesse, 153
Columban, 57
Commerce, 409
Confederation formed, 119
Conrad I., 77; II., 88; III., 99
Conradin, 114
Constance, siege of, 304
Clairvaux, monk, preaches Crusades, 99
Clovis, king of the Franks, 54
Crusades, 98

D

D'Affry, 372, 376
Davel, Major, 319
"Delices, Les," 326; theatre destroyed, 328
Diesbach, Nicolas von, 206
Divico, 20, 23
Domo d'Ossola, 188
Dornbühl, victory at, 158
Drachenried, engagement at, 353
Drusus, 25, 32
Dufour, General, 393, 401, 415

E

East Frankish realm, 72
Eberhard the "Quarrelsome," 143; of Kyburg, 161
Education, 388, 412
Eidgenossenschaft, the, 118
Eight States League, 139, 166
Einsiedeln, 82, 134
Eishere the Giant, 62
Elizabeth of Habsburg, 133
"Empty Pocket," Frederick the, 181
Ensisheim, peace of, 197
Erlach, Ludwig von, 350
Erlach, Rudolf von, 164

Ernest II. of Swabia, 82
Escalade of Geneva, 302
Eschenbach, 133
Escher, 358, 375
Ewiger Bund, 129
Exports, 410

F

Farel, reformer, 275
Faucigny, 380, 402
"Faustrecht," the, 107
Federal Assembly, 396
Federal Council, 396
Federal Tribunal, 396
Felix Martyr, 42
Fellenberg, educationist, 374
Ferney, 326
Feudalism, 103
Fichte, 338
Fontana, 234
"Foul Peace," the, 175
Franche Comté, 215
Franco-German War, 417
Franks, the, 54
Fraubrunnen, skirmish at, 350
Frederick von Staufen, 93
Frederick I. (Barbarossa), 105
Frederick II., 127, 150
Frederick III., 190
Frederick the "Empty Pocket," 181, 185
Freiburg, 161, 221
French Revolution, 343
Fridolin St., banner of, at Naefels, 177
"Friedel" (Empty Pocket), 185

G

Galba, 25, 35
Gallia Comata, 31
Gall, St., 57, 62, 182, 241, 346
Geneva, 245; "Children" of, 273, 285; besieged by Savoy, 276; occupied by Bernese army, 277; Calvin's rule in, 284; escalade of, 302; Fatio's reforms, 322; admitted into league, 380; Geneva Convention, 415

Geschworne Brief, 155
Gessler, 121, 123
Giornico, victory at, 189
Glarean, scholar, 254
Glarus, 141; 1st Landsgemeinde, 175; defeats Austria, 177; defeated at Rapperswyl, 353
Goethe, 341
Golden League, 294
Gothard, St., pass, 187; tunnel, 412
Götterdämmerung, 50
Gotteshausbund, 184
Grandson, battle of, 208, 211
Graubünden, 184, 234; religious feuds, 305; massacre in, 307; Austrian occupation, 308; independence recovered, 311
Grauholz, conflict at, 351
Gregory VII., Pope, 91
Greifensee, 194, 317
Greyerz, 162, 164
Grey, Lady Jane, 298
Grey League, 184
Guillermins, the, 282
Gümminen, 161
Gundobad of Burgundy, 52

H

Habsburg Castle, 113
Habsburg-Austria, family of, 113
Habsburg-Laufenburg, 113
Habsburg, house of, 113, 114; kings of Germany, 115
Hadrian, Pope, 60, 63
Hadwig, 81
Hærige, the, 48
Hagenback, Peter von, 204, 205
Haller, 334, 336
Hallwyl, Hans von, 212
Harpe, La, 347, 359, 367, 372, 384
Hartmann, 108, 161
Harsthörner, 209
Hatto, Bishop, 66
Heer, Professor, 8
Heierli, 11
Helvetia, 13, 31, 32
Helvetians, 14; government, 17; feuds with Germans, 18; victory

over Romans, 20; defeated at Bibracte, 24; made associates by Rome, 25; split into two sections, 36
Helvetic Club, 347
Helvetic Republic, 352
Helvetic Society, the, 340, 342
Henry I., the "City Founder," 80
Henry II. of Germany, 87
Henry III., 88, 90, 105
Henry IV., 91, 93
Henry VII., 134
Hericourt, Siege of, 208
Herodotus, 8
Hertenstein of Lucerne, 213
Hildgard, Princess, Abbess of Zurich, 70
Hirtzel, 339
Hohe Frau von Zurich, 149
Hohenstaufen line, 107; extinction, 114
Hooper, Bishop, 297
"Horned Council," 229
Hotze, 360
Hug, Dr. Arnold, scholar, 416
Huns, 44, 45
Huss, martyr, 198

I

Im Grund, 219
Imports, 410
Initiative, the, 403
Innsbruck, 186
International Postal Union, 415
Italian Wars, 237

J

Jacques, St., battle of, 191, 193, 195
Jenatsch, 307, 309; stabbed, 310
John XXIII., Pope, 185
Judith, 72
Julien, St., treaty of, 274
Juvalta, Anna, 307

K

Kaernthen, Arnulf of, 76
Kappel, first battle, 264; second ditto, 267
"Kappeller, Milchesuppe," 262
Keller, Dr. Ferdinand, 3, 414
Keller, novelist, 154
Keller, poet, 414
Kern, Swiss envoy, 400
Klaus, Bruder, 221
Klingenberg, Henry of, 153
Klopstock, 337, 338
Kloten, 38
Knonau Castle, 186; rising at, 227; Ludwig Meyer von, 340
Knox, 287
Köchly, scholar, 416
Königsfelden, Monastery, 133
Korsakow, 360, 361
Kyburg Manor, 82; counts of, 89; rise of family, 104; fall, 166

L

"Ladle Squires," the, 274
Lake dwellers, 5, 9, 11
Lake dwellings, 3; construction, 5; probable dates, 11; ditto in East Yorkshire, 12
Landammann, installation of, 249
Landenberg, 121
Länder, the, 218
Landsgemeinde, 247
Latin right, 35
Laupen, 97, 163
Lausanne bishopric, 271
Lavater, 340, 359, 361
League of Perpetual Alliance, 119
Lemanic Republic, 349
Lenzburg, counts of, 89; family, 104
Leopold, 135; defeated at Morgarten, 136
Leopold III. of Austria, 168; defeated at Sempach, 172
Letzinen, the, 162
Leventina, 188; rising in, 316
Libertines, 285
Ligue à la Cassette, 316
Linth canal, 375
"Lion of Lucerne," 346
Locarno refugees, 295
"Long Diet," 378
Lorraine, kingdom of, 200

Lothair, 73, 96
Louis Napoleon, 389
Louis Philippe, 389
Louis the Child, 76
Louis the German, 70
Louis the Pious, 71
Louis XI., 195
Louis XIV., 312, 313
Lucerne, 140
Luneville, peace of, 367
Lützelburg, Henry of, 133
Lyons, 32

M

Maehren, the, 76
Malleolus, savant, 198, 253
Mamelukes, the, 273
Manesse, 142, 153
Manufactures, 410
Marignano, 218, 240
Martel, Charles, 58
Massena, 360, 361
Maximilian, 232
Mayence, diet at, 93
"Mazze," the, 183
Mediation Act, 369
Meilen, 3
Meistersinger, 251
Melchthal, Arnold von, 120
Mermillod, Bishop, 402
Milan, 187, 189, 238
"Milchsuppe," the, 264
Military system, 398
Minnelieder, 153
Misox, 295
Monk of St. Gall, 62
Morat, battle of, 212
Morgarten, battle of, 131, 135; another engagement at, 354
Müller, historian, 124
Murten, *see* Morat
Mytenstein, the, 121

N

Naefels, battle of, 175
Nancy, battle of, 215
Napoleon and Switzerland, 370
"Natifs," the, 323
"Negatifs," the, 322
Nellenburg, counts of, 89

Neuchâtel, 209; rebels against Prussia, 323; admitted to league, 380; troubles in, 399; Prussia renounces claim to, 402
Neueneck, engagement at, 350
"Nibelungenlied," 51
Nicolas von der Flüe, 219
Nidan, Count of, 164
Nidwalden, 129
Notker, chronicler, 62; Monachus S. Gallensis, 75
Novara, siege of, 239
Noviodunum, 33

O

Obwalden, 129
Ochs, Peter, 347, 352, 358, 367
Octodurum (Martigny), 35
Omer, St., treaty of, 204
Orcitrix, *see* Orgetorix
Orgetorix, 17; his treason and death, 21
Otho I., 80
Ottokar of Steyermark, 116
Otto of Strassberg, 135; death, 136
Otto von Freysing, 151

P

Papal see, alliance with, 238
Paracelsus, 301
Paris, peace of, 377
Paulus Diaconus, 64
Peasants' revolt, 311
Pepin le Bref, 58
Pestalozzi, 331, 339, 356, 366, 374, 385
Peter Martyr, 295
Peter of Savoy, "Second Charlemagne," 108; Savoy palace, 109; war with Austria, 110; death, 111
Pfäffikon Lake, 6
Pfyffer, "Swiss king," 293
Philip of Savoy, 111
Pius II., 203
Planta, John von, 305; Rudolf, 307
Polytechnikum at Zurich, 398

428   INDEX.

Population, 418
Postal Union, the, 415

R

Railways, 410
Rapinat, 364
Rapperswyl, counts of, 104; skirmish at, 156; John of, 156; battle at, 353
Raron, barons of, 182, 183
Rauraci, 14, 33
Rauracian Republic, 345
Reding, 191, 194; advocates Reislaufen, 226
Reding of Schwyz, 353, 359, 367
Referendum, the, 403; of two kinds, 405; its working, 406
Reformation in East Switzerland, 254; in West Switzerland, 267
Regensburg, peace of, 145
Regula Martyr, 40
Reichsfreiheit, the, 126
Reinhard, 376, 379
René of Lorraine, 208, 215
Rengger, 365
Rhætians, 14; campaign of Drusus, 26; joined with East Switzerland, 32; fall of Goths, 55
Rheinfelden manor, 91; battle of, 310
Richard of Cornwall, 109
Robenhausen, 6, 8
Rohan, Duke Henry de, 309, 310
Romans, 20; Bibracte, 23; conquer Valais, 25; Rhætia, 26; policy, 30
Romaunsh dialect, 14, 26
Rotach, 181
Rothenburg, 168
Rotzloch, battle of, 355
Rousseau, 325; birth, 328; writings, 329; "Contrat Social," 331
Rudolf der Alte, 113
Rudolf of Habsburg, 113; elected King of Germany, 115; policy, 116
Rudolf II., 74
Rudolf III., 82, 87

Rudolf IV., 145
Rudolf, "Rector of Burgundy," 91
Rudolf the Guelf, 73
Rudolf the Silent, 113
Rudolf von Erlach, 164
"Rufst du mein Vaterland," 178
Rütli, the oath on, 120, 122

S

Sabaudia (Savoy), 51
Salis, Von, 305
Salodunum (Soleure), 35
Sarnen, the "White Book" of, 124
Savoy, 98; Palace in Strand, 109; defeated at Visp, 182; loses Lower Valais, 208; and Freiburg, 216; and Vaud, 277
"Savoyards," the, 273
Sax-Misox, 183, 188
Schaffhausen, 204, 236
Schauenberg, 350, 355, 360
Scheffel's "Ekkehard," 81
Schindellegi, battle of, 354
Schinner, Matthaeus, 238
Schirmverwandte, 180
Schmalkalden wars, 291
Schosshalde, battle of, 158
Schwyz, 119; charter of liberties, 127; joins league, 128; war with Zurich, 190
Sempach, battle of, 166; Winkelried's death, 170
Sequani, the, 41
Servetus, 286
Sforza, Ludovico, 238; Maximilian, 239
Siebner Concordat, 387, 391
Sigismund, 55, 185
Sigmund of Austria, 204
Simplon Road, 376
Socinus, 295
Solernon, Abbott of St. Gall, 76, 77, 80
Solothurn, 159, 221
Sonderbund wars, 392
Soult, Marshal, 361
Staël, Madame de, 332
Stäfa, insurrection in, 346

INDEX.

Stanz, meeting at, 217, 219; covenant of, 221; siege, 355
Stapfer, 365, 370
Staufacher, 120
"Stecklikrieg," the, 368
Steyermark, 116
Strasburg, 203
Strauss, 391
Stuppa, 313
Stüssi, 191, 193
Subject lands, 179
Suwarow, 360, 361
Swabia, 71, 73; John of, 133; wars, 235
Swiss guards massacred, 345
Sylvius, 204

T

Tagsatzung (Diet), 250
Tatwil, Austrian defeat at, 142
Tavelli murdered, 182
Tell, 122, 123
Tell, historian, 301
Tellenplatte, 123
Theiling of Lucerne, 227
Theobald, bishop, 66
Theodoric the Great, 51, 53
"Thermopylæ of Switzerland," 137
Thun, 97
Thurgau, 204
Ticino, 187, 241
Tigurini, the, 14, 22
Tirano, skirmish at, 308
Toggenburg, 93, 190
Torberg, peace of, 146
Toygeni, the, 14
Tremouille, General, 239
Trivulzio, 239, 241
Tschudi, historian, 124, 252

U

Ufenau Island, 192
Ulrichen, battle of, 182
Ulrich of Kyburg, 108
Unitarier, 366
Unterthanen Laender, 180
Unterwalden, 119; divided, 129
Uri, 119; severed from Zurich Abbey, 126; chooses Ammann, 127

Uristier of Uri, 209
Ursus (and Victor) put to death, 42
"Uster, Day of," 385
Uto Castle, 115

V

Valais, 14; joined to Savoy, 32; joins league, 182; rising in, 345
Valangin, Count, 164
Valisians, 14, 25
Valtellina, 241; massacre in, 307; joined to Lombardy, 346; to Austria, 380
Vaud, 216, 269; lost to Savoy, 277
Vazerol, diets at, 184
Vercellæ, battle of, 21
Vercingetorix defeated, 25; death, 29
Verdun, treaty of, 72; ditto, 200
Vespasian, 34
Victor (and Ursus) put to death, 42
Victoriden, the, 55
Vienna Congress, 378
Villemergen, religious strife, 311; second ditto, 316
Vindonissa, 35
Viret, reformer, 276
Visconti, the, 187
Visp, battle of, 182
Vitellius, 37
Vogelinseck, battle of, 181
Volkslieder, the, 251
Voltaire, 325; at Ferney, 326; influence, 327
Voralberg, 190

W

Walchen Romaunsh, 184
Waldmann, 212, 213; his life, 222; policy, 225; conspiracy against him, 227; sentence and death, 228; compromise, 229
Waldshut feud, 204
Waldstätten, the, 3, 120, 140
Walter Fürst von Attinghausen, 120

Wart stabs Albrecht of Habsburg, 133
Wasserkirche (Zurich), 68, 224
Weiss, 349
Wengi, Nicolas von, 268
Werdenberg, counts of, 105, 176, 181; revolts, 316
Werner of Kyburg, 104
Werner Staufacher, 120
Wesen, 175, 177
West Frankish realm, 72
Westphalia, peace of, 311
Wieland, 337
William IV. of Burgundy, 95
Willisan destroyed, 169
Wimmis stormed, 162
Winkelried, 171, 173
Winkelriedstiftung, the, 415
Winterthur, 74, 132
Wyss, Prof. Georg von, historian, 69

Y

Yorkshire, lake settlements in East, 12
Yverdon, 97

Z

Zaeringen, house of, 95, 96; dissolution, 101
Zehngerichte (Bund), 184
Zschokke, novelist, 374, 384, 414
Zug, 142; excluded from league, 145; readmitted, 146
Zugewandte, 180
Zum Ranft, 219
Zünfte or guilds, 225
Zuricum, 17
Zurich, 60, 66; abbey founded, 70, 75; diets, 90; Reichsvogtei, 94; attacks Winterthur, 132; joins league, defeats Austrians, 142; Lenzburgs and Zaerings, 149; a poet's corner, 155; "Mordnacht," 156; war with Schwyz, 190, 193; gives up Austrian Alliance, 197; revolts against Waldmann, 228; war with Forest, 264; religious refugees, 295; educational pre-eminence, 398; largest Swiss city, 420
"Zurichputsch," 390
Zwingli, 255; birth, 257; called to Zurich, 258; abolishes Reislaufen, 260; establishes National Church, 262; with Zurich army, 264; killed in battle, 267

www.ingramcontent.com/pod-product-compliance
Lightning Source LLC
Chambersburg PA
CBHW032009300426
44117CB00008B/956